Online File Sharing

It is apparent that file sharing on the Internet has become an emerging norm of media consumption—especially among young people. This book provides a critical perspective on this phenomenon, exploring issues related to file sharing, downloading, peer-to-peer networks, piracy, and (not least) policy issues regarding these practices. Andersson Schwarz critically engages with the justificatory discourses of the actual file sharers, using Sweden as a geographic focus. By focusing on the example of Sweden—home to both the Pirate Bay and Spotify—he provides a unique insight into a mentality that drives both innovation and deviance and accommodates sharing in both its unadulterated and its compliant, business-friendly forms.

Jonas Andersson Schwarz is a Lecturer in the Department of Culture and Communication at Södertörn University, Sweden.

Comedia

Series Editor: David Morley

Advertising International
The Privatisation of Public Space
Armand Mattelart; translated by Michael Chanan

Black British Culture and Society
A Text Reader
Edited by Kwesi Owusu

The Consumerist Manifesto
Advertising in Postmodern Times
Martin P. Davidson

Cultural Sniping
The Art of Transgression
Jo Spence

Culture after Humanism
History, Culture, Subjectivity
Iain Chambers

Culture in the Communication Age
Edited by James Lull

Cultures of Consumption
Masculinities and Social Space in Late Twentieth-Century Britain
Frank Mort

Cut 'N' Mix
Culture, Identity and Caribbean Music
Dick Hebdige

The Dynasty Years
Hollywood Television and Critical Media Studies
Jostein Gripsrud

Family Television
Cultural Power and Domestic Leisure
David Morley

A Game of Two Halves: Football, Television and Globalisation
Football Fandom, Television and Globalisation
Cornel Sandvoss

Hiding in the Light
On Images and Things
Dick Hebdige

Home Territories
Media, Mobility and Identity
David Morley

Impossible Bodies
Femininity and Masculinity at the Movies
Chris Holmlund

The Known World of Broadcast News
International News and the Electronic Media
Stanley Baran and Roger Wallis

Media/Theory
Thinking About Media and Communications
Shaun Moores

Migrancy, Culture, Identity
Iain Chambers

The Photographic Image in Digital Culture
Edited by Martin Lister

The Place of Media Power
Pilgrims and Witnesses of the Media Age
Nick Couldry

The Politics of Heritage
The Legacies of 'Race'
Edited by Jo Littler and Roshi Naidoo

Spectacular Bodies
Gender, Genre and the Action Cinema
Yvonne Tasker

Stuart Hall
Critical Dialogues in Cultural Studies
Edited by Kuan-Hsing Chen and David Morley

Teaching the Media
Len Masterman

Television and Common Knowledge
Edited by Jostein Gripsrud

Television, Audiences and Cultural Studies
David Morley

Television, Ethnicity and Cultural Change
Marie Gillespie

Timeshift
On Video Culture
Sean Cubitt

Times of the Technoculture
From the Information Society to the Virtual Life
Kevin Robins and Frank Webster

To Be Continued . . .
Soap Operas Around the World
Edited by Robert C. Allen

Transnational Connections
Culture, People, Places
Ulf Hannerz

Video Playtime
The Gendering of a Leisure Technology
Ann Gray

Watching with The Simpsons
Television, Parody, and Intertextuality
Jonathan Gray

Media, Modernity and Technology
The Geography of the New
David Morley

Media Events in a Global Age
Edited by Nick Couldry, Andreas Hepp, and Friedrich Krotz

Relocating Television
Television in the Digital Context
Edited by Jostein Gripsrud

Branding Television
Catherine Johnson

The Photographic Image in Digital Culture
2nd Edition
Edited by Martin Lister

Available in hardback:

Transmedia Television
Audiences, New Media, and Daily Life
Elizabeth Evans

Teletechnologies, Place, and Community
Rowan Wilken

Online File Sharing
Innovations in Media Consumption
Jonas Andersson Schwarz

Online File Sharing

Innovations in Media Consumption

Jonas Andersson Schwarz

Routledge
Taylor & Francis Group
NEW YORK AND LONDON

First published 2014
by Routledge
711 Third Avenue, New York, NY 10017

Simultaneously published in the UK
by Routledge
2 Park Square, Milton Park, Abingdon, Oxon OX14 4RN

Routledge is an imprint of the Taylor & Francis Group, an informa business

Library of Congress Cataloging-in-Publication Data

Schwarz, Jonas Andersson, 1978–
Online file sharing : innovations in media consumption / by Jonas Andersson Schwarz.
pages cm — (Comedia)
Includes bibliographical references and index.
1. Peer-to-peer architecture—Social aspects. 2. Computer file sharing—Technological innovations. 3. Social media. I. Title.
TK5105.525.S39 2013
384.3'3—dc23

ISBN: 978-0-415-85430-6 (hbk)
ISBN: 978-0-203-74442-0 (ebk)

Typeset in Sabon
by Apex CoVantage, LLC

For Laura and Suzanna

Contents

Acknowledgments

I would like to thank my PhD supervisors Sarah Kember and David Morley; all of my other colleagues at the departments of Media & Communications at Goldsmiths and at Södertörn University College; all of you who have had to bear with me while finishing this work; all of you who managed to distract me; and all of you who kindly let me use the floor space and facilities that were required to do this work. Large parts of this work have been made possible thanks to Swedish research foundation Riksbankens jubileumsfond.

A special thank you goes out to all the world's file sharers—especially those of you who were so kind to lend me your opinions and viewpoints; not only my formal respondents but all of you who I have in some way or another engaged with over the course of the last decade. I owe you one.

1 Introduction

> People don't even know we're a company. They think we're two teenagers in a basement in Sweden. (Matt Mason, Executive Director of Marketing, BitTorrent, Inc., in Wortham 2012)

The aim of this book is to make for a deeper critical perspective on the current phenomenon of mass-scale file sharing on the Internet. By focusing on the example of Sweden—home to both outlaw file-sharing site The Pirate Bay (TPB) and sanctioned corporate streaming service Spotify—insights will be offered into both infrastructure and the ways personal inclination is premised on a general disposition that follows from the collective experience of such infrastructures. "Sharing" has become one of the most telling pastimes of our digital, networked age. However, as digital literacy involves both innovation and deviance, it accommodates sharing and copying in rather divergent ways: Today sharing is manifested in ways that are both uncontrollable and unyielding, as well as compliant and business friendly. One of the things that this book will show is how these two modes of sharing are related.

Peer-to-peer-based (p2p-based) file sharing has been a mainstay of popular culture since the turn of the century, as well as the subsequent debacles around applications such as Napster, Limewire, and Kazaa. It should be noted that corporate attempts at harnessing the rapid spread of MP3 technology was only later captured in innovations such as the iTunes Store in 2003, Spotify in 2008, and a vast range of other services such as Rdio, Wimp, Grooveshark, and Soundcloud that will not be discussed in this book. Since the emergence of BitTorrent in 2001, online file sharing no longer entails only music files, but movies, software, and e-books alike. The phenomenon has been an integral part of online life for more than a decade, and from my own and other researchers' findings it is apparent that unregulated file sharing has become an emerging norm—if not even a new condition to media consumption—especially among young people. In countries such as the United States, the United Kingdom, Sweden, and South Korea, access to high-speed broadband is commonplace, and the file sharers who I have interviewed and surveyed, and who speak out on various online forums, hold that file sharing is as natural an element online, as trees would be in the forest.

My own approach has been to critically engage with the justificatory discourses of the actual file sharers, taking Sweden as a geographic focus, and to interview file sharers from other countries as well, at the same time following the mediated debates closely, both in Sweden and abroad. What my research has aimed to show is how file sharers justify their own media use in the face of the activity's portrayal as a deviation from the conventional acquisition of media content. Further, a strong trust was noted among my respondents, in that unmitigated copying after all would have positive side effects that are, on the whole, beneficial to society. The potential downsides of file sharing were either avoided or met with counterarguments, but only occasionally denigrated—in fact, most of the file sharers who I interviewed offered coherent answers in defense of their behavior.

Where as this book will elaborate on debates that are largely international in character, and conclusions will be made that have general application, the example of Sweden will be illuminating also for international readers. In the last five years, Sweden has been home to both illegal operations such as the infamous Pirate Bay website and to well-known thriving business start-ups—such as Spotify—which utilize online sharing in rather different ways. What is less well known, however, is that the engineers behind Spotify honed their skills by crafting pure-play file-sharing applications (µtorrent) and that the Swedish founder of the voice and messaging service Skype, Niklas Zennström, similarly began his career in 2001 by founding Kazaa, a file-sharing program based on p2p technology, which in May 2003 was the world's most downloaded software application.

This, in turn, makes for a potentially much wider discussion, as Sweden is an ideal case study on tendencies that have—for the last decade or more—been apparent throughout the developed world but are significantly strong in this country: individualization, increasing digital access and literacy, a typically modern inclination to efficacy, and a general trust in the state as an overarching system. Further, by having invested more heavily in broadband connectivity, countries such as Sweden and South Korea have had infrastructural conditions that have benefited mass-scale file sharing in more decisive ways than the United States or the United Kingdom.

Put simply, during the last decade, the unrestricted duplication of digitized media content between autonomous end-nodes on the Internet has become an extremely popular pastime—largely involving music, film, games, and other media copied without the permission of the copyright holders. The arguments put forward in this book are not that file sharing should be seen as a phenomenon that is a priori opposed to the current, neoliberal, capitalist world order. Rather, more often than not, it hinges on the individual end user's desire to acquire entertainment and to maximize both pleasure and efficiency. As Giarin, Nuccio, and Montagnani (2012) have noted, convenience and gratuity lies at the heart of consumer behavior, both in the legal and illegal modes of online consumption. Although illegal services enable a lot of nonmainstream material to be exchanged, most of the material circulating in the BitTorrent ecosystem is not necessarily alternative or independent material. Further, such "alternative" content tends to consist of copyrighted, commercial products of the cultural industries, albeit with more narrow target audiences or commercial potential. Although the argument has been made—most successfully by Anderson (2006)—that the Internet makes possible a long tail of obscure or alternative content, it should be noted that, from a civic point of view, there would be nothing inherently different from file sharing as a mode of acquisition than legally sanctioned alternatives. Nevertheless, in allowing for this consumer agency to come about—in aggregated, not entirely foreseeable ways—file sharing has dislodged certain established industries (most conspicuously, the sales of audio CDs) while creating potentials for entirely new ones. At the same time, file sharing is being harnessed in ways that act as opposition to various centers of established, institutional order, while potentially reinforcing other forms of power and domination.

Using the recent years' developments in Sweden as a case study, in which notable actors in the file-sharing economy have surfaced, this book will thus critically expound on contemporary debates around copyright and digital infrastructure. Making a clear overview of the area while at the same time connecting the subject to political philosophy, this book is intended to appeal to both undergraduate students and more erudite readers. Among the many things that I would like to argue for in this book is the peculiar resilience of file sharing in the face of legal suppression. Several observations attest to this—not only the various statistical indications that p2p-based file sharing has continued to grow during this last decade when looking at sheer volumes of data (p2p traffic still remains high, having become surpassed by real-time streaming video only in later years), but also when inquiring about the justificatory attitudes and opinions of file sharers themselves, as a growing subfield of new media studies has begun mapping this cognitive landscape.

This is, to all intents and purposes, a new book: Only around a third of it is based on my PhD thesis (Andersson 2010). As for my own approach, it is not my intention to revisit those debates on intellectual property rights (IPR) regulation and opposition that have already been covered by others such as Lessig (1999; 2002; 2004), Vaidhyanathan (2001; 2004), and Benkler (2006). Also Burkart (2010) and David (2010) center their narratives around the legal "tug of war" over file sharing in the United States. Although some legal context is given as it is important, my book is less of an enumeration of copyright laws than it is a "media anthropology" of file sharing, similar to that of Coleman (2012), Kelty (2008), and Söderberg (2011) on open-source/hacker communities. It does not comprehensively map or explore cyberliberties activism such as that of Dmytri Kleiner's Telekommunism or

Michel Bauwens' P2P Foundation, nor is it a book about piracy in third-world countries; a (currently under-researched) field that has been explored by for example Sundaram (2009), Karaganis (2011), Liang (2005), and Pang (2006). The methods employed are less ethnographic than they are discursive. I focus not only on the ways argumentation is constituted—the justificatory motives and rationales among file sharers as a particular form of media audience—but also on the political economy enabling this sharing and forming obstacles to it.

It does not strive to romanticize activism; on the contrary, I am interested in precisely those modes of media consumption that do *not* presuppose an activist viewpoint. Moreover, I am inclined to use the term *consumer* as well as *content* when talking about culture. Many commentators, such as Fleischer (2008b), have argued against these terms—on good grounds, as such concepts are partially unsettled by file sharing. But given the proportions regarding degrees of user activity—very few upload and arguably even fewer contribute by creating their own professional content—the consumer-producer diagram is still often justified. Regarding the argument that "with copying, nothing disappears," and that cultural goods are used but not "used up" in the same way as other goods—nor are gardens, buildings, or furniture, but we can still talk about consumer markets of such things. In fact, some cultural goods can be said to be used up at the act of consumption, for example, those films that are only viewed once.

It really is a book about ethical management in an era of networked accumulation. By this I primarily refer to a Foucauldian understanding of how the self is managed. As this is a self whose agency is amplified by technology—to the degree that ordinary consumers also become (unwittingly or not) occasional activists, partial producers of structures that, in turn, effectuate a dissent toward the ruling establishment—an understanding of a self-reflexive, reactive management of the self can also be read as a template for voluntary regulation in an era marked by individual freedom and empowerment.

It is a work of media structuralism, of injecting the burgeoning field of media ecology with a more system-centric approach. It is also an account that tries to maintain an awareness of the deeply paradoxical nature of agency in this current era of media consumption, as citizens are not only consumers but equally co-producers and co-distributors, becoming occasional activists—while this is, nevertheless, only a partial performance enacted in those brief instances when their agency is in fact restricted by the particular infrastructural setup of the system (being required to upload while they are downloading). For this reason, and the earlier reference to ethical management, the book should be of interest to policymakers who seek more progressive approaches to squaring civic needs and desires with organizational equity.

Lastly, it is also a piece of contemporary history, outlining interesting aspects of the weird and wonderful stories about Piratbyrån and TPB, alongside the equally amazing story of Spotify.

1.1 SOCIAL ONTOLOGY AND NORMS

Much has already been written about copyright, piracy, file sharing, and the legal regimes pertaining to these things. However, not all of this is written in hindsight, and even less is grounded in philosophical analysis of the standpoints and arguments involved. Hence, the perspective adopted here will be inspired by Nissenbaum (2004) and her references to social ontology.

Nissenbaum argues that the conception of hacking has changed over time: an "ontological transformation of hackers from heroes to hooligans" (2004: 211). For her, the very nature of a social role is contextually defined, and since the technocultural context shifted throughout the last third of the twentieth century, so has the image of what constitutes a hacker.

> Hacking is now imbued with a normative meaning whose core refers to harmful and menacing acts, and as a result it is virtually impossible to speak of, let alone identify, the hackers that engage in activities of significant social value. (Nissenbaum 2004: 213)

In the manner that hackers have been characterized as "sociopaths, thieves, opportunists, trespassers, vandals, peeping toms, and terrorists" (Nissenbaum 2004: 204), so have file sharers. These normative terms that our language is full of have relevance not only to the discursive analysis of metaphor and law (see Larsson 2011; 2012c; 2013; Larsson & Hydén 2010) but for the reflexive ways in which file sharers understand themselves as well (Andersson Schwarz & Larsson 2013). Much of the intervention that activist groups such as Piratbyrån has enacted has been to recapture language such as this; instead of speaking of *downloading*, these activists made a point of talking about a more reciprocal *file sharing*, instead of *theft* they spoke of *sharing*, and so on.

Social ontology (Searle 1995) is defined by conventions, practices, and institutions of social life; sets of rules differently codified—some of them hard-coded, such as the protocols and applications of the Internet, and some of them soft-coded, such as norms and conventions. I would, however, argue that Searle puts too much emphasis on the social aspect of ontology. Much more suitably for our area at hand, Latour (1993; 2005) has showed that the line between the human and the nonhuman aspects of agency is hard to draw, especially when it comes to phenomena that are so characterized by technical mediation and aggregated structural complexity. Searle emphasizes "collective intentionality," but I would just as well emphasize "collectives by design"; the weight engendered through the system setup. Ontology is never really only social; however, the prefix is nevertheless useful to signify material configurations that have effects on the social world, and vice versa.

Halbert (1997) hypothesizes that the shift in the public evaluation of hackers is the result of a conscious movement by mainstream voices of governmental and private authority to demonize and portray hackers as abnormal, deviant bullies. She also mentions Ross's (1991) interpretation that because hackers expose and threaten the resilience of infrastructure, mainstream culture links the hacker counterculture with sickness and disease.

The shift toward the depicting hackers as harmful could also be attributed to the greater shift in governance toward neoliberal economic policy and, later, neoconservative security policy in which exploits that lack obvious economic motivation are suspect and exploits that directly threaten social order are seen as acts of terrorism. It could equally be attributed to the normalization of those infrastructures that, ironically, were originally built through hacker exploits. Nissenbaum explains how narratives of transcending frontiers and homesteading in the infosphere were superseded by a narrative of normalization, as a second enclosure movement was enacted: "Private property leached into and became central to all the multiple layerings of the online world" (2004: 201).

If the Internet, by the shift of the millennium, was seen as an increasingly commercially appropriated (enclosed, gated, regulated) space, it is not surprising that the unregulated file sharing that ensued was seen as a "remnant of the old anarchy" (Nissenbaum 2004: 203). The ethos of *free sharing* has been interpreted as heroic by many commentators, as it calls into memory those legendary exploits that, by and large, made the digital environment into what it is today.

What is perhaps more interesting in Nissenbaum's account, however, is how shifts in social ontology entail marginalization:

> Although shifting the meaning of hacking does not immediately cause those identified with the earlier hacker ideology to disappear, it causes them *effectively* to disappear into what Bowker and Star call the marginal residual: namely, atypical members of a category that do not fit salient characterizations. Lodged at the margins, these hackers lose their robust identity and with that goes recognition of their ideas, ideals, and ideologies that comprise an alternative vision for a networked society. (Nissenbaum 2004: 211)

In actual fact, she writes, hacker exploits had at the same time already begun to suffuse the mainstream technoculture that was allegedly hostile to it: Tim Berners-Lee was inspired by a hacker ethos; hacking provided blueprints regarding how to manage design processes; the commercial software world adopted open-source approaches; a hacker ethos suffused also those broad political coalitions that defeated the Communications Decency Act in 1996 and the Stop Online Piracy Act (SOPA) and Protect IP Act (PIPA) fifteen years later. Paradoxically, although the original meaning of hacking became untenable, key aspects of social organization were characterized by hacking writ large.

Tellingly, in the new millennium, the hacker exploit has also become an influential approach to management and entrepreneurialism. In Sweden,

Palmås (2011a) has written about how entities such as TPB upset established notions of what constitutes an economically viable innovation, as well as how economic innovation has social and political effects. In our present era, perhaps the most efficient form of political intervention is not to conduct protest in conventional, argumentative, text-based form but to construct new infrastructures altogether by way of exploits that are, in certain aspects, entrepreneurial.

These are tendencies that could equally be seen to be happening with file sharing, if file sharers are lodged at the margins while the new norm—streaming—takes center stage. This book is an investigation as to whether this is currently the case.

1.2 THE TECHNOLOGICAL AND THE POLITICAL

At the beginning of the past decade, Barry (2001) argued that the space of government is increasingly dissociated from the ways national populations relate to national territories. In contemporary technological society . . .

> government operates not just in relation to spaces defined and demarcated by geographical or territorial boundaries but in relation to zones formed through the circulation of technical practices and devices. Practices of government are as much oriented towards the problems of defending, connecting and restructuring such technological spaces, as with older concerns with the defence and demarcation of physical territory. (Barry 2001: 3)

He writes about the management of a technological society: "an era obsessed by a series of interconnected technological problems." While society could not be argued to be more or less technological than before, he maintains, questions relating to technology "have acquired a new sense of urgency and centrality in contemporary political life" (ibid.). This requires a technologically endowed citizen; not only does contemporary society ask its citizens to have the skill, knowledge, and capacities to be able to fully engage with the world, as will be seen, but also many of today's problems and disputes stem from the fact that civic control and prowess of highly advanced technologies come with their own opportunities and controversies. In a technological society, civic engagement turns on expertise. The argument could—and should—be made that political power, as a relational manifestation of the relative influence of individuals in contemporary Western society, is perhaps better exerted in their capacity as consumers and as subjects having technical prowess (e.g. an Internet user), rather than as voters.

We need to remember, he notes, that *the political* is a much wider category than that of (parliamentary) politics. The political, as Barry sees it, is "an index of space of contestation and dissensus" (2001: 7). He also notes that there can be an excess of politics, if and when countless spaces are opened up and turned political.

> A democratic politics is not one which demands that every issue should be made a political issue; it is a politics which claims that anything can be political in principle. Whether to make something a political issue, and how to resolve an issue which has been made political, is a matter of judgement. (Barry 2001: 7)

As we will see, spaces are opened up and turned into politics, but these spaces can fold and become dormant again. The mass media of course plays a pivotal and, it should be added, highly biased role here. The intense debate on copyright and file sharing during the last decade has in some ways politicized features of everyday life that had, prior to digitization, been largely taken for granted and absent from public debate. The public awareness of things such as trade agreements, copyright legislation, patenting, and infrastructural policy was recently made apparent in the massive outpouring of dissent toward the proposed ACTA and SOPA/PIPA legislation worldwide. That the interest in these issues was so geographically widespread is testament to the transnational, technological nature of contemporary government that Barry calls our attention to. The protestation against legislative proposals—by invoking the nature of the technologies that this legislation seeks to govern—is a form of protest that is typical for this technological society. As Barry points out, technical controversies are forms of political controversy. The contestation of technical designs and practices may open up new objects and sites of politics (2001: 9).

At the same time, technological conditions prescribe behaviors; they become normative by way of their design and circumstances. Pressure is not only exerted from the polity, as "national governments, international organisations and firms argue that the scientific and technical literacy of a population is a measure of its value as a workforce" (Barry 2001: 4). It is exerted from the system toward the user; the user is required to learn certain things and act in certain ways. When it comes to file sharing and copyright, activist groups such as the Electronic Frontier Foundation (EFF) reckon that the awareness of certain technical and political conditions will help foster more rational policies toward the increasingly digitized cultural ecosystem—all the while, lobbyist efforts from parts of the established cultural industries act to foster attitudes that are more understanding toward the changing conditions for these industries. And indeed, the systems that make possible the exchange of illicitly copied cultural material are, at least in their current configuration, partial to those subjects who have the knowledge and expertise to be able to access them.

As an upshot of this, Barry warns for the ways in which technological conditions tend to beget metaphors (2001: 14). Throughout the history of ideas, society has been likened to a vast array of mechanisms and organic concepts (evolutionary degeneration, the body politic, systems and structures, machines and apparatuses), and such metaphors are often inevitable, but demand interrogation. Similarly, Mansell (2012) grounds her critique of the online digital ecology in a concern that the values and ethics of stakeholders in this ecology turn upon *social imaginaries* that are very different. The particular usefulness of her approach is that she trains us to the paradoxes that these social imaginaries constantly have to negotiate. This is of great interest to me, because file sharing provokes many of these paradoxes of digital infrastructure to reveal themselves.

Reflexivity and a critical approach is vital to better understand the practical, collective, and often uncertain realities that our technological imaginaries intend to depict—everyday reality is much more complex and untidy than simple metaphors or clear-cut imaginaries would have it. Such an approach also has to be taken self-reflexively, toward one's own concepts. Hence, it is my intention to try to complement some of the more conventional ways of imagining file sharing with alternative metaphors and conceptions. Many of these rely on empirical observations that my work is based on, and I hope to lay claim to the same constructive approach to empiricism that both Barry and Mansell lay claim to. Lastly, I have tried to be wary also of my own generalizations; to me, this is the key to a reflexive and, in that sense, scientific approach.

1.3 SWEDEN: A STRATEGIC CASE STUDY

During the last decade, Sweden has seen a significantly lively mass-media debate around file sharing. Arguably, the debate has been relatively comprehensive compared to other countries, not least given the wide popularity and controversy of sites such as TPB, the relative visibility of the Swedish Pirate Party (SPP) before and after the time of the Pirate Bay trial, and the role of TPB as linchpin as a symbol for the transnational pressures emanating from the US and European Union (EU) trade interests within IPR.

What has been particularly lively has been the intellectual climate, in part thanks to voices loosely affiliated to the casually organized think-tank/activist hub known as Piratbyrån (The Pirate Bureau) and later instantiations of a similar kind, such as the lobby group Juliagruppen (the Julia Group), the transnational activist network Telecomix, and the hazy, philosophically tinted Kopimi imperative. Some leading exponents of these formations would be Rasmus Fleischer (blogging in Swedish on *Copyriot*), Karl Palmås (who runs the blog *99 Our 68*), Christopher Kullenberg *(Intensifier),* Magnus Eriksson (blogging under various guises such as Blay and Monki), and Isobel Hadley-Kamptz, who all have provided erudite, although somewhat disorganized, critiques of copyright and digitization. Several other bloggers and commentators contribute with variably politicized and often well-informed writings.

Some of the anonymous bloggers and online commentators tend to formulate rather libertarian, acerbic critiques, whereas Fleischer and Kullenberg represent a standpoint based in critical theory, strongly influenced by continental philosophy (Nietzsche, Spinoza, Deleuze, Heidegger, and Marx) and media materialism (Kittler, McLuhan, Latour, and object-oriented ontology), while Palmås and Hadley-Kamptz are more politically liberal yet equally eclectic in terms of theory. Several of these bloggers are academics and are rather extensively published by now (Fleischer 2009b; 2012a; Kullenberg 2010; Palmås 2011a; Hadley-Kamptz 2011), to such an extent that during 2009 they were criticized in Sweden's second biggest newspaper for being sectarian (Wirtén 2009).

From my knowledge of the English-, Swedish- and German-language public spheres, many of the Northern European academics, Pirate Party representatives, activists, and journalists tend to formulate critiques that have in many ways been more socially acute than many of their US counterparts, especially if one considers newspapers such as the *Guardian, Süddeutsche Zeitung,* and *Svenska Dagbladet.* This has all contributed to relatively sophisticated debates in which simplistic neoliberalism or "Net libertarianism" is shunned. Similarly, derogatory tropes such as likening record company executives to robber barons—or, conversely, likening "pirates" to terrorists—have been relatively absent from the debate. The notion, for example, that frequent file sharers tend to be frequent media consumers as well was picked up on in Sweden before it started to become widely noted by key representatives of the European copyright industry; one of the early academic reports on file sharing in Sweden (Findahl 2006) featured arguments that the record industry representatives also soon began picking up on.

At least since 2005 (when my research began), national newspapers and public service broadcasters have covered the topic rather extensively—not to speak of the debates enacted in the online blogosphere, where Piratbyrån became an interface between continental discussions about compensation systems such as "cultural flatrate" and the broader Swedish debate, which really broke into the mainstream in the spring of 2005. According to Fleischer (2008a: 99), the reasons for the intensification of the debate were two: A very controversial antipiracy raid against an Internet service provider (ISP), Bahnhof, and the implementation of the EU InfoSoc directive in Sweden. The following year this debate reached yet new levels of intensity after the raid against TPB. By that time, Piratbyrån was no longer alone in pursuing copyright criticism in Sweden; loose networks of bloggers and politicians (both on the left and right) voiced opposition against the war against piracy.

Alongside the 2009 Pirate Bay trial, two books on file sharing were published in Sweden: Rydell and Sundberg's book (2009) is the journalistic, dramatized story of TPB, while Ernst's book (2009) contains a series of interviews with various members of the Swedish political and cultural establishment regarding unauthorized file sharing and digitization. These were preceded by a more academic, theoretical critique of the Swedish file-sharing debate (Söderberg 2008) and followed by an anthology edited by myself and Snickars (2010) in which several of the abovementioned academics participated.

It appears that a generational divide runs through the file-sharing debate. Söderberg (2008: 208) notes how Swedish center-right politicians who defend intellectual property argue that a whole generation has become fostered to disregard the principle of property rights and how this is problematic for a rights-based liberal market economy. This normative acceptance for certain forms of property becomes further undermined, Söderberg argues, when noting the new business models that prosper from the file-sharing services and the potential profits that other sectors of the entertainment industry make thanks to illegal distribution channels. When a Swedish 31-year-old was sentenced in May 2008 for making available music and films, he recounted his experiences on a personal blog, and soon sympathizers voluntarily donated money to him to cover fines and legal expenses. Söderberg (2008: 35) notes that this reflects a public attitude to perpetrators that differs significantly from other types of crimes.

Yar (2008: 609) mentions "the apparent inverse relationship between age and propensity to commit copyright offences. . . . Historically, youth have been the subject of successive waves of social anxiety or moral panics, which focus upon the threat that young people supposedly represent to morality, body and property." Cultural studies have a long history of accounting for this generational dilemma, and the often hectic debates in the comments sections of online editions of Swedish newspapers (such as *Svenska Dagbladet*) during the period when TPB figured in these papers attest to a large congregation of people expressing concerns over the ongoing, widespread file sharing.

However, it would be hard to argue that these scattered expressions would constitute a moral panic or a false appearance of the same thing—as unregulated file sharing appears to enjoy a similarly strong support on the same forums. Lindgren (2010) has analyzed how newspapers reported on issues of file sharing and online piracy during 2005–2010 compared to how blogs reported on the same issues. According to his analysis, the core concerns of the news discourse were business models, copyright law, and the policing of copyright violations, whereas the core concerns in the blog discourse tended to focus less on such clear-cut issues and more on morality in general. What appears to be different is the mode of framing the issue, not necessarily the incidence of disapproving views on it.

As with my own approach, Yar turns to Boltanski and Thévenot's concept (2006) of discursive resources and strategies that actors mobilize to justify their normative claims in which rhetorical performances are seen as attempts to establish the legitimacy of a given point of view and its affiliated arguments. "Given the inherent plurality of such repertoires, there are always alternative justifications available which favor alternative norms and claims" (Yar 2008: 610). If the propensity for file sharing is not to be primarily attributed to age, rather it could be attributed to ability and a general identification with the respective roles that the technological assemblage of p2p-based file sharing assigns to the actors involved.

1.4 MAKING USER AGENCY VISIBLE: A REFLEXIVE TASK

Practices that have earlier taken place mainly in the private realm—on a vast scale but dispersed as singular events, separated from one another in space and time, and largely unaccounted for—are now made visible, searchable, and partially traceable, generating statistics that enumerate online popularity. Still, much of the accumulation online remains opaque or nebulous, as interactions remain largely anonymous and occur on such a vast scale that they can never be fully surveyed in real time. In this sense, civic sharing of cultural products has become overt. As it takes place on what is practically an industrial scale, between perfect strangers and no longer only between friends or acquaintances, it has—to some observers, especially those who have claims to controlling the products shared—become unpalatable, a moral aberration. This book is not about those observers, but instead focuses on those who actively participate in this mass sharing. Here, another aspect of visibility becomes central to understanding the preferences, prejudices, and justifications of the file sharers involved: The potential side-effects of sharing—here, I am referring not only to the potential damages to sales, but also to more existential aspects of cultural life, such as the expectations on gratification and materiality of cultural products—are, by and large, hidden from view.

Assessing the side effects and externalities of one's behavior most often involves a probability equation in which behavior that takes place in separate, private instances has to be considered not in isolation but in (vast) aggregation. What does it mean that hundreds of thousands, even millions, of consumers watch TV and listen to music in such radically de-centered and largely immaterial ways? What new norms and expectations are generated? These are questions that are likely to employ scholars of media and communication for generations to come.

The fieldwork that this book is based on comes from two systematic ventures into different file-sharing communities, resulting in in-depth interviews by means of e-mail exchanges. The first batch of interviews took place in 2006, as part of the overall fieldwork for my PhD thesis and the second batch took place in 2012, as part of research funded by the Bank of Sweden Tercentenary Foundation (Riksbankens Jubileumsfond).

The selection of respondents in my 2006 study was deliberately small: twelve Internet users, all of them Swedish, ranging between the ages of 15 and 42. Four of them were female. There was no illusion of seeing them as representative of the overall Swedish population; instead, the task was to find out what constituted a user and how this user is constituted in regard to a greater generality. Interviews were conducted by means of a continuous e-mail exchange, generating considerable data. The small size of this case study was complemented by extensive analysis of the discourse, by reference to technology and theory. My approach deliberately avoided framing the issue along predefined tropes of law, copyright, or pirates and instead allowed the respondents to elaborate on the discursive justification for unrestricted file sharing in a wider sense. The networks referred to in this study were primarily BitTorrent, DC++, FastTrack (Kazaa), and SoulSeek.

My 2012 study focused on a closed and, among film buffs, highly treasured, well-respected cinephile community. As vast amounts of movies are redistributed thanks to the BitTorrent tracker around which this community is centered, I have decided to let the name of this forum and tracker be anonymous. None of these users were Swedish; the respondents were located in Germany, India, Croatia, the United Kingdom, the Netherlands, and the United States. I also performed a few complementary interviews with users found on more open file-sharing forums, such as EZTV (these users were located in Sweden, the United States, Canada, and New Zealand). In addition, I conducted an extensive content analysis of the open answers in the so-called Research Bay survey: a global file-sharing survey with more than 75,000 respondents, conducted by the Lund University Cybernorms research group (Svensson, Larsson & de Kaminski 2013). This quantitative analysis is developed in Andersson Schwarz and Larsson (2013). All of the respondents remain anonymous, and biographical information about most of them was only available by means of interpreting their own discretionary, e-mail-mediated accounts. In the following, any personal data other than gender and age has been withheld, and names/aliases have been altered.

It is my general belief that cultural consumption is always productive—yet hampered by infrastructural settings that make for a relatively weak agency or durability at the site of reception. In some ways, what makes file sharing controversial is precisely that it enables such powerful redistributive and productive capacities yet allows these capacities to subjects whose field of vision tends to be restricted to that of the civic sphere and does not comprise an industrialist point of view.

Hence, it is important to note that my interpretation of these file sharers was to see them more as citizens and consumers rather than as representatives of pre-defined collectives, or as activists, because the activist element has been stressed in so much of the previous literature on file sharing. Nevertheless, there is of course a gliding scale between active, productive consumption, and activism. Most of my 2006 respondents were found through the Piratbyrån online forum; some, but not all, were affiliated to this forum as moderators. Likewise, some of the respondents found in the 2012 study are probably not representative of the overall population of file sharers. However, statistical representativity is not the point of qualitative research. What I will focus on in this book is one of many dimensions in the respondents discourse, namely the more general, shared experience of "networked individualism" (Wellman 2002) and the civic approach to issues of copyright and intellectual property as exemplified by p2p-based file sharing and the systemic position in which consumers find themselves, given the relative abundance of illegal content on offer and the ubiquity of connections. Hopefully, this will make for an analysis that can go beyond and transcend the mere observation of a discursive "copyfight." My account should be read as a reflexive analysis of the interpretations that I, as a researcher, make of other people's discursively mediated interpretations, in the vein of "thick description," as proposed by Geertz (1993). This will, inevitably, be colored by my own direct experiences, nevertheless with the ambition of being independent and maintaining a critical distance.

1.5 READING AGAINST THE GRAIN

Jameson (1981: 286–292) has called for a criticism that goes "beyond good and evil," trying to see both the negative and positive potentials in cultural texts. Regarding the area at hand this is particularly acute, since also the actors involved in the copyfight discourse tend to take on positions that either fall into a celebratory "positive hermeneutic," or an overly suspicious, often conspiratorial "hermeneutic of suspicion," or a more dejected "negative hermeneutic" that sees only problems and refuses to admit any Utopian potentials whatsoever. Jameson proposes a dual hermeneutic, a "both-and" criticism in which texts are read in terms of their ability to express Utopian impulses as well as affirming the status quo.

Ricœur (1970: 32) has famously asserted that the legacies of Freud and Marx (especially in the Althusserian reception of the latter) are characterized by a "hermeneutics of suspicion." What is notable with the turn to platform politics—the social ontology engendered by media infrastructures—is that it becomes more relevant to talk about "false configurations" than "false consciousness," since both sides of the current debate tend to invoke very concrete, structural arguments in support of their cause; more of an invocation to "base" than "superstructure" in Marxian terms. However, what will hopefully be shown in this book is that also more subjective, mental categories are affected by the surrounding ecology and the ways in which this ecology is grasped; platform politics hence make for a re-politicization also of the private realm.

Thus, it is always instructive to read the oppositional views that elucidate the "grain" of a stream of arguments; Levine (2011) is one such account—his view lacks all the usual ingroup praise on the sleeve, and although I too will criticize many of his arguments, it is instructive to begin here as it will reveal some of the dynamics of the debate.

He begins by noting how certain industries are bearing the brunt of free online distribution. Conventional, national TV broadcasting (e.g., NBC) is suffering, as is the newspaper industry (e.g., the *Washington Post,* the *Tribune*)—two industries that rely on advertising and that provide privileged content that is not leeched and illicitly distributed for free. As we will see, however, this mainly goes for those broadcasters and newspapers who rely on an ambition to reach the entire nation; subscription-based broadcasters such as HBO and newspapers that charge for content (e.g., the *Wall Street Journal, Financial Times,* and the *Economist*) fare better. However, the current success of these latter examples might not be as attributable to narrowcasting per se as it is to target audiences with more purchasing power.

Further, we see industries that are somewhat exposed to a current race to the bottom regarding item pricing; primarily, the DVD and book markets. Here, I would add, Amazon acts both as a price deflator, lowering profit margins, and equally as a boon to bulk sales, increasing turnaround. The effect of pure-play file sharing, as we will see with the much more well-documented but nevertheless incompletely verifiable case of CD sales, is much harder to fully assess. Levine, however, asserts that file sharing in effect constitutes a race to the bottom; dragging down prices both of online advertising and products sold.

The key touchstone of this debate, however, is whether such marginal-cost competition—in some sectors, on some markets—is a be-all and end-all when taking a macro view of the entire culture industries as a whole. Not only is consumer purchasing power freed up, and channeled differently, when some markets die hard (as in the case of CDs), but at the same time, lower profit margins can lead to higher overall turnaround (as in the case of Amazon) and thus continue to engender equitable markets. Still, I am wary, too, of those simplistic correlations that show that extensive file sharers also consume culture extensively; this argument is merely saying that people who are generally interested in culture tend to both file-share and buy stuff. It could still be the case that they would buy even more if they did not file-share.

Levine (2011: 4) focuses on something important that many cyber-liberties activists might not be comfortable to admit: The argument of "free" has an economic agenda behind it. The real conflict online is between the entertainment industries (content producers) and the technology companies (ISPs, platform providers such as Google and Amazon, hardware producers such as Apple, and new distributors such as Netflix) that thrive on distributing this content—legally or otherwise. During the last year, this has also been picked up on by some Swedish colleagues of mine (Snickars & Strömbäck 2012; Jakobsson 2012). In this context, Google's self-professed role of guarding free speech online is not less determined by a crass, commercial profit motive than the pro-copyright lobbying of the IPR interests would be (Levine 2011: 79–109).

Another really valuable insight is Levine's corrective to Stewart Brand's commonly invoked maxim "information wants to be free." Brand's original quote actually reads as follows:

> On the one hand information wants to be expensive, because it's so valuable. The right information in the right place just changes your life. On the other hand, information wants to be free, because the cost of getting it out is getting lower and lower all the time. So you have these two fighting against each other. (Levine 2011: 4)

This is a much more value-neutral observation than what is found in the often radically charged uses of the shorter version of the maxim. The shorter version has a clear activist thrust, both in the sense that information is presented as an anthropomorphized agent with active will, desire, or purpose and in the sense that humans, as conscious agents, have an active role in maintaining the dispersal of said information. It echoes what Hayles (1999) observes as the main cultural condition of virtuality: the perception that (decontextualized) information is "more mobile, more important, more *essential* than material forms" (p. 19, her emphasis). This normativity will turn out to be significant for the individual justification of continuing to copy files in the face of disapproval and denigration.

In 1990, Richard Stallman restated the concept but without anthropomorphization:

> I believe that all generally useful information should be free. By "free" I am not referring to price, but rather to the freedom to copy the information and to adapt it to one's own uses. . . . When information is generally useful, redistributing it makes humanity wealthier no matter who is distributing and no matter who is receiving. (Denning 1990)

Here, information is loaded with a purpose that is clearly utilitarian; not, however, in the strictly economic sense that copyright industries and the legislative complex have tended to frame intellectual property in recent years. We will return to the distinction between a traditionally liberal understanding of copyright (based in utilitarianism) and a neoliberal understanding (based in economism).

However, pundits such as Anderson (2009) seem to argue that there is a teleological trend toward diminishing marginal costs, making "free" not just an option, but "the inevitable endpoint" (p. 173). Similarly teleological accounts of sharing will be found below. For me as a sociologist, this self-assured zeal among many of those technologists who praise file sharing is interesting. How can they be so self-assured, and why the common lapse into totalizing arguments? The assertion that "everything" is a certain way and that it is "inevitable" must rely on more than a mere observational stance (reflecting the totalizing aspects of digitization) and a rhetorical assertion (a strategic reply to those who want to curb unmitigated file sharing). Levine gives an example of this autistic impulse by noting Google cofounder Sergey Brin's befuddlement as to why an author would choose *not* to put his book online for free. Brin's assertion seems to be that the mere act of making something accessible would render it popular and, automatically, profitable. Information idealists seem to believe that cultural distribution is all "pull" and forget the fallible realm of human affairs: reporting, editing, marketing, and "pushing" a product, since hardly anyone would find it otherwise. As I will expand on later, perhaps it is the industrial connotations of the latter term—"pushing" content—that is tricky for citizens to accept, especially with the added narrative of greed and ostentatious profits in the cultural industries.

However, the great stumbling block for accepting Levine's otherwise thoughtful criticism is when he argues for turning what he characterizes as a massive "online free-for-all into a free market" (2011: 7), because the attempts of doing so have been so largely sweeping, ill fitting, and sometimes all-out draconian (at least in some legislatures; in Sweden the actual cases against private individuals have actually been very few). The nature of the digital infrastructure makes it immensely hard to effectively and comprehensively curb illicit file sharing without imposing an Orwellian control society. The ease of copying, and the ease by which the smallest leak can engender files that are endlessly recirculated present what I will call "the Pandora problem" (see Chapter 2). Here, Google-affiliated pundits such as Patry (2012) provide proposals—essentially, asking for a reconfiguration of copyright from the bottom up—that are, after all, more progressive than those more predictable, path-dependent proposals of Levine (2011) and Keen (2007).

Put simply, regarding the potentially authoritarian impositions needed to curb file sharing, this is after all where I—as many other cultural studies academics alike—split ways with Levine, although I would easily agree with him on many of the various problems with the current situation. For me, the biggest problem with unmitigated file sharing is that it engenders altogether new, unmitigated market mechanisms, which tend to fall into patterns of networked aggregation in the shape of so-called power-law distributions, favoring the endlessly long tail of obscure independents as well as the small handful of vastly popular blockbusters but disfavoring the group between them. The blockbuster economy thrives on financial muscle, and the amateur economy on enthusiasm and adaptation, while these "middling middles"—driven by talent—risk falling behind and bringing whole genres and art forms with them (see Section 2.8).

There is one more point regarding the highly granular, vastly interconnected scale-free networks that comprise the flooding world markets engendered by digitization. Based in a conventional management culture where target audiences are thought to cluster around the probable median, critics such as Levine do not seem to be able to embrace emergent phenomena and the notion of aggregating value out of countless transactions that each have infinitesimal profit margins: While Levine (2011: 11) holds that online newspapers are ruined as a result of the race to the bottom regarding the value of online ads, actors such as Google nevertheless manage to generate value through its AdWords and AdSense programs, based on an algorithmic mode of extraction. Spotify similarly does so with its remuneration model for individual plays. It is quite wrong, as Levine seems to argue, to say that infinitesimal profit margins will not engender any viable business models at all. However, this new mode of extraction is of course problematic in itself: It only benefits the biggest of players. Much like Shapiro and Varian (1999) predicted, those who own or control the platforms become the rentier capitalists of this new era. Further, it does not engender particularly pleasant advertising experiences, as low-valued inventory makes for poor-quality ads (Morrissey 2012). What is more, it is based on a managerial mindset that demands culture to be metered down to the most granular level. As I will argue later in the book, this has grave philosophical implications.

Further, Levine (2011: 9) is right to criticize the simplistic recourse to "rights" among file sharers, when their arguments are found to defend inane examples such as the alleged "right" to download *Iron Man 2*. But this is nevertheless a disingenuous way of sidelining the argument: It is, after all, manifest that a dimension of civic rights has been lacking in all but one legal directive in the EU over the past two decades, and that the US legislation is, if possible, even less committed to civil rights such as the right to privacy, the right to access to vital information, the right to assembly, and so on. In Europe, it has only really been the Data Protection Directive in 1998 that seeks to account for the civil interest first and foremost. The US has no single data protection law comparable to this directive. Instead, the approach taken is one of little federal intervention and a combination of reactive legislation and industry self-regulation. Recently, a Federal Trade Commission (FTC) proposal promotes a framework by which "consumers can compare the data practices of different companies and exercise choices based on privacy concerns, thereby encouraging companies to compete on privacy" (FTC 2012: 61). Those formal acts and regulations that govern personal privacy are patchy and have been formed on an ad hoc basis; in general, the constitution is thought to safeguard free speech and (implicitly) privacy (see Movius & Krup 2009 for a further discussion). In addition to the 2001 Patriot Act—that effectively works to the detriment of privacy with regard to governmental surveillance—a range of privacy-related acts have been issued (Movius & Krup 2009: 174; Vogl 2013[1]). To compare, since the Copyright Act of 1976 went into effect (in 1978), the US has expanded the copyright law fifteen times on issues related to "stopping piracy" (Masnick 2012). See Section 2.1 for a further discussion.

Levine seems to think that the Digital Millennium Copyright Act (DMCA) was too much of a compromise benefiting the technology companies, as it allows for so-called safe harbors, freeing ISPs from liability if copyrighted works are transmitted over their networks and enabling a culture where actors such as YouTube can benefit from uploaded music or video, as long as they remove it when asked (2011: 10). A similar principle exists in the EU under the Electronic Commerce Directive (2000/31/EC), which was implemented in Sweden as a law concerning e-trade in 2002. It is not my intention to go into details about the DMCA here—numerous people have commentated on it and criticized its vagaries, from Litman (2001) to Khanna (2013)—however, suffice it to say that the standpoint typified by Levine is miles apart from those cyberliberties proponents who point to the dysfunctional elements of the DMCA and wish that the compromise would have been more toward civic accountability than a business-to-business affair.

1.6 MY STANDPOINT

In this book, I will elaborate a methodological approach of discerning and critically assessing different justificatory regimes (industrial, domestic, and so on). Hence, it is illustrative also to make explicit my own personal standpoint: my own reliance on particular, justificatory regimes.

First and foremost, the primary justificatory regime that I align myself with is that of an archivist mode of interpreting culture in which file sharing is, in many ways, seen as a way of maintaining or safeguarding a sprawling, living archive of cultural content. Further, as a cultural studies scholar interested in media audiences and the particular situatedness of such audiences, I also align myself with a more vernacular approach, where civic access and consumer freedom are paramount.

Would this make me partial to the accounts of the file sharers and activists whose arguments I dissect? Not if we consider the disinterested utilitarian standpoint that I also ground my arguments in: One of the things that I observe among these pro-sharing accounts is the ways they risk overlooking the long-term effects or unexpected externalities, such as that of an increasingly sclerotic media economy in terms of equitable models for media production despite an outward appearance of continued, or even increasing, diversity.

This critical approach can in fact be traced back to a radicalization of the archivist standpoint, since the concern for a rich, variegated output of cultural works would have to go beyond mere concerns for free flow and domestic, decentralized storing of such content to actually engage with the conditions and incentives for cultural production. It is a common historical experience that an unmitigated free-for-all rarely has particularly progressive effects on those forms of cultural production that rest on a temporary respite from the aggressive totalism of a de-territorializing world market. Clearly, regulation has a role to play here—the key question is how to organize such regulation without falling into an equally totalitarian rule or an overly lax neoliberal conception of industry self-regulation. Further, my own perspective also involves a radicalization of the vernacular approach of civic agency in that I am wary of the technocratic aspects inherent not only to the corporate management of culture in an era of cloud storage and spotification but also to the technocratic aspects inherent to unmitigated file sharing alike.

2 Initial Orientations / Outlining the Conflict

Observations and Potentials

–Are you from Sweden?

–No, I'm from Internet.

The *celestial jukebox* was a term coined by Goldstein (1994) referring to a "system by which we could quickly and cheaply download any text, video, or sound that fit our fancy"—a utopian notion of media convergence and convenience (Vaidhyanathan 2005: 135)—but equally, a libidinal machine, both driven by and realizing human desires. To the surprise of many people, pundits included, it manifested itself sooner than what was thought possible.

The only problem was that this manifestation was entirely illegal at the time; only later, the formally administered, legally sanctioned sphere was able to catch up and establish services equally convenient and convergent. This book is an attempt at retelling this story, with an eye to social ontology and material processes that unsettle and destabilize the question of what constitutes the political. It is also an attempt at provocatively asking what types of sociality and which forms of distribution of resources are made possible by digitization, both in its formally illegal mode and its legal one.

Digitization can in many ways be seen to engender a radicalization of many things that are inherent to society at large. Land (2011) has brought forward the notion of *accelerationism*: Rather than halting the onslaught of capital (such as by defending a welfare state or defending the right to work), accelerationism is a philosophical and political strategy that strives to exacerbate its processes to bring forth its inner contradictions and thereby hasten its destruction, to accelerate them beyond the control of the established gatekeepers of capitalism. The roots of accelerationism are found in the post-68 reception of Nietzsche and materialism in French philosophy (e.g. Deleuze & Guattari, Lyotard) alongside the Italian operaismo movement (e.g. Negri, Virno), two genealogies that were revisited in the 1990s theory fiction of Nick Land, Iain Hamilton Grant, Sadie Plant, and the Cybernetic Culture Research Unit. Central to these theories is also the famous distinction, developed by DeLanda (1996) via Braudel (1982), between markets (bottom-up, granular, self-organizing networks) and anti-markets (oligopolistic, capital-accumulating, predatory control regimes). This genealogy can be criticized; Brennan (2006) shows how this way of thinking is to engage in a very risky pact with neoliberal development. The hopes that the system will eat itself might, at the end of the day, only serve to further exacerbate neoliberalism.

Illegal file sharing can be said to be accelerationist in that it challenges the capitalist system by over-affirming it. Capitalism generates a desire for movies, but instead of enjoying a small sample after paying for it with money earned through labor, the file sharer misappropriates the system by consuming everything at once. I will not expand on the deep philosophical baggage that accelerationism comes with, but it is worth mentioning in connection to the concept of networked accumulation that I will develop.

In an era of file sharing instead taking place through encrypted tunnels, darknets, and virtual private networks (VPNs), Fleischer (2010a; drawing on Fuller 2005: 23) has proposed a strategy parallel to accelerationism: *escalationism*. This concept is more similar to the classic hacking strategies such as finding security holes, making exploits, and building darknets that elude control. Eriksson (2010) characterizes it as a way of harnessing desires generated by capitalism, but implementing them in ways that are not capitalist.

Therefore, he argues, escalationism is a politics of probability in which one acts in areas where possible future conflicts or crises could arise. This very clearly relates to the hacker teleology described by Nissenbaum in chapter 1.

> Once the crisis is manifest, escalationism is no longer possible in that particular field. The paranoia that comes with these tactics is well-known in the hacker world and succinctly illustrated by *Terminator*. Sarah Connor must destroy Skynet before it is built, since once it is constructed it is too strong to resist. But is it really the guy who builds chess computers who is building the Skynet of the future? Must he be killed, and his equipment destroyed? A possible non-paranoid escalationism would not propose destroying Skynet before it is actualized, but to prepare in advance for the day Skynet is built (in whichever form it will occur). An unexplored possibility in the Terminator universe is that Skynet has redundant causality [a teleological development] and therefore will come about through any number of processes (that's probably something that Nick Land would have agreed on). TV drama assumes that Sarah Connor must look for *exactly that* person who is building Skynet, but in actual cases of development of technology, this occurs through entire actor-networks that are partly independent of the efforts of particular individuals. This is important for Internet politics. What does it mean, for example, to possibly be able to stop agreements like ACTA, when the forces that give rise to it still exist? What makes an agreement like ACTA possible? How can individual victories be used to

> dampen those forces instead of waiting for the next bad thing to happen? (Eriksson 2010, my translation)

Perhaps this preparatory, risk-averse approach is typical for welfarist countries. Later in the book we will come to know the activism of Eriksson, Fleischer, and other Piratbyrån affiliates as a distinctly Scandinavian approach to cyberliberties activism, in that it retains a welfarist impulse.

A third concept that seizes on the inherent amplificatory power of digitization is the notion of *contagionology*, coined by Kullenberg and Palmås in an essay with the same title—in short, a re-appropriation of a "forgotten" school of sociology:

> Tarde argued in favour of an epidemiological conception of society. However, his points of departure were not very successful. The modern bio-political states were unable to find proper use for his style of reasoning, partly because Tarde argued against ascribing social processes any pre-defined logics and categories, and partly for the lack of instruments of quantification and statistics. Even though quantification may not be necessary for sociology, it has become attractive for governing hierarchical and stratified societies.
>
> Instead the twentieth century became Durkheimian, since his demarcation between social and natural facts rendered a domain of knowledge which was measurable and quantifiable, while simultaneously securing solutions to the bio-political goals of modern states. (2009: 1)

The emergence of digital technology reactivates a Tardean conception of society, not only through the panspectric surveillance diagram (explained further in Section 7.3) but also in the ways digitization enables both duplication and tracking of social phenomena. Tarde's micro-sociology is sharply contrasted to theories presupposing a general consciousness (Marx), a norm system (Durkheim), or principles of organization (Weber); for Tarde, imitation is the essence of the social. Behaviors spread through societies (human as well as nonhuman) by means of actors repeating other actors. However, repetitions only exist as potential variations. No repetition is ever fully identical with the original but is always a displacement and a variation. In Deleuzoguattarian terminology, Tarde "stresses the primacy of molecular intensities over the striations of molar aggregates and statistical reduction of complexity" (Kullenberg & Palmås 2009: 2).

What prompted these authors to revisit Tardean ontology was the turn to Tarde initiated by Latour (2005), Latour and Lepinay (2009), and Barry and Thrift (2007). As Latour has pointed out, digitization makes manifest many of the elements of Tarde's "universal repetition": Computer viruses work through a logic of contamination (Sampson 2011) and replication; piracy is enabled through the ease of near perfect duplication; innovation works by way of processes of imitation and adaptation; and digitization prompts new social practices such as remixing and upgrading. Later in this book, this contagionology is related to cyberliberties activism and the concept of Kopimism: "The 'copy me!' imperative is not only to be understood in ethical terms. It is at least as important to understand it in ontological terms" (Kullenberg & Palmås 2009: 6).

At the heart of pirate politics lays a potential that I would call the Pandora problem: the simple fact that a leaked piece of content, no matter how minimal, will potentially be duplicated and multiply—very much like in the tales of Pandora's box or the genie in a bottle. This is interesting since it prohibits those approaches to regulation that operate by raising the bar for engagement and rely on a Gaussian, probabilistic calculation that a significant majority of interactions will be averted. Instead, it prompts a totalitarian, all-or-nothing-like approach to regulation: If only one genie is let out of the bottle, it will spread and multiply—hence, no genies can be allowed. The Pandora problem is attributable to a combination of the accelerationism and contagionology inherent to digital data.

The problem is that, in reality, trying to adopt such regulation is of course deceptive, often undemocratic, and potentially regressive. Further, this all-or-nothing nature of digitization is repeatedly invoked also by those who defend the current status quo of unmitigated sharing: The file sharers I interviewed held that since total blockage is both impossible and undesired, no regulation should be attempted. The all-or-nothing nature thus prompts an equally totalizing mirror image; the deceptive ideal of an entirely free flow of culture. What I will show is that this mode of circulation also engenders undemocratic distributions, taking the form of extreme long-tail curves (Pareto distributions). What will also be expanded on are the various forms of governmentality that this entails, given that networked individuals are invested with a huge degree of freedom and (relational) power—a latitude that is a function of the size and scope of the overall system and a latitude that is, statistically speaking, unequally distributed, but nevertheless prompts a mode of regulation that hinges more on voluntary self-regulation than on command-and-obey structures from above. I will not make a huge detour into the land of Foucault, but as many of the theorists briefly mentioned here, he will figure in the conceptual background.

Tellingly, complex networks of interrelating agents tend to cluster in so-called scale-free or small-world ways, forming distributions that are similarly unequal. The network society thesis, formulated by Castells (2000) contains an ontology (a way of devising the nature of society) that, in turn, can be seen to be radicalized by Latour's actor-network ontology. Actor-network theory (ANT) suggests that the world is populated by hybrids, but that hybrids disturb the ways modernity envisages society (Latour 1993). Hence, the hybrid ontology of the world is repeatedly underplayed, hidden from view, and unacknowledged. One example is how the field of sociology tends to presuppose that the social is an exclusively human affair, while what can actually be said to make society durable, to separate our civilization from that of (equally sociable) baboons is the ways in which we invest our sociality into material forms.

For Latour, what constitutes modernity is indeed this tendency to categorize the world, to demarcate allegedly separate dominions:

culture—nature
human—nonhuman
private—public

Latour (1993) stipulates that this great ontological split of modernity entails an "act of purification"; constantly ongoing and repeatedly performed by social actors. What will be shown in this book is how file sharing—as an absolutely unique case study in hybridity—acts to upset a range of such dichotomies.

2.1 LEGAL CONTEXT

This book will place file sharing in the context of a small, highly technically developed, highly consumerist society at the periphery of the US-EU power axis. As a case study, the focus on Sweden will reveal various tendencies that can be transposed onto Anglo-American debates. As we will see (Section 5.6) specific US-based interest groups representing multinational companies can be suspected to have directly pressured the Office of the United States Trade Representative (USTR) to influence Swedish politics and law to benefit those trade groups by placing Sweden on the Special 301 Watch List: a blacklist not intended to directly sanction US trade partners but to name and shame them.

We will also see how the harmonization of EU law forces certain binaries of copyright law in the open, such as the distinctions between private and public and between legal and illegal. Further, we will see how file sharing is highly concurrent with the idea of an autonomous, individualized media consumption. We will also see how pirate politics in many ways illustrate the turn to a more neoliberal, less welfarist, post-social democrat way of conducting politics, while many of the conclusions actually made by people affiliated to TPB echo a welfarist approach to policy. Tellingly, both the politics of the traditional Right (combining a concern for maximizing market conditions with conservative values and outright moralism) and the traditional Left (combining, as we will see, a corporatist union- or sector-based subsidization of culture with a bell-curve interpretation of society, poorly adapted to the more extreme mechanics brought about by contemporary network society) involve statist, authoritarian modes of regulation that fall out of favor with cultural consumers such as those examined here.

This crisis between self-imposed, voluntary regulation and authoritarian, statist regulation is also seen in the current, EU-wide crisis of social democracy and in the current neoliberal approach of re-regulating the economy by means of further regulatory frameworks. This allows us to understand the market model of broadcasting regulation, and it also allows us to understand the turn toward Net neutrality. European Commission directives demand that competition authorities must pre-assess public service broadcasters' new inventions to consider whether they distort markets or not (European Commission 2009: §88; Donders & Moe 2011). Similarly, Marsden (2010) has outlined the market concerns implicit to the uneasy balancing act between various regulatory frameworks regarding Net neutrality (co-regulation, industry self-regulation, or even regulated self-regulation).

Further, exposure to globalized markets is often said to exert deregulatory pressures, but the penetration of globalization is not equally distributed; nor is it in any way an a priori force that should be presupposed (Hafez 2007). Rather, as we will see, it can be traced back to explicit trade interests and disparities in terms of power and influence—domestically as well as transnationally. Following, I will briefly outline the industrial context to the file-sharing debate, as the trade interests of the United States have resulted in an "upwards ratchet" of global IPR legislation (Sell 2008). Support for this claim can be seen in the balance of trade in cultural services between the United States and the EU. It can also be seen in the appearance of mechanisms created by the US Congress to formalize bilateral and multilateral trade agreements with strong antipiracy and anticounterfeiting terms, as well as in plurilateral trade agreements, such as the Anti-Counterfeiting Trade Agreement (ACTA), that are negotiated at executive levels with foreign ministries.

In Sweden, the act of downloading copyrighted material that has been made available without the consent of the rights holder—that is, not only redistributing said material—became illegal in July 2005, in accordance with the Directive 2001/29/EC of the European Parliament and of the Council of May 22, 2001, on the harmonization of certain aspects of copyright and related rights in the information society, also known as the EU Copyright Directive (EUCD) or Information Society (InfoSoc) Directive. So-called private, domestic copying became restricted to a much smaller group of people. Moreover, the original copy has to be legally acquired. As we will see, this enforces a norm of what is private and public. Since the enactment of the InfoSoc directive, several individuals have been prosecuted, also in Sweden (where legal cases were rare prior to 2005). Many of the current prosecutions are not related to BitTorrent, however, but to earlier applications such as Direct Connect that tend to make the participants more trackable (Goldberg & Larsson 2013).

In the United States, the precedential nature of the legal landscape makes it more ambiguous, but in the case of *Capitol v. Thomas* (previously named *Virgin v. Thomas*), the jury instructions in a retrial in June 2009 mentioned both violation of the copyright owners' exclusive *reproduction right* (the act of downloading copyrighted sound recordings on a peer-to-peer network, without license from the copyright owners) and their *distribution right* (distributing copyrighted sound recordings to other users on a peer-to-peer network, without license from the copyright owners), but there was ambiguity regarding which of these violations would have actually motivated the verdict in this retrial. Generally, what has been accentuated in US tort law is whether actual financial harm would be induced on the copyright holders, and the defense attorneys in *Capitol v. Thomas* thus made the argument that the plaintiffs had not, in fact, been able to prove actual harm incurred by the defendant—only by file sharing in general. According to this line of reasoning, what would have to be proven is whether the making available of files on a p2p network would constitute distributing more copies and—further—that there would be a trickle-down effect akin to being at the top of a pyramid of distribution that would cause multiplicative damages to copyright owners. The claim that there are such cascade effects, often voiced by the copyright industry, is most likely a deliberate strategy serving to set precedents that would induce an upwards ratchet of fines; for example, the retrial in *Capitol v. Thomas* actually resulted in fines of $1.92 million for the willful copyright infringement of twenty-four songs (on average, $80,000 per song), but this verdict was later appealed.

An important conclusion I am making in this book is that both sides of the copyfight seem to make references to potential network effects. The contention that one single act of making available would have trickle-down effects—in the vicinity of $80,000 per song redistributed—could be argued to be as tenuous as the dispute that one single act of downloading would lead to exposure that, in turn, precipitates further consumption that would, on average, weigh up the potential negative effects of this illicit download. Larsson (2012b) examines the inflated cost of file sharing from the viewpoint of sociology of law; two key reasons for prosecutors to inflate claims in this way is to, on the one hand, generate publicity and instill fear and, on the other hand, force the accused sharers to settle the matter outside of court, thus avoiding the risk of legal precedents that weaken the industry position.

Following the discussion on Barry (2001) in the chapter above, it could be argued that the EU is itself a technology—it is a structure and an invention that redefines and creates altogether new possibilities of governance (2001: 213). Media policy in the EU is interlinked through a range of regulatory documents relating to everything from media distribution, media content, IPR, public service, and general trade rules on competition, corporate ownership, and concentration (enacted through agreements such as TRIPS). Further, seemingly unrelated supranational decisions and rules also affect media policies (e.g., harmonized tax rules applied to culture and the media; issues of data protection and retention; and health, consumer, and environmental policies affecting advertising). A common theme to this regulatory discourse is the dichotomy of civic concerns (on the one hand, plurality—on the other, a common European cultural heritage) versus market concerns (maintaining a strong internal market, stimulating competition within the EU, and protecting it from strong external influences such as Hollywood); see Christensen (2008).

Generally, media policy within the EU has always acted to balance market interests with civic ones, although the case can be made that market concerns have begun to weigh more explicitly (Hesmondhalgh 2007). Contrastingly, the United States has a tradition of refusing to ratify United Nations (UN) pacts; it does not fully recognize moral rights within copyright law[1]; it deliberately shunned UNESCO negotiations on human communicative rights during its twenty-year refusal to confer with this UN agency (Mattelart 2011); and it aggressively pursues a policy regarding civic access to the Internet that flies in the face of UN instructions that "three strikes" policies in fact violate basic human rights (La Rue 2011: 14). Both Geiger (2009) and Grosse Ruse-Khan (2009) have argued that civic rights should be used as a balancing force to a potentially ever-expanding IPR ratchet, not least since

> fundamental rights and human rights represent ethical values which enjoy widespread consent and acknowledgement under international law. In the context of globalization, they offer a "human" legal framework for the advancement of intellectual property, which so far has been regarded exclusively from an economic point of view. (Geiger 2009: 40)

Within the multilateral regulatory landscape, a more civic approach to IPRs—rather than the one-sided market approach embodied by the Office of the United States Trade Representative (USTR)—can be attributed primarily to the UN, for example, in its emphasis on human rights applied to communication and the media (Mattelart 2011; Shaver & Sganga 2009), but also in parts of the EU and its emphasis on public value (see Jakubowicz 2011) and "the cultural exception" (Palmeri & Rowland 2011). The historical heritage, underlying the Berne convention, of *droit d'auteur* (splitting copyright into moral as well as economic rights) remains strong in several of the EU's constituencies and can—at least potentially—act to moderate multilateral agreements. On the other hand, no clear definition of allowed, fair uses exists in the European tradition; various fragmentary permits are listed, under different laws, depending on medium or purpose (photocopying, photography, databases, artworks, quotations in text, and so forth).

Copyright means that the artist/producer grants someone the rights to reproduce copies of the artifact that he/she has created, normally in return for a negotiated fee. Digital rights management (DRM)—the technological protection systems against the disallowed access to or copying of a copyrighted artifact—are already in place in, for example, DVDs, eBooks, video game consoles, Internet streaming, and password-protected sections of websites. Burkart & McCourt (2006) explore the interaction of DRM and personalization services—sometimes called CRM (customer relationship management)—in the operation of the celestial jukebox, an underlying business model for new media that has come to engulf practically all interactive media experiences. CRM-DRM remains the underlying logic of the celestial jukebox, they argue, embodying surveillance and traceability in its core system architectures. In fact, the idea that artists would be the main holders of copyright is rendered moot by the fact that, in actual practice, these rights are held by publishing companies that act to collect fees when, in turn, consumers seek to access, purchase, or hire copies of the artifact. If consumers wish to own a legal copy, they normally must pay the negotiated amount.

However, this too becomes problematic as copyright traditionally holds exceptions for secondary uses (such as the exchange of secondhand CDs). Although it is perfectly legal throughout the world to resell CDs or books you have bought, when it comes to digital files, most countries have restricted this right of secondary use to only cover personal backup copies and the like. In the United States, this right to resell is referred to as the first sale doctrine, which gives people who lawfully own copyrighted material the right to sell their copy to a new owner who can decide to keep, give away, or sell it. This is in line with international praxis. However, first sale law does not provide anyone with the right to make additional copies (Anderson 2008; Giese 2004).

The DMCA criminalizes the act of circumventing an access control (a technology, such as a password or encryption, that controls who or what is able to interact with the copyrighted work), whether or not there is actual infringement of copyright itself, but the act of breaking copy protection ("cracking" it) for personal or fair use would not be prohibited. It is a violation of the DMCA to provide tools to others that circumvent copy controls, but it is not a violation of the DMCA to engage in the act of circumventing copy controls. The EU InfoSoc Directive, however, prohibits circumvention also of copy protection measures, making the European legislation potentially more restrictive. Cracking copy protection, as in the earlier example, would in fact be illegal under InfoSoc. By using DRM, record companies can restrict reselling of content sold that would, in fact, have been legal had the content not been in the shape of a file (as computer files, as we know, have to be copied every time they are reused). There is, therefore, a great irony to DRM: It is largely inefficient for keeping copy-protected content out of the hands of warez sites and torrent search engines, yet it inhibits secondary markets for such products.

In fact, DRM hinders such markets twice. First, for users who try to stay legal and sell only used copies of games, music, and movies they have purchased, the DRM scheme needs to be bypassed in each case, by each user. Actually, DRM even makes criminals of those who do break the DRM to sell their files. Second, the market for secondhand legal products is undermined by the circulation of ripped, illegal copies that are available practically for free, often even being technically superior in that the unwieldy DRM authentication step is removed, or—as in the case with ripped DVDs—without unnecessary prerolls, ads, and menu extras.

For music CDs, DRM fell out of fashion as a result of Sony-BMG's root kit fiasco of 2005, explaining the subsequent discontinuation of copy protection on audio CDs by major companies (Grassmuck 2010: 32). Meanwhile, DVDs and Blu-ray discs have DRM built in by default, whereas commercial music files and computer software see even further entrenched DRM regimes because of the establishment of Internet-connected machines. With cloud-based products and services such as Steam, Xbox Live, or Netflix, convenience is increased—users can often access their files from anywhere, using any machine, and have full access to their accounts—but legal secondhand markets are even more restricted here. Games bought on Steam, MP3 files bought on iTunes Store, or *World of Warcraft* characters are to be regarded more as subscriptions limited by a particular time span and access restrictions than products that buyers can freely dispose of as long as the physical carrier endures.

2.2 DISCOURSES ON FILE SHARING: DIFFERENT FORMS OF BIAS

Similar to much of the contemporary discourse on the governance of the Internet, the debate around p2p has had a strong US bias, especially regarding questions of legality, economic redistribution, and future prospects of the entertainment industry. The discourse recurrently makes reference to two particular antagonists: On the one hand, the representatives of the entertainment industry or the law-enforcing establishment, often explicitly supported by the Recording Industry Association of America (RIAA), the Motion Picture Association of America (MPAA), or the International Federation of the Phonographic Industry (IFPI), depicted as being engaged in a veritable battle with, on the other hand, the activists of the Net, often libertarian by ideology, and partially synonymous with the hacker/cracker/warez communities that willingly describe themselves as pirates, file sharers, or geeks in general. The latter groups congregate in online fora such as TorrentFreak, ZeroPaid, Techdirt, Slyck, and Slashdot. TorrentFreak is a blog dedicated to original reporting on file sharing, started in November 2005 by Lennart Renkema under the pseudonym Ernesto van der Sar, alongside Andy "Enigmax" Maxwell, and Ben Jones who joined in 2007. Rickard Falkvinge, founder of the SPP, is a regular contributor.

Although I would make the argument that both economism and utilitarianism are agnostic to the sectorial and unionist interests the copyright industry embodies and thus can be used to argue both for and against unmitigated copying, the pro-copyright argument is based on a conservatory ethos: the

Lockean ideal that cultural producers should be able to benefit from their labor. Yar (2008) has deconstructed the mythological nature of this ideal.

Yet, paradoxically, there appears to be a conservatory thrust also among the copyleftists, in the sense that they in many ways argue for a reversal of the expansion of copyright law to a previous state, something that seems to be paralleled by a rather artisan ideal of culture, which commentators such as Keen (2007) has criticized as a "cult of the amateur." These issues appear to become increasingly acute the more technology becomes characterized by two extreme poles of openness and closure. This impulse is related both to the ideal of the First Amendment and to the romanticized notion of an untarnished vernacular culture of horizontal sharing, invoked by Jenkins (2006), Bruns (2008), and others. It can be criticized as prioritizing free flow as an alleged default—the highly mythological "idea of a pure global communication" (Lovink 2003: 24), which becomes "overrun by 'dirty' market forces and even more 'evil' government regulators" (p. 52). This notion idealizes digital communication—it ignores the highly institutionalized, protocol-governed structure of the Internet (Galloway 2004) and assumes it to be akin to a natural, premodern state of similarly free flows of culture.

What a number of authors, including Lessig (1999; 2004) and Vaidhyanathan (2001; 2004), have in common is that they take as their principal examples those spheres of agency where a certain stance is pronounced among the actors involved: that of deliberately creating alternative platforms of peer production or business models of user-generated content or of using platforms such as blogs and wikis for expression (grassroots media production). Strangelove (2005) advances the proposition even further in his diatribe against the established copyright regimes, suggesting a polarity between allegedly "active" (radical) and "passive" (pacified) use, through embracing and arguably overestimating the "expressive freedoms" of Internet users, much like Lunenfeld (2011) has done later. Strangelove deliberately wants to counter what he sees as dominant narratives of a pacified, commercialized media audience through arguing that "culture jamming" and anti-corporate activism would be the most prominent elements of online youth culture, emphasizing the "individual's new role as a content producer" (Strangelove 2005: 6) with a significant "ability to create and disseminate cultural products" (p. 7).

Michel Bauwens (2002), one of the founders of the P2P Foundation and an articulate proponent of p2p, presents a similar narrative of comparing the new, innovative practices of cooperative intellectual work by today's "class of knowledge workers" with the solidarity of the labor movement that originated from the industrial working class of the past. He cites several commentators to argue for an analytical extension of the idea of p2p as a technical paradigm to the socio-cultural sphere at large. As in Lévy's "collective intelligence" thesis (1997), Bauwens argued for a form of "evolution's arrow,"[2] pointing toward a future of mass cooperation, self-organization, and sharing. When he quotes Dutch academic Kim Veltman in stating that "the advent of Internet marks a radical increase in this trend towards sharing," it seems to me that what is presented is a teleological account of technology, a predestined history.[3]

There is, I would argue, an activist bias inherent in much of this espousal of p2p as an emancipatory technology that sometimes borders on the quasi-religious. Much of it comes from an assertion that many file sharers, cyberactivists, and Net libertarians seem to make: that they are being actively persecuted by a looming, nefarious media industry that forces any alternative formation to become hard-lined and creative in inventing new ways to keep sharing. This assertion is somewhat misguided, however, when one comes to reflect on the fact that the very same media industry is striving to find similar ways of creatively harnessing user agency. Indeed, the whole Web 2.0 hyperbole was exactly about this. Already in 2006, just as the boom in social networking sites (SNSs) was taking off, Henry Jenkins noted that Web 2.0 enterprises are in effect instantiations of media corporations increasingly picking up on insights from fan forums and grassroots media activism. What is adopted, he argues, is increasingly a strategy of collaboration rather than an outright prohibition of these consumer-led movements (Jenkins 2006). In the later, more critical view typified by scholars such as Mark Andrejevic, Trebor Scholz, and Christian Fuchs, this harnessing is equated with exploitation. The media industry is seen here to effectively appropriate decentralized consumer agency for both creation and circulation of media content to come about, and it does so in ways that rarely involve direct remuneration to these decentralized authors. Media corporations appropriate vast amounts of user labor without making it clear who will benefit monetarily from this (Jenkins 2007). This has more recently been picked up on in theories like the "openness industry" thesis (Section 2.9).

Further, the noncommercial aspect of the activist bias risks overstating the alleged altruism of file sharing. Indeed, it is useful to regard p2p-based file sharing as a vital part of the radically increased media convergence that is taking place as a result of the rapid digitization of consumption, production, and distribution. Convergence brings about multiple ways of accessing media content and "ever more complex relations between top-down corporate media and bottom-up participatory culture," Jenkins argues (2006: 243). With the entirely digital modes of consumption and distribution that we see on the Internet—both legal and illegal—consumer and producer roles are blurred and occasionally clash, as media consumers become more like participants and co-creators of transmedia narratives, infrastructures, and communities, and traditional media producers try to harness this participatory agency. The argument is congruent with Anderson's (2006) concept of a long tail of accessible media back catalogues, which assumes a savvy media consumer actively seeking out content and recommending it to peers.

What is appealing about Jenkins's account is that—in contrast to much of the literature on hacker culture (Jordan & Taylor 2004; Atton 2004; Strangelove 2005)—it is based on fandom rather than political radicalism. Fandom fosters participation and knowledgeability, but not necessarily activism. The active, creative re-appropriation of media forms here comes from the love of particular subcultures, particular works or authors, particular forms of media, rather than from any allegedly oppositional political stance relating to the political organization extraneous to these media. And in those modes where use necessarily becomes more politicized, what is acknowledged are infrastructures that do not force users to take a specific political standpoint, but instead favor modes of use that generate possibilities for occasional activism, such as the "smart mobs" of Rheingold (2003) or the "adhocracies" of Doctorow (Jenkins 2006: 251).

The productive forces inherent to consumption are utilized through the accumulation that digital networking makes possible. New infrastructures are built around unpaid user activity—something that could be labeled a regenerative form of entrepreneurship that does not take into account whether the infrastructure that is constructed is legal, illegal, or somewhere in between. This is one of the key arguments of this book. In the semi-legal hubs exemplified throughout the book, the activity of building a functioning service or site tends to have taken precedence over the activity of negotiating licenses and allowances for it to come about; this latter activity came *after* the first one, not the other way around. Much as TPB managed to build new infrastructure around the scattered activities of individual file sharers, Spotify managed to build a rogue archive of mp3 files that users could remotely access via streaming protocols, before reaching a deal with record labels and ultimately succeed to make the service legit.

Further, these new infrastructures engendered have, as we will see, implicit rules of engagement, or prescriptive agencies, which can be said to foster tacit assumptions, such as, for example, that a wide range of cultural content should be available entirely for free—which prompts novel ways of approaching cultural economy, such as much more elastic pricing schemes or, alternatively, more holistic proposals such as cultural flat rate. Another assumption that is fostered could be that what is downloaded and consumed is not really official, never fully accountable—an observation that could be used both as an excuse for one's illegal behavior and, additionally, as a template for novel ways of valuing digital media. Ultimately, one could take the much more novel view, espoused by the members of Piratbyrån, that there is a deep, ontological difference between infrastructures of *access* and infrastructures of *community*, even *communion*. The Kopimi movement (see Section 5.4) testifies to this central distinction.

In the typically American Net libertarianism of Rheingold, Bauwens, Lessig, and others, the term *community* is regarded as foundational to society. The roots of this particularly American technologically progressivist communitarianism are traceable not only to McLuhan but to Etzioni's (1968) visions of an active society of mass participation and community-based media (cf. Mattelart 2003: 89–91). Toffler (1980) expressed similar visions of an impending de-massification of the media thanks to all-encompassing digitization. Söderberg (2011: 79–83) shows how the notion of an information society is linked to the post-industrial society thesis (Bell 1976), which, in turn, is akin to historical materialism in that it presents a new grand narrative designed to rival Marxism (Barbrook 2007). Further, the forecasting of a rise of a networked mode of production—espoused by Benkler (2006) and Raymond (1999)—has longer roots as well and is wedded to a notion of the end of ideology (Bell 1962) where differences between traditional liberalism and socialism are thought to fade, through the onset of an technocratically managed consumer society of abundance and convenience. Post (2009) relates the ideals of the open Net to the Jeffersonian legacy of civic autonomism and many of the self-sustaining communes of the hippie era—blueprints for online communities such as the WELL—idealized the heritage of settlers and precarious self-organization on the frontier. See Burkart (2010: 82–85) for a good overview of this New Communalism.

It is therefore perhaps not surprising that analysts are trying to seek this quality in online milieus, ever since Rheingold's virtual community thesis of 1994. Perhaps this is why the amorphous mass phenomenon of p2p is often described in the activist terms the way I outlined it, fueled by the narrative seduction that is offered by the often anecdotal tales of de facto instances of innovation and establishment on the digital frontier. Activism implicates a strong emphasis on individual agency and serves well to tell those stories of groundbreaking innovation that the historiography of culture is so keen on capturing—in the same way art historians always value the first of whatever style of expression or advertisers always focus on the early adopters. Similarly, as Burkart (2010: 97) points out, "critical theory looks for empirically identifiable expressions of social conflict, and then discovers, to the best of its ability, whether they are cases of oppositional agency, and whether they are linked to political and economic changes."

Perspectives that strive to emphasize opposition or resistance are problematic, because they risk missing the complex phenomenon of the resistance infrastructures themselves "spilling over," having externalities: As we will see with cases such as TPB, although the intent was to build an alternative distribution system, it could be argued to have actually reinforced the primacy of the entertainment industry in unexpected ways. At the same time, however, these infrastructures also spread distributed forms of activism-by-proxy, as preferred uses and behaviors become embedded in the emergent infrastructure by those who build the applications and configure the networks. Hence, another narrative is needed for capturing the experience of making do with what is already in place: both the alternative hubs and the larger, variegated economy they are embedded within.

Sweden makes for a telling corrective to well-worn narratives of resistance. In Chapter 5, I will show how this country is characterized by a mode of self-reliant individualism that is, compared to other countries, extreme. Still, the same individualism is premised on a reliance on the state, on forms of collectivism that from Anglo-American perspectives might appear confusing, if not deeply paradoxical.

2.3 TECHNOCULTURAL IMAGINARIES

According to Ross (1998) and Miller and Slater (2000: 16), two types of libertarianism are typical among technologists: a more free-market-oriented neoliberalism and a Net libertarianism, more closely related to postmodernism and its recognition of the arbitrary, relativistic nature of information. The main difference between these flanks, since the commercial appropriation of the Net from the 1990s onwards, pivots around the idea of proprietary software and the attachment of monetary value to information (Ross 1998: 9). The doctrines of free information and the unfettered, disembodied nature of the Internet (akin to the idea of cyberspace as a place apart duly criticized by Miller and Slater) are strong. Combined with an "untrammeled individualism" (Ross 1998: 10–13) and a hedonistic embrace of the abilities and freedoms of the end user, much of the discourse surrounding the Internet ignores the physical efforts, the material conditions of production, that are necessary for the preservation of the systems in question, a tendency being illustrated by Barlow's (1996) widely acknowledged "Declaration of the Independence of Cyberspace". This tendency seems to transpire also into the more recent discourses on p2p, Web 2.0, and social networking.

Furthermore, Ross argues, this ignorance sometimes translates into a general phobia about any regulation or government activity—not just those relating to new media—which is ironic, since state policies everywhere have not only restricted but also governed and even facilitated the shape of information industrialism.

One can thus see how Net libertarianism and rudimentary neoliberalism might be more closely interrelated than initially expected, especially given the convenience and individual gratification underpinning the establishment of p2p implementations. However, the example of Sweden will also attest to a more social-democrat, collectivist approach. Barbrook (2005) noted, early on, how the Net can be found to accommodate both untrammeled neoliberalism and anarcho-communism, and endless examples could be listed that would attest both. It is not my intention to go through them here, but one thing should be noted: Within the motley crew behind TPB, both anarcho-libertarian leanings (Gottfrid Svartholm Warg) and eco-socialist ones (Peter Sunde) can be found. Later, the site came under management by the Swedish wing of the Pirate Party. It would therefore be unwise to say that a service such as TPB would have been tainted by one ideological leaning alone. Once again, piracy tends to become what one makes of it—as the term remains vague, it can be charged with those political connotations that are most expedient to the observer. We will return to this expedient character of piracy later in the book.

Further, there is another paradox. Although no notion of freedom is absolute, Miller and Slater conclude, it takes the form of a normative structure, a social order (2000: 16). As with other discursively mediated concepts, the nature and ideal state of freedom are subjects of negotiation in which the most powerful exponents often are the ones that take semiotic command. This tends to obscure how freedoms are always normative, negotiated, and constructed. The copyfight thus appears to be a conflict not so much between freedom and constraint (as if these were simple, self-explanatory, singular concepts) but rather as a range of conflicts between different models of order and normativity (Miller & Slater 2000: 18), relating to what kind of freedom should be granted to the end user. Both sides of the debate imply that p2p brings about decentralization and diffusion of power, emancipating the user and disturbing the established order of the entertainment industry. Nevertheless, the core of the debate seems to hinge on whose vantage point to adhere to.

Latour allows us to conceptualize the material aspects of agency: what can and cannot be done with the Internet, and what the Internet lends itself to. At the same time, conceptualizing technological agency as an imaginary is something that begets different orders of reflexivity—what agents consider that they can do with the Internet; the ways they imagine their own scope of action; the ways they reflect on the what everyone else are thought to know.

2.4 "DOWNLOADING" AS METAPHOR

Since the turn of the millennium, *downloading* has been a recurring topic in the mainstream media, as well as in everyday conversations, where the illegality of the phenomenon—acquiring copyrighted content without the permission of the copyright holders—has taken center stage. As we have seen, words are political as they shape the ways we conceptualize social reality. I would hence agree with the activists in that it is more etymologically correct to speak of *file sharing* instead of downloading as, by default, most such downloading makes the user simultaneously upload while being in the process of acquiring the file. File sharing unsettles the ontological status of consumers, producers, distributors, and cultural objects alike; it unsettles the notion of what it is to be a consumer, a producer, and a distributor and, more importantly, what the digitized cultural object actually is.

Yet, the term downloading implies not only a direction and a topology—the user is located *below* the entity that is accessed, and the data flowing to this user is moving *downstream*, as if pulled by gravity and coming from a higher place. The nature of most domestic Internet connections follow this diagram: ADSL connections, for example, offer downstream speeds that tend to be ten times as high compared to their default upstream speeds. The etymology of downloading, as a term, is closely intertwined with the client-server model of computer networking and its presupposition that users access databases by way of dial-up connections. As I will show in the initial chapters of this book, file sharing as it is commonly understood today has been preceded by various modes of internetworking: the server-to-server model of the early Arpanet and other proto-Internet instantiations, such as Usenet, in the 1970s; the BBS scene and Fidonet of the 1980s and 1990s in which users interfaced with databases through modems directly dialing telephone-based switchboards; and the dial-up model of the 1990s in which subscribers dialed their ISPs who in turn acted as gateways to the wider Internet. In Chapter 6 I will make the argument that not only has p2p-based file sharing started to be replaced by so-called cyberlockers, or one-click hosting sites, in recent years, but also a lot of pure-play p2p-based file sharing appears to be premised on a client-server-like model: Users tap into repositories such as TPB, where vast collections of torrent links are hosted and then start their torrent clients, "tapping into" an already ongoing circulation, a torrent of data. Hence, I would like to maintain the following arguments:

First, file sharing is, among the file sharers whose accounts I have taken part of, associated primarily with acquisition and only secondarily with sharing and redistribution.

Second, it is a form of copying that seldom has malicious intent; it is enacted out of positive effects for the content shared, rather than as a form of retribution toward particular industries or artists. It is markedly different from the conventional use of the term piracy in that it—unlike historical piracy, both actual and imagined (Johns 2009; Selman 2008; Wilson 1991)—does not involve active violence and/or bodily harm; the only potential damage is to certain preexisting sectors of the economy.

Third, file sharing, in the everyday meaning of the term, differs from counterfeiting in that it does not entail a profitable business for the person engaging in it—which is not to say that the avoidance of paying can sometimes (in those rare cases where the artifact would otherwise have been bought) act as a form of monetary gain; nor that institutional actors can make money out of facilitating the actual hubs or spaces where this civic sharing takes place; nor that, for everyday users, some kind of value is of course extracted from the file-sharing transaction.

Because of all this, the term *piracy* is deeply problematic when referring to file sharing, for reasons that will become apparent throughout the book. The term file sharing is a broader, and technically more correct term than downloading, and it is less morally charged than the term piracy.

2.5 "PIRACY" AS METAPHOR

The definition of piracy has, according to Litman (2001), changed over the relatively few years that it has been used to describe the activity of copying. Today, the metaphor is used to describe any activity that involves some kind of unauthorized copying, despite the fact that much of this copying is legal. Ironically, a lot of new behaviors and business models in the present media landscape rely on what might previously have been based on strategic responses to such counterfeiting; Hill (2007) lists such responses. A critical reading of these responses would ask when the responses themselves become permissive to further copying (by yielding to requirements of increased openness, free material, lowering prices, etc.). Hill notes how piracy can be made to signify any one of these four examples:

1. Active counterfeiting of goods, with clear profit motive
2. Duplication of goods, with clear profit motive
3. Duplication of goods, without profit motive
4. Consumption of pirated goods.

Even among institutional actors, these definitions are not clear-cut. The Pirate Bay trial shows that it is in fact hard to determine whether many of the more professional, dedicated file-sharing hubs are susceptible to point two or three, as a certain degree of profit is required for running costs. Hill (2007) includes the last of these points—consumption of pirated goods—in his definition of piracy and points to four contributing factors among consumers:

1. social consensus (peer pressure, norms)
2. feelings of inequity (value relative to price, lack of fairness)
3. low concern with the ramification of one's actions toward society in general (moral development having reached what he calls the postconventional level)
4. lack of moral intensity (magnitude, proximity, probability of effect).

While the first three points can be attributed to age, all of these points can be related to the psychology of what Suler (2004) has labeled "the online disinhibition effect"; the tendency among Internet users to do things they would have had a more ambiguous attitude toward if they were to perform them without the cloak of (semi)anonymity and the other distancing mechanisms that the online experience entails.

A working hypothesis, when assessing the file sharer discourse critically, would be to note how it takes place in a situated context, where externalities and side effects are generally only approached by the users through resorting to probabilities—often supported by anecdotal evidence and statistical indicators. We will return to this issue of visibility and probability later.

Another discovery that Litman has made is that the definition of piracy has changed over the relatively few years it has been used to describe a copying activity. She has argued that piracy used to describe people who made and sold large numbers of counterfeit copies—the first of the four points listed earlier—and that today, the metaphor is used to describe any activity that involves some kind of unauthorized copying (points one to three). As she puts it, not all of this is illegal: "The content industry calls some behavior piracy despite the fact that it is unquestionably legal" (Litman 2001: 85). This shows how metaphors can be socially renegotiated and expanded, and how this expansion can be affected by power structures at play (Larsson 2011). As both Yu (2003), Litman (2001), and many others have noted, copyright law is "long, wordy, complex, cumbersome, counterintuitive, and internally inconsistent" (Yu 2003: 133). Especially on the Internet, copying precedes and far outweighs the regulation of it. Pang (2006) cuts to the core of the problem: *Copying* is, in fact, a wider cultural phenomenon than those instances of culture that are regulated by intellectual property management.

This argument underpins also those more recent accounts that emphasize the unregulated, unruly undertow of digital life; there is an entire subfield of media studies that emphasizes the libidinal, hedonic aspects of unregulated information ecosystems and the productive aspects of vernacular media usage. Authors such as Deuze (2012), Pasquinelli (2008), Boon (2010), Fuller (2005) and anthologies such as Parikka and Sampson (2009) all underline the libidinal undercurrents of the economy; much of this theory comes out of a genealogy in continental philosophy that emphasizes human affect and desire. Lyotard (1993) has criticized Deleuze and Guattari in that their emphasis on "desiring machines," "immanence," and "pure production" cannot be sustained because there are no illegitimate uses for desire; it has no moral compass. The invocation of desire can also be criticized, as the recent reappropriation of Land (2011) shows, for being overly anthropomorphic.

Numerous other authors have specified the ways in which civic, not-for-profit copying of cultural artifacts becomes controversial, often arriving to the conclusion that file sharing—as a "disruptive technology" (Oram 2001) that destabilizes certain earlier sectors of the economy such as copyright licensing, sales of recorded music, film, and computer games, and software development. However, as we will see in the coming chapters, although a lot of the discourse on file sharing during the last decade has pointed to the latent undoing of entire preceding capitalist structures, more often than not the actual implementation of it is more similar to existing capitalist infrastructures than its proponents would admit. The content shared is mainly the same content that the entertainment industries want us to covet. Local file-sharing communities emulate market strategies of barter and trade, ratios and barriers to entry, while nevertheless maintaining a sharing that is radical in its near total disavowal of monetary reimbursements. Meanwhile, commercial operations such as Spotify and Facebook utilize p2p networking as a mere technical means to efficient data transfer, "under the hood," while being tied to a centralized broadcast model in terms of usability. The example of Grooveshark is more conspicuous in that this is essentially a p2p service masked as a streaming service (Lindvall 2011a; 2011b). In these later cases, p2p is merely a way of making current operations more efficient in terms of agility and speed at the point of delivery.

If the rhetoric of the proponents and opponents of file sharing is to be taken as an even more recent example of piracy, it becomes clear that the term takes on a secondary meaning. The arguments by the abovementioned authors of the pre-Internet era can be said to be characterized more by the traditional, literal meaning of the term, while its secondary, more rhetorically malleable meaning connotes a pirate *imaginary* or *persona*. The pirate becomes an archetype that can be applied differently according to how one wants to frame the issue. In fact, the choice to label illegal file-sharing piracy has had some rhetorically productive consequences for the file sharers themselves.

2.6 THE ECONOMIC IMPACTS OF FILE SHARING

The debate about whether unmitigated file sharing reduces the market for music and other creative content is perennial. It is not my intention here to elaborate on this debate; I will briefly touch on some insights. Various studies have different conclusions. Generally, a direct causal link between widespread unauthorized file sharing and falling CD sales is hard to establish. However, the two tendencies have coincided since the shift of the millennium. Levine (2011: 268, n74) lists several studies that indicate an impact from file sharing. More extensive summaries of research come from Pollock (2006), Grassmuck (2010), and Tschmuck (2013).

A central question is that of sectorial impact compared to macroeconomic impact. A study commissioned by the Dutch government (Huygen et al. 2009) concluded that the economic implications of file sharing regarding general welfare were, on balance, strongly positive in both short and long terms. Conversely, however, file sharing was found to probably have resulted in a decline in sales of CDs, DVDs, and games. Levine pricks several of the rosy accounts of the allegedly limited impacts of file sharing, especially the often quoted paper by Oberholzer-Gee and Strumpf (2004), who have later conceded that file sharing appears to have had effects on music sales. A key insight Levine provides is that music has become much more of a hobbyist venture and that the "long tail" of obscurity is endemic: Out of seventy-five thousand albums released in the United States in 2010, sixty thousand sold fewer than a hundred copies, and many of those sold fewer than ten (Levine 2011: 65).

Over the past decades, movies, software, and video games have also been subject to copying and piracy, yet these industries seem to have remained less blemished by file sharing. It is also important to note that drops in record sales occurred also in the late 1970s and early 1980s and that CD sales in the 1990s may have been abnormally high as individuals replaced older formats with CDs. However, during 2004–2009, sales of newer releases declined more than sales of older ones and declined more in countries with high degrees of file sharing, indicating an impact by file sharing (Levine 2011: 63). There have been periods of boom in the 1920s, 1940s, late 1950s, 1960s, and 1990s—all of which were followed by periods of slump in the 1930s, late 1940s, and early 1950s, 1970s, and also in the 2000s (Freedman 2003). In virtually all of these historical periods, Lessig (2004: 69) notes, technology was seen as the problem to which bans and legislation were the answer; a mode of regulation that is premised on a split between the technological and the allegedly nontechnological in which measures are thought to be imposed onto technology from the outside, as if it were. Freedman (2003) similarly asserts that the music industry, when faced with technological uncertainty or declining sales, historically tends to turn to "discourses concerning copyright and intellectual property as a means of controlling its environment and adapting to changing market conditions" (p. 175). The video games industry has taken a more lateral approach in which the solution has been to restrict the hardware either by proprietary formats such as cartridges and specially engineered consoles or by effectively allowing for a significant degree of home copying alongside selling computer games and software on duplicable floppy discs and (later on) CD-ROMs. Liebowitz (2006a: 151) correspondingly lists several economic studies on software piracy in which "the existence of unauthorized users creates additional value to the purchasers of legitimate copies and thus might increase the profits of the seller." Gayer and Shy (2004) and Curien and Moreau (2005) also attempt at formulating more holistic models of the impact of file sharing on revenues from music and software by accounting for various network effects.

The video games industry is revealing in that it has, over the course of the last decade, changed emphasis in the business models for many of its products, so that revenue is generated mainly from subscriptions to multiplayer communities, such as in the famous *World of Warcraft* series. Freedman (2003) lists the two typical counter-efforts as being litigation and the development of new (proprietary) services. These latter services, harnessing the network effects, can include subscription services, financing by advertising, sales of extraneous products (concerts, merchandise, etc.), and price discrimination (leveraging different prices on different parts or versions of the content) (Söderberg 2008: 187; Anderson 2009). This is also concurrent with early findings by Shapiro and Varian (1999), namely that if you control the platform (the operating system), you can skim money out of every single transaction being made on this platform. Whether the platform is given away for free to users is secondary. Windows is the most widely pirated operating system in history; a dissemination that, according to this view, hardly damaged Microsoft in the long run. Shapiro and Varian emphasize the importance of building a network around one's product, making each node dependent on this network, thereby advancing various forms of "lock-in" effects. Interestingly, we will see that pirates such as Sunde and critics of digital life such as Lanier (2013) in effect embrace similar, extractive platforms in their embrace of remunerative systems.

Within the field of econometrics, Liebowitz (2006b) has argued that of the various plausible factors for explaining the drop in CD sales in the last ten years, file sharing would, however, most likely be the main one. He bases this in a comparison of various music genres in which the genres exposed to high volumes of file sharing also showed a larger drop in sales. In a later study (2011), he examines the econometric studies that seek to explain the share of the decline in CD sales that could be attributed to file sharing. The mainstream view in the papers he collects is that file sharing would have been responsible for almost the entire decline in CD sales since Napster. He argues that while it is generally accepted that a large majority of empirical studies have found that file sharing has caused a decline in the sales of prerecorded music, the size of the estimated piracy-induced decline is hard to assess—largely because of the lack of a metric across differing empirical methodologies, different time periods, and different geographic regions. He proposes that the share of the sales decline explained by file sharing should be used as key metric.

In Liebowitz's analysis (2006a), the incentive to buy CDs has dropped significantly when exposed to the same songs, albeit in lower technical quality, online, and for free. "In fact, the alternative to file sharing might not be the purchase of CDs, but instead might be the activity of listening to radio" (Liebowitz 2006a: 153). Interestingly, the recent proliferation of streaming services such as Spotify has made this analogy even clearer.

It is nowadays uncontroversial that avid file sharers also tend to be avid consumers of culture in general. File sharing might stimulate a higher exposure or sampling of music, increasing demand (Liebowitz 2006a; Andersen & Frenz 2007). Karaganis, Grassmuck, and Renkema (2012) have shown that the average American file sharer has a music library of almost 2,000 songs. Of these, 760 would be legitimately purchased (38 percent). In contrast, those who say they are not p2p users (but do collect digital music files) had an average library size of 1,300 songs. Of those, 582 were purchased from legitimate sources (roughly 45 percent). However, studies of this kind do not show whether file sharers would have actually purchased even more music from legitimate services, if it was not for the p2p networks.

During the period between 2005 and 2008, the British press began to acknowledge much of this: The entertainment industry was thought to have weathered the economic crisis purportedly instigated by unauthorized file sharing, and certain sectors of this industry were in fact doing well (Gibson 2005; 2008; Keegan 2008; Wallis 2008). More importantly, a realization about the commonness of unregulated file sharing (especially among younger people) seems to have led many cultural commentators to have accepted unauthorized file sharing as a part of the contemporary cultural landscape.

Already in 2005, British consumer research agency the Leading Question found that those who admittedly downloaded or shared unlicensed music on a regular basis also spent significantly more money on legal services.

The average spending on legal downloads among these groups was £5.52 a month, compared to the average monthly expenditure on digital music among those who were not illegally file sharing, which was only £1.27 (Gibson 2005). Paul Brindley, the agency's director, commented:

> There's a myth that all illegal downloaders are mercenaries hell-bent on breaking the law in pursuit of free music. In reality they are often hardcore fans who are extremely enthusiastic about adopting paid-for services as long as they are suitably compelling. (Gibson 2005)

During this period, even representatives of the music industry began acknowledging this. Glen Merrill (formerly Google's chief information officer, later digital strategist for EMI) said: "There is academic research that shows file sharing is a good thing for artists and not necessarily bad. [. . .] We should do a bunch of experiments to find out what the business model is" (Gibson 2008). Similarly, the ubiquity of unregulated copying led Disney co-chair Anne Sweeney to state that piracy "is just a business model" to be competed with (Wistreich 2006), signaling a different attitude toward unregulated file sharing where Disney regards itself as the mainstay for putting out content in the first place, lending them primacy in the life cycle of products.

Another use of statistics would be to infer a ratio from the estimated relative sizes of illegitimate to legitimate downloads, which is then extrapolated to expose the impossibility of industry estimates (Larsson 2012b). This is illustrative as a means to show how the numbers certainly are rigged and that, equally, such statistics do not hold in terms of validity and reliability: Since the first factor (the estimated relative share of downloads that are legal versus illegal) is undetermined, the figures are always bound to be estimates. For a range of reasons, this becomes spurious; no total overview is possible. The sharing is regionally diversified, constantly shifting over time. Further, illegal sharing is subject to definition. What counts as a download, exactly? What about duplicate versions of the same file that are downloaded, for example? Further, how are numbers of downloads related to actual consumption? We know that there is an unknown number of downloads where the artifacts are in fact never consumed.

> [IFPI] is still putting it around that illegal music downloads outnumbered tracks sold by a factor of 20:1 last year, as if that bore any relation to lost sales. Only a tiny proportion can in any realistic way be attributed to downloads. Or do they think that CD sales should be something like 20 times higher? (Keegan 2008)

Regarding the regulatory landscape, in their review of all copyright-related directives within the EU between 1990 and 2005, Montagnani and Borghi (2007) argue that economic disputes have strongly influenced all directives.[4]

> A review of recitals accompanying the directives reveals a huge recourse to arguments directly or indirectly connected to economic-utilitarian views, and only sporadic and largely insubstantial use of personality right rationales. (Montagnani & Borghi 2007: 233)

Jakobsson (2012: 72) notes that allegedly "economic" and "utilitarian" arguments—even though they are linked in the earlier quote—are not the same thing. Utilitarian arguments can be made in support of things such as heritage, research, and education—that is, on grounds other than sheer economic benefit. While the Anglo-American copyright tradition is normally said to be utilitarian, the European is said to rest on the *droit d'auteur* tradition. He argues that it would be the economic disputes rather than the utilitarian ones that indicate an influence of a neoliberal rationality in recent years; this is in line with Hesmondhalgh's (2008) observation of copyright serving neoliberal interests and Foucauldian understandings (Brown 2003; Burchell 1993; Dean 2009) of neoliberalism as primarily a mode of regulation serving the artificial arrangement of entrepreneurial, competitive subjects (proactively trying to generate markets) rather than the naturalistic impulse of traditional liberalism (retroactively trying to safeguard markets that are thought to be naturally occurring).

As we have seen, the legislative process regarding IPR within the EU is marked by an ongoing concern between civic values and market values; however, the pressure from foreign trade interests forces a bias toward market concerns. Although the EU-wide harmonization of copyright directives has primarily been based on the concept of "adequate legal protection as a means to increase production" (Montagnani & Borghi 2007: 214), using this to solely argue for a strengthening of copyright would, however, be a perverse reading: Increased productivity could just as well be to rid the market of the loss of economic efficiency that results "due to the creation of unnecessary monopolies over non-rival resources such as cultural and information goods" (ibid.). Even a strictly economic approach toward cultural regulation need not be synonymous with the clinging to copyright maximalism; it could just as well be agnostic to copyright, if copyright is found to impede overall economic efficiency.

2.7 EXTERNALITIES AND WELFARE EFFECTS

According to the industry view, if the rights holder does not wish for someone to have ownership of a copy of the artifact without paying a fee, and a person nevertheless copies it without paying a fee, then that person would have infringed on that artist's legal right and has stolen an amount of money from that artist by overriding the transaction required for a legal copy. According to the civic view, however, only very rarely would an actual copy acquired from a file-sharing network otherwise have been purchased.

Once again, we are seeing the structural problem of delimitation, as the civic economy is in fact a wider economy (Pang 2006) than that subset of the cultural economy that is strictly managed by econometrics (i.e., by invoking measurable, calculable monetary returns). This larger "general economy,"[5] explored by sociologists, anthropologists, and philosophers (e.g. Braudel, Bataille, Mauss, Bourdieu) is premised on other logics than mere revenue maximization (capitalist extraction of monetary value) alone; it draws on the notion of a gift economy (determined by familial bonds, psychosocial factors, and communal exchange) and the notion of a shared commons. Burkart (2010) invokes Habermas (1987) when framing the ways industrial logic eats itself into everyday life as a "colonization of the lifeworld." Nevertheless, as we shall see, also this wider cultural lifeworld contains elements of utilitarian, value-maximizing thinking, some of which is accentuated by file sharing. Titmuss (1971) has shown that economic logics are determined by the ontological status of the product that is disseminated. As with the fallacy of externalities in neoclassical economics, the perceived nature of a disseminated product is not only a matter of disagreement among the agents involved. The settlements around what a product is and how it is therefore thought to be managed actually determine how it is managed (Callon 1998).

If one takes a more holistic view on the entertainment industry, the general exposure generated by file sharing makes it likely that the artists get remunerated in alternative ways (through merchandising, DVDs, radio/TV airplay, concert tickets, or sponsorship deals). This was argued for in some early accounts (Silva & Ramello 2000), and it seems to have become more of a mainstream view in recent years. Here, network effects, convergence, and cross-ownership should also be accounted for—something that, of course, makes simple statistical overviews hard to make. This helps explaining why the debate so often returns to probabilities and estimates. Effects can be noted in the live music, software, hardware, and telecommunications industries, which are all said to have benefited from file sharing, at the expense of the recording industry (Cammaerts & Meng 2011).

Grassmuck (2010) discusses papers that employ a so-called welfare analysis—the sum of consumer surplus and producer surplus, accounting for so-called network effects (i.e., an increase of consumers' valuations of a product with the number of other consumers who adopt the same product). Bayaan (2004) was one of the first papers to apply this mode of analysis to the music industry, looking at the gains or losses not only of firms but of other actors as well. Grassmuck points out that *price differentiation* (he takes the example of how Nine Inch Nails released an album in a variety of packages) is better suited to this dynamic than *flat product pricing* (one-size-fits-all CD prices). The increase in the size of the network resulting from copying increases the valuations of high-valuation consumers, enabling the firm to sell them at a higher price than it could charge without copying (Takeyama 1994: 160).

Rob and Waldfogel (2006) have been approvingly cited by IFPI (2010). They hold that file sharing allows consumers to engage in a do-it-yourself form of price discrimination. Albums that tend to be low valued are not candidates for being purchased in the first place, but if the prices for legal consumption can be held down under a certain threshold, a lot could be gained, especially since the marginal cost for production is low anyway. Aggregate welfare would be increased if more of the actual consumption could be harnessed and accounted for—and price elasticity is one way to recap these "grey zones" of media consumption that would otherwise be unaccounted for. In retrospect, it is clear that ad- or subscription-based models such as Spotify are sensible alternatives, at least when it comes to music, which is a product that is enjoyed in repetition; movies are a different kettle of fish in that they are normally only consumed once.

Two problems with radical price elasticity, however, could be that (a) revenues accrued from network effects mainly benefit large artists, where the network is large and consumers stand to benefit from greatly valued exclusives and collectables and (b) pricing stands in a direct causal relationship to aggregated demand that, again, only benefits those acts where demand is high. The advantage with the traditional record label model is that artists signed are granted marketing budgets and thus the possibility to spark further demand. Historically, this model has worked through profitable blockbusters subsidizing a range of potential acts (most of them, however, ultimately failing). Arguably, this latter model makes for safe harbors for more ambitious creativity—something that risks falling by the wayside in a world of happy amateurs and virtually no record contracts available for budding artists.

New, Internet-based fund-raising platforms such as Kickstarter are attempts that act to remedy this matter: They allow for a crowd-funded safe harbor by asking ordinary Internet users to back projects in advance, in exchange for a tangible reward or one-of-a-kind experience. An ambitious budget can be established, by giving advance promises of exclusive, status-laden products or services (tickets to pre-screenings, being mentioned as a sponsor in the ending credits, limited edition, perhaps signed copies of the product, a personal note of thanks, custom t-shirts, etc.), but it is too early to say whether—and if so, in what ways—this will act to engender new demand or merely funnel the existing demand. Further, will actors such as Kickstarter be a boon to creativity that is not marked by utilitarian, philistine expectations of "delivering what is expected"? It is of course important to note that the record label model of patronage was riddled with problems, but the excess that high profit margins allowed for also meant possibilities for risk taking, sometimes idiosyncratic creative effort; the existence of "golden eras" within music and film should attest to this.

2.8 NETWORKED ACCUMULATION AND THE "DEATH VALLEY PROBLEM"

In recent years, an insight has emerged—in management theory (Andriani & McKelvey 2011), anthropology (Hart 2004; 2010), economics (Anderson 2006), and sociology (Lehmann et al. 2007) alike—that a world premised on networked complexity begets so-called power-law distributions and a market or population characterized by that form of accumulation has somewhat different characteristics than populations characterized by Gaussian (so-called normal curve) distributions. A key premise if this book is that this type of networked accumulation takes place through and within legal markets and illegal ones alike.

A Gaussian distribution (often called a *normal* or *bell-curve* distribution) describes any variable that clusters around its central tendency; it describes parameters that are causally unrelated from one another and tend to fall into statistical patterns based on random variation (one example being human height or shoe size). Gaussian models, however, fail to account for the emergent properties of systems that derive from connectivity within or among systems. A Paretian distribution (often called a *power-law* or *long-tail* curve), on the other hand, takes place when positive-feedback processes result in extreme outcomes occurring more frequently than normal, bell-shaped, Gaussian-based statistics lead us to expect.

As Andriani and McKelvey (2011) have explained, there are several explanations to power-law distributions. They typically hinge on interdependence among data points and a possible ensuing positive feedback or other scale-free processes:

> Herein lies the problem for "normal" science: most quantitative research involves the use of statistical methods presuming *independence* among data points and Gaussian "normal" distributions. The many findings of natural and social PL phenomena, however, indicate that *interdependence* is far more prevalent than "normal" statistics assume and the consequent extremes have far greater consequences than the "averages" in between. (Andriani & McKelvey 2011: 96)

Power laws seem ubiquitous: they characterize earthquakes and hurricanes, and they appear (as fractals) in leaves, coastlines, and music. The frequency of words used in natural language and the distribution of molecular reactions in cells can be plotted as long-tail distributions. Cities, when ranked by population, often fall into power-law distributions, as does the size of firms and the popularity of Web pages. The long tail distributions described by Anderson (2006) are typical manifestations of a power-law distribution.

> The "new science of networks," growing out of the physics of complexity, has been announced by authors such as Albert-Laszlo Barabasi

> (2002) and Duncan Watts (2003). Just as, in the late 19th century, the normal distribution seemed to lend unity to statistical patterns emerging in a number of apparently unrelated fields, such as criminology, astronomy and plant genetics, now the power-law distribution appears in fields as disparate as the worldwide web, stock markets, air transport, Hollywood actors' networks, electric power grids, urban hierarchies and molecular biology. (Hart 2010: 70)

Kampmann Walther (2007) shows how Castells (2000) also seizes on these newfangled notions of human organization in his conceptualization of the network society. However, there is a difference between social networks in general, characterized by a normal distribution of individuals in which the overwhelming majority of people are relatively weakly connected and a few moderately powerful nodes appear (so-called small world networks) and systems in which a few nodes possess a gigantic number of links (Kampmann Walther 2007: 28). According to Urry (2004), the former can be called an *egalitarian network*, while the latter is an *aristocratic pattern*. While we need to approach the new social physics of complexity with caution, I would argue that in an era of an increasingly networked sociality, the former begins to increasingly take on mechanisms traditionally attributable to the latter.

Kampmann Walther takes global brands as an example, showing (very much similar to Andriani and McKelvey) how management in a field characterized by Paretian distribution is related to controlling networked complexity. In networked economics, the manufacturing of a few powerful nodes makes all the difference. TPB should equally be read in the context of this.

Castells nevertheless heeds the risk of turning all this into a grand metanarrative. Although the multidisciplinary field of "complexity theory" should "ideally be considered as a method for understanding diversity" (Castells 2000: 74) and should direct our attention to the self-organizing character of nature and society—the small world phenomenon being one such principle—one should not let this become solely determining. Thanks to their complexity, networks contain liberating as well as constraining tendencies; in a network ontology also the resistance happens in and through the network. Complex networks have "qualities"; they have a powerful "materiality"; and yet they seem to elude our complete understanding (Kampmann Walther 2007: 30–31).

Power-law distributions that are acted out within the field of human affairs—aristocratic pattern—could be said to describe primitive accumulation (Harvey 2005), the principle of preferential attachment, which literally means "the rich get richer." While Pareto is credited with discovering the 20/80 rule (the idea that 20 percent of the people own 80 percent of the wealth) Hart (2010: 70) argues that the premise of inequality contained in this rule was, however, not adapted to the ideology of national society in the twentieth century. If we contrast this with the emergence of the world society of increased global trade, transnational communication of the early twenty-first century—with the added note that this de-territorialization takes place under the aegis of multinational corporations and a mobility of capital that has shifted the wealth distribution toward an extreme end—it is highly likely for civic counter-politics to emerge as a reaction to this conspicuous inequality.

While occurring in natural processes, there is nothing natural with Paretian modes of aggregation in human affairs; in fact, for world markets to come about, certain infrastructural arrangements need to be in place. I would argue that p2p-based networking is one such infrastructural arrangement—a radicalization of certain underlying properties of the Internet.

Further, the question of agency (explored in this book) is brought up when noting the nonhuman aspects of networked accumulation. If left to its own devices, the system could be claimed to beget these systemic effects. But if we interpret accumulation from a Marxian perspective, we see that there is nothing natural to a blindly technocratic system. Hence, a defeatism of p2p networking also becomes a defeatism of the aggregated macro effects of such networking. To seize on the vagaries of networked accumulation is to argue for a regulationist perspective in which human agency has a role to play for systems not to run amok.

One example is how Google has based its entire model for mapping and indexing Web pages on a model of networked accumulation but equally allows for human intervention by means of algorithms for targeted advertising. As Sergey Brin and Larry Page invented the Google search engine, they developed an algorithm for grading links, PageRank, which also formed the basis for Google's search results. PageRank uses the vast link structure of the Web as an indicator of the value of each individual page. Google interprets a link from page A to page B as a vote (A voting for B). But Google does not only measure the amount of links that a page receives; it also analyzes the page where the link was established. Links from pages that are themselves important weigh more heavily and thus enable the pages they link to become equally important. PageRank was originally a further development of Eugene Garfield's system, Science Citation Index (SCI), for ranking scientific articles.

Thus, the PageRank algorithm ranks Web pages based on the preferential attachment between them; the resulting listings are images of the extreme Pareto distribution of the Web, as a handful of Web pages are ranked extremely high, becoming preferred in the search results, while the vast majority remain obscured. However, Google can be said to at the same time act to alleviate the unfettered long-tail market in that it allows for actors along the obscure end of the long tail to advertise themselves, alleviating this lack of visibility. Through Google AdWords and AdSense, introduced in 2000 and 2003, individual advertisers can bid on targeted ads on a cost-per-impression (CPM) or cost-per-click (CPC) basis, allowing also for very small actors to find very targeted audiences. Sure, the ability to advertise is largely based on financial clout, but not entirely: Through a strategically clever use of such advertising smaller actors can also gain an advantage.

While primitive accumulation is found in the online sphere, also the (partial) solution to it would be to add layers on top of the primitive infrastructure; editorial selection, gatekeeping, manual moderation, advertising, and curation can all help alleviate power-law tendencies. By incorporating user-based ranking of links and different types of content, hierarchies can be introduced that make different sites and pages take priority over others. Hyperlinks upset and undermine hierarchies, because they directly make available the information contained, overriding infrastructure. At the same time, editorial linking can build new, potentially progressive hierarchies.

Piratbyrån's Eriksson (2007) has observed two central tendencies connected with network complexity. The first, dubbed the Death Valley problem (McCracken 2006), comes down to the observation that the long-tail economy benefits two types of actors. Multinational corporations survive by taking large market shares through massive marketing and through supplementing their income through peripheral goods and services such as merchandising. The others who do well are the amateurs, driven by enthusiasm and empowered through falling production costs. However, the "fat middles" (professional, semi-influential companies and producers often driven by talent) are struggling. Historically, the relative access to resources within this group has fostered continuity and autonomy, and likewise, they have never operated solely out of strict requirements to make profit and appeal to the broadest masses possible (Eriksson 2007).

The second phenomenon he points to is that talent, innovation, and authorship has to be understood as a collective function (much as the Foucauldian notion of the author function), in other words, as an upshot of the system—its density, efficacy, and comprehensiveness being central to both creation and diffusion. Arvidsson and Peitersen (2013) argue that creative clusters operate in this way, while Watts and Dodds (2007) have shown that diffusion through social networks likewise thrives more on network density than on the "myth of special people" (the idea that diffusion relies on certain, particularly well-connected singular nodes; Watts 2011: 94–98).

The reaction to superabundance, Eriksson (2007) argues, should be therefore not to regress to the idea of the singular author or talented individual, but to organize, administer, interconnect, aggregate, filter, and contextualize the collectively distributed creativity. The talents sought are not creative authors but creative administrators.

File sharing marks a contradictory response to this order: partly a confirmation, partly a reversal of it. Cyberliberties activists, Hart (2010: 71) argues, actually tend to accept that power-law distributions exist, as long as equal opportunity is allowed for. At least as long as choices can be made freely, Paretian inequality is acceptable; one might say natural or even normal. Also the argument regarding price elasticity seems to be premised on adopting to the long tail as the new normal. Here, the distribution of cultural artifacts is not the problem; the problem is that pricing is not adapted to the variegated demand that this entails. Price elasticity, it is argued, would allow for more transactions as the tiny minority of consumers who are highly invested in the content would pay generously whereas large majorities of more peripheral consumers could be harnessed through much more modest prices.

At the same time, the act of evading the traditional market mechanism through illegally downloading corporate blockbusters becomes a tenable moral choice for the file sharers in that they are found to recognize and personally reflect on the calculating, risk-averse nature of Hollywood franchises, even seeing the movie industry as rentier capitalists. The financially profitable extreme end of the Pareto distribution here becomes the moral touchstone in that firms are seen to make sizable profits despite peripheral leakage. The reflexive component of Pareto society is that knowledge about the distribution guides consumer behavior: If a movie is a blockbuster, it is more likely to be easily found on TPB, whereas obscure material requires more effort to be found, also on the illegal networks. Similarly, when consuming blockbusters in this way, one's monetary expenses can be diverted toward more local or, for other reasons, more treasured products.

The file-sharing network—as any world market—has no center and can grow in all directions; it is "scalable" as computer scientists tend to say. It nevertheless has hubs, and it is also those hubs that are seized on by regulators to make interventions. File-sharing networks, too, follow a power-law distribution: A few nodes are extremely well-connected—hubs in the network—whereas the vast majority are peripheral, tiny specks.

I engaged in a polemic with Fleischer (2010b) on these aspects of file sharing. He opposed my observation that file sharing can have regressive elements in that it might buttress the negative spiral in favoring that which is already known, thus counteracting serendipity. I wholly agree with his retort, that different applications, different networks, and different protocols make for differing extents of this problem: Soulseek allows for serendipity by allowing users to browse other users' folders; hosting sites such as Rapidshare, Megaupload, and Mediafire beget extraneous clusters of music blogs where highly sophisticated recommendations and editorial selections thrive; and private torrent trackers similarly specialize, sometimes to an awesomely impressive extent. Editorial functions exist in traditional mass media, as well as blogs and communities, and in affiliation with some of the file-sharing applications.

However, most public torrent sites remain highly agnostic to this function; they thrive on a search function which only benefits that which is already popular. Charts and lists do exist, such as the Pirate Bay charts, but they only remedy the problem very slightly. Further, the hollowing out of traditional publishing or of the curation that the traditional artists and repertoire (A&R) model makes possible can be seen as negative byproducts of unmitigated file sharing. Later in the book, we will see how both illegal file-sharing sites (such as TPB) and legal streaming services (such as Spotify) have begun to experiment, in recent years, with adding different types of editorial functions to the underlying p2p substrate.

One study (Blackburn 2004) indicates that file sharing would have had positive effects on CD sales for relatively unknown artists, whereas it had negative impact on those who were already popular. He estimated that the best-selling quarter of albums was affected negatively, while the remaining three-quarters were affected positively. However, since the top quarter represents such a high share of the accumulated sales, the aggregated effect on overall CD sales was negative. Further, Burkart (2010: 72; Burkart & McCourt 2006: 131) has noted that two-thirds of the musicians surveyed in the Pew Internet and American Life Project in 2004 responded that they were not significantly worried about the effects of file sharing on their income. Most active artists are unaffiliated to the majors, are affiliated but not making money, or work with indie labels (however, many of the artists in these two latter groups tend to at least be marketed, something that they would not be if they were unaffiliated), or they self-release. These findings still only indicate what has been argued: The obscurer ends of the long-tail distribution would be favored by file sharing.

At the same time, the weakened music market during the 2000s meant that major record companies became extremely risk averse, resulting in the function of developing new artists (A&R) increasingly becoming a responsibility of artists themselves—rather than the previous model of record labels signing and marketing several artists of whom only a minority actually become successful and profitable (Wikström 2006). Music was forced to become an increasingly deskilled, precarious venture. I will later show that there are, however, signs of this situation shifting in Sweden—mainly as a result of the emergence of streamed media and Spotify as a new, profitable music platform in this country. Still, this is not to say that this new model is without problems.

2.9 INDUSTRIES: A MACROECONOMIC CONTEXT

How can a media industry thrive on transparency instead of closure, on commons instead of enclosures, or on free dissemination of digital content instead of controlled sales of it? Jakobsson (2012) explores the notion of what he calls the "openness industry." He identifies three types of companies. The first are companies that exploit user-generated content on their own websites and find ways to generate incomes on the dissemination rather than on the content itself, for example, by serving ads next to this content. One example is YouTube; another one would be TPB. The second type are companies that only act to distribute, index, and make searchable and accessible copyrighted content on the Internet. The prime example would be

Google, not only the search engine, but several of its other services, such as Google Books and Google Scholar. The third type would be those companies that do not handle copyrighted content themselves but produce and/or sell products or services intended to do so. One example would be manufacturers of mp3 players.

All of these types of companies benefit from a weakened copyright regulation, as this weakening would increase the circulation of digital content on the Internet. Jakobsson argues that the openness industry has been supported by the neoliberal development of transnational policymaking in recent decades, whereas the copyright tradition is instead based on classical liberal ideology (and its foundations found in the writings of John Locke). In the classical paradigm, the labor of creative individuals enjoys protection in the marketplace, through regulation of ownership and property. The roots of IPR are deeply embedded in liberal ideology. Neoliberal ideology is somewhat different; it is more recent and tends to regard phenomena in more instrumental, pragmatic ways. If a loosened copyright regime makes it possible to develop markets and entrepreneurs, it is not only consistent with neoliberal ideology to loosen such regimes but even necessary. From a market-optimizing point of view, unhealthy monopolies would corrupt the marketplace.

The openness industry is therefore analogous with neoliberalism, as it leaves the market to determine the level of copyright protection applicable to digital content—governments or legislature should not favor any of the two types of industry in advance. Another prerequisite for the openness industry is to upgrade the creative potential seen in mass aggregation; Through enumerating and collecting vast amounts of data points, the productive potentials in scattered acts of consumption can be harnessed. This is akin to Hayek's (1978: 108) concept of catallaxy, and similar lines of thinking are present in Lanier's (2013) endorsement of Nelson's distributed social contract in which individual contributions could be tracked and emergent order would arise through the mutual adjustment of many such inscriptions. This is, essentially, an inversion of the Platonic ideal of expert rule, as reason is not seen here as an essence or property residing among a select set of a priori experts, but instead seen as an upshot of the distributed, aggregated intelligence of the crowd. What proponents of such radical democratization risk missing, however, is—following Sunstein (2007)—whether the criteria for taking on decisions are quantitative (an equitable model of direct democracy, which, however, risks collapsing into naked populism) or qualitative (an evolutionary model of survival of the fittest ideas, risking to collapse into meritocratic autocracy).

This is a markedly different approach to value creation compared to the lonely professional writer, film maker, or songwriter protected by copyright. The currencies that the openness industry thrives on are attention and popularity; it offers contributors a place in a community but not necessarily leverage to have their contributions discovered by more people, by means of dedicated marketing. The model for editorial discovery in the openness industry is radically inductive; it relies on algorithms to extract emergent trends among the population in terms of what content should be given center place (crowd-sourced charts, automated recommendations, etc.), whereas the copyright industry relies on actively marketing a selected number of acts based on the estimation that most of them would make successes and recuperate the initial expenses. In this sense, the copyright industry would thrive on a more deductive model, in which editors, curators, and researchers second-guess what would make a hit, rather than mirroring patterns in the marketplace by means of cybernetic feedback loops.

Historically, EU-level Internet policy has been shaped by a strong dedication to copyright protection. At the same time, the EU also shares an agenda for opening up markets. This becomes pertinent in Jakobsson's (2012: 152) analysis of materials from the European Commission, where a key problem for the emergence of an open, EU-wide online market would be posed by the copyright organizations for music, film, and literature. These organizations often represent national interests and create monopoly situations that run counter to EU-level market ideals. A central question in these hearings is whether there could be such a thing as "an open enclosure" or "a fenced commons." Are these incommensurate propositions, or is a middle way possible, and what type of regulatory landscape would such a compromise require? I believe that the task will be partly eased by better understanding the civic standpoints found among media audiences.

In the United States, the Democrat Party is often said to rely on campaign funding by entertainment companies such as Comcast, Disney, and Time Warner. The MPAA along with the RIAA and the US Chamber of Commerce were the main lobbyists for Congress to pass the Stop Online Piracy Act (SOPA) and the Protect IP Act (PIPA) in 2011 and 2012. The overlapping influence of Hollywood was manifested by former senator (D-CT) Chris Dodd, who—in his capacity of being CEO of the MPAA—publicly urged politicians to back SOPA/PIPA or otherwise lose campaign funding from said industry. Meanwhile, several House Republicans (Darrell Issa, Ron Wyden) opposed SOPA and managed to get House Majority Leader Eric Cantor (R-VA) to stall the bill because of a lack of consensus. It is important to add that the Republican US presidential candidates, as well as the Obama administration, publicly opposed SOPA.

The allegedly strong links between the Democrat Party and the entertainment industry need to be reconsidered, however, in the light of recent campaign contributions made by the communications and information technology industries. Although TV/movies/music lobbyists contributed almost $9 million to federal candidates in 2012, these contributions were outweighed by the total contributions from computers/Internet and telco industries: approximately $16.5 million.[6] The contributions from the latter sector was biased toward Republican Party contributions by a factor of three to two, whereas the entertainment industry exposed less bias: 48 percent to Democrats and 52 percent to Republicans (OpenSecrets.org 2013).

Regarding telcos, the United States remains a mainly domestic market—where, sadly, veritable "information empires" reign (Wu 2010), beset by market failures such as profit inflation and lack of equitable consumer choice (Crawford 2013). However, although US exports in the computers/Internet sector have been rapidly growing—with companies such as Apple constituting what has been called a rebirth of US-based manufacturing—the US content industry is still a significantly strong actor in terms of global exports. Of world exports in cultural services 75 percent comes from the United States (32 percent) and EU countries (42 percent) combined. Nevertheless, the difference between the two entities lies on the import side, such that the United States shows a surplus of $9 billion and the EU a deficit of $2 billion (OECD 2008: 26). The US exports accrue almost half of the world's royalties and license fees for patents, trademarks, and copyrights.

In Europe, it is generally thought that the telecoms industry holds more political power than the content industry and should be able to stave off any incursion from the smaller creative industries. Yet, in the case of the Telecoms Package, apparently tiny collecting societies were able to exert a disproportionate amount of political influence (Horten 2012: 70), partly as they received support from large global firms of a similar size to the large telco firms, partly as they formed strategic alliances and devoted to the cause.

In Sweden, the relative difference in size regarding the telecoms industry versus the entertainment industry is considerable; the Swedish ICT industry involves companies such as Ericsson and TeliaSonera and has a turnover of around $95 billion, whereas the Swedish music industry has a turnover of just under $1 billion. ICT exports alone are around $24 billion, while music exports total around $150 million. The share of turnover going toward export is therefore notably higher in the ICT industry (25 percent), whereas the share is 15 percent in the music industry (Portnoff & Nielsén 2012).

At the same time, the Swedish music industry is relatively strong compared to other national music industries, especially when seen per capita. If one relates the copyright revenues generated in the domestic market to the population, Sweden emerges as one of the world's most successful countries. Swedish copyright revenues amount to $20.6 per inhabitant and year—almost twice as much as Great Britain's $11.7, which, in turn, is nearly twice as high as the United States and Canada at $6 per inhabitant (Portnoff & Nielsén 2012: 18). This adds to a self-image of Sweden as having a strong, innovative music industry. Of course, the emergence of actors such as Spotify can act to both gain from and reinforce this image, while enjoying the infrastructural support of a highly broadband-saturated environment.

3 Personal Justifications / Learning from the File Sharers While Criticizing Them

> I can see piracy as a form of civil disobedience. But, most people engaging in piracy aren't thinking in such terms of reform. They just want stuff for free. I guess we could say that the imbalance in copyright is a direct result of the imbalance of civic virtue among the people today. (sign. "Mark," commenting Bode 2009)

> I think most people are struggling like me in defending file sharing morally. Even if the author isn't losing anything and even if you'd never buy the work anyway, it feels a bit wrong for many of us. (VT, m21, 2006)[1]

What is sought in this book is a reflexive, socially embedded model of autonomy. Peer-to-peer-based file sharing is a great example of how the latitude of the individual node stands in direct relation to the size and quality of the aggregated collective. Tellingly, a social-democrat conception of liberty—as we will see, typical for Sweden—is premised on a very similar systemic setup. Further, as was noted in the Introduction, since no concept of freedom is *sui generis*, this conception of freedom should also be scrutinized as being constructed, normative, and repeatedly negotiated.

As has been argued by Vaidhyanathan (2004), the new regimes engendered by maximalist copyright regulation laid bare those aspects of everyday life that would have otherwise remained dormant:

> Was I a thief all along? If I cared less about music, I would have recorded fewer cassettes, but I would also have purchased fewer albums. Before the rise of peer-to-peer music distribution, I don't remember anyone asking these questions. I certainly never asked them about myself. (p. 42)

The increasingly technocrat management of culture, and accelerating reminders about the nature of IPR legislation that go along with it, prompts ordinary citizens to ask reflexive questions about the nature of consumption and circulations in ways that these were almost never discussed twenty years ago. Burkart (2010) has argued that this shift was operationalized in 1998, with the implementation of the DMCA altering the premises for what constitutes the economic and legal category of a consumer. In Sweden, a similar tendency will be shown to have been implemented with the adaptation to the EU Copyright Directive in 2005. Now, it was no longer unambiguously legal to share music among a hazy circle of loosely defined friends; instead, the law stipulated that the nature of private consumption be thought of in a particular way.

What I found in a lot of the file-sharer argumentation that I took part in during the last decade is that it serves to justify the role of the individual by invoking totalities (the overall unstoppability of the phenomenon) and externalities (observations that the side effects are not harmful enough to warrant criminalization). As Latour (2005: 56) has pointed out, actors constantly criticize each other and other agencies, accusing them of being fake, absurd, and irrational. Following these dismissals of the actors involved, one can follow the way in which the landscape of the new media circuits of distribution is in effect construed.

Hence, my arguments are largely structural, not ethnographic in the conventional sense. In the following chapter, I will continue to show not only how the notion of the p2p network as an indicator of worth, or a significant mass of other users, was a central constituent of the file-sharer discourse but also how the nature of technology was invoked, time and again, prompting me to explore the ways in which the Internet can be ontologically conceptualized in Chapter 6. Second, as any perspective of such embeddedness is viewpoint dependent, I will criticize these viewpoints where need be. Third, I will outline some guidelines that policy makers and Internet regulators can learn from this.

I take file sharing, in the conventional sense, to be a civic phenomenon, taking place in the crevices of domestic, everyday media use. With "civic" I primarily refer to the individual's own experience of being a citizen; this experience was, among my respondents in the 2006 study, framed more as a sense of universal autonomy, or by one's access to a commons, than by traditional institutions of civil society.

Standpoint theory has taught us that also the researcher's viewpoint is restricted and biased. However, by paying attention to and critically engaging with the peripheral views of sometimes marginalized individuals, more objective accounts of the world can be assembled (Harding 2004). This notion of different viewpoints depending on vested interests also applies to the representatives of industry or commerce. Within certain industrial orders of assessment (depending on sector) the same phenomenon might be perceived to have more clearly detrimental or beneficial effects, while potential externalities are dismissed as outside of the horizon for analysis (Callon 1998; Barry & Slater 2005). Thus, both file sharers and representatives of the copyright industry can be expected to hold limited views of the issue, as an altogether eclectic or all-encompassing personal view would render a purely partisan standpoint nigh impossible.

What was noted in both my 2006 and 2012 studies was that the file-sharer discourse invokes and incorporates the notion of a general economic benefit for society—a concern that it prioritizes over the concerns of particular sectors, such as that of the record industry. It can nonetheless be read as a mode of reasoning that assumes market principles to be the most universal ones, yet does so from a populist point of view in which "the customer is always right"—that is, where the rights of individuals, as citizens-consumers, outweigh those of industrial actors. Admittedly, this all underplays the communitarian or activist aspects of public life; this is most likely a result of the selection in terms of geography and personal disposition of respondents. Some of the participants in the 2006 study were found through Piratbyrån, and some of the 2012 participants were found through another, much more secretive and exclusive forum. To minimize bias toward communitarianism, I deliberately did not exclusively approach activists. Yet, because of research design, the selection is likely to be biased anyway; participants in qualitative interviews do not tend to be representative of the general population.

The respondents in my 2006 study ranged between 15 and 42 years of age. All of them expressed a partiality for free and unmitigated file sharing, noting that their range in taste and cultural exploration had been significantly widened by it. Several of them envisaged a society-wide gap, regarding whether a person would be at all aware of file sharing or not. This knowledgeability of the phenomenon would in most cases depend on whether one has actual experience of it or not.

They were all relatively advanced computer users—several of them self-taught. They would envisage the Internet as a vast resource for knowledge and problem solving. VG (m22) moderated a discussion board and ran his own server for file sharing (including a public BitTorrent tracker). ES (m17), SZ (m31), and VT (m21) were Piratbyrån moderators. SZ was quite politically committed (primarily opposing what he described as the potential terrors of surveillance, criminalization, and control), whereas VT appeared to be more technologically knowledgeable, pragmatic, and moderately in favor of (a nevertheless limited) copyright. AG (m32) was a professional cultural producer, listing his experience as scriptwriter, writer, musician, and cartoonist. Further, both PG (m24) and PN (m15) could be labeled as "tinkerers" and hobbyist cultural producers.

They could all be said to share a progressivist, utilitarian view, especially LB (f42), who ran a BitTorrent website. Her view of cultural economy was akin to social Darwinism in that she seemed to advocate a notion of "survival of the fittest" regarding technical protocols and paradigms. This reminded me of software designers, who often judge software applications depending on their usability and the extent of their uptake. In the hacker ethic, openness and a wide user base make for beneficial mutational potentials ("given enough eyes, all bugs are shallow"; Raymond 1999: 41). For harnessing resources, p2p makes good sense systemically, LB argued.

Only a small percentage of my respondents were female. In another study on Swedish file sharing (Findahl 2006), 71 percent of respondents were male and 29 percent female. In the mass media debate around file sharing, a stereotypical trope has been the notion of a computer-savvy, relatively young man standing in as a metonym for the file-sharing community at large. Piratbyrån and TPB have had young, male spokespersons such as Fredrik Neij, Gottfrid Svartholm, Peter Sunde, and Rasmus Fleischer. Also, in dramatic events such as the raid on TPB, the proponents and representatives of unregulated file sharing were all male. It is hard to discern whether this public imagination had influenced the consensus that was found, initially among the pilot study respondents, that the typical file sharer was, primarily, a young (however, not necessarily male) person, from a developed nation. After a long e-mail exchange, I deliberately asked one respondent: Does it all boil down to the right for some privileged, computer-savvy, young male computer user in the Western world to be able to acquire as much free material as possible? Or would you describe it differently?

> Yes (very leading question but I agree). Because the only reason for me having access is through the young knowledgeable man, my little brother! Which could prove the point you're making. (LS, f25, 2006)

LS's younger brother was the person who initially introduced her to file sharing. Pilot study respondent AN (f27) told a similar story: She was introduced to the phenomenon by, in succession, a (male) student at her halls of residence, her boyfriend's younger brother, and her uncle. LS explained how she felt that "the 'grown-up' world" would see it as more controversial to do something that is presumably illegal, including file sharing. She also connected the reluctance about the phenomenon in this allegedly older age group to "virus fear" and a general lack of technical knowledge. However, AN's account disproved the exclusive prevalence of young people when she referred to her 45-year-old uncle, who "happily downloads anything." Once again, knowledge and skill were seen as the central factors, rather than age or gender predispositions. The consensus seemed to be that someone who has the ability and inclination to file-share would be expected to do so.

3.1 PREVIOUS RESEARCH ON FILE SHARERS' OWN MOTIVATIONS AND ATTITUDES

As has been shown by García-Álvarez et al. (2009) and Cenite et al. (2009), the morality of accessing culture depends on the social, economic, and cultural context in which an individual has been raised. Cenite et al. (2009) draw on Lessig's (2004) observation that file sharing can take place for a number of reasons, not always replacing a sale. However, their study makes the problematic presupposition that file sharing is premised on gifting. From one perspective, this point of view is highly understandable.

But, as these critics have pointed out, we might be talking about distinctly different forms of capital and different forms of valuation and accumulation. What, after all, makes file sharing markedly different from mere symbolic exchange is that here de facto accumulation is possible on an entirely different scale and in more functional ways than in traditional forms of symbolic value. Further, what is judged is not the person per se but the folder containing the data; the emphasis can thus be argued on instrumentality rather than identity. Some of my respondents remarked on how having a vast archive, and valuing the accumulation of files for the sake of accumulation itself, can be said to be a form of "data hoarding"—often with the purpose to transform the glut accumulated into strategic benefits, such as invites and download allowances. With this in mind, the notion of file sharing being synonymous with disinterested gifting should be met with caution.

What about strategic gifting to gain interpersonal benefits within one's community, then? I will make the argument that file sharing is only in some instances taking place in settings where the individual is placed in a file-sharing *community*, in the traditional sense. The proposition that file sharing is automatically related to gifting in this strategic sense is problematic, because it too needs to be contextualized: It is valid for some file-sharing protocols/applications but not necessarily to BitTorrent or cyberlockers. Napster, for example, as it is described by Giesler and Pohlmann (2003), might be seen to have generated an altogether different experience of inter-user reciprocity and gift giving. Cenite et al. (2009), similar to Mlcakova and Whitley (2004), confirm many of the pragmatic arguments for file sharing and the rhetoric of reciprocity and sharing.

García-Álvarez et al. (2009) reviewed the literature on the consumer ethics pertaining to copying software. Besides noting differences in "gender, age, religious orientation, knowledge of copyright, availability of original software and personal benefits" (p. 245), as well as cultural differences in moral arguments, the intention to copy was nevertheless "related to the perceived equity or fairness of relationships or exchanges with others—that is, to the perceived ratio of what was received in relation to what was brought to the exchange" (ibid.). The authors conclude that differences in approach were found, depending on, for example, whether the respondent had good experience of public libraries or not (this experience depends on home country). The authors emphasize *differences* in the moral arguments, and they show how these are determined by differing biographical experiences of subjects. In contrast, what I am interested in is the nature of the arguments—the *consistencies*—rather than the respondent who utters them.

Mylonas (2012) emphasizes the civic potentials inherent to unmitigated file sharing. His analysis shows that civic elements may be developed through p2p practices, but they rely on material social experiences, ideological issues, events, and social and communicative relations that are, in some ways, external to the realities developing through technologies and digital networks. Drawing on the example of file-sharing practices in contemporary Greece, he emphasizes the communal experience and self-organization of its participants.

I will return to this civic dimension of p2p-based file sharing in Chapter 7, but suffice to say that my observations in Sweden differ rather radically from the Greek experience in that Sweden has not suffered the austerity measures that southern European countries went through in the aftermath of the economic crisis that began in 2007. Hence, the sense of urgency and antipathy toward transnational corporations and neoliberal policies does not appear to be as acute in Sweden.

Japan is a contrasting example, as their CD market has remained more stable than other national markets (Levine 2011: 63), probably a result of the early establishment of mobile Internet connections and to the prevalence of CD rentals. The p2p users in Condry (2004) felt that downloading was illegal but justified it by their antipathy toward music labels. Only recently, record labels in Japan have announced that they would discontinue the use of DRM, which has so far been common in the Japanese audio CD market.

Psychometric studies such as Chen et al. (2008) indicate that utility, pragmatism, and value maximization are more pressing factors when choosing between buying and downloading music than ethical considerations. The authors extrapolate "ideologies of freeware" and p2p as a consumerist opposition to the music industry, as the range of content on offer was thought by respondents to be increased thanks to file sharing. Shang et al. (2008) similarly found the norm of consumer rights to be decisive, yet emphasize behavioral aspects such as neutralization techniques and cognitive dissonances as well. The authors argue that when asked, people may apply neutralization techniques, such as "appealing to higher loyalties" or "denying the victims" (Sykes & Matza 1957) to match the norms of the behavior they prefer. Hill (2007) similarly discusses the lack of moral intensity (magnitude, proximity, probability of effect) that typifies a lot of online behavior, and Moore and McMullan (2009) found a disparate range of neutralization techniques among file-sharing university students.

It has not been my purpose to speculate on the inner motivations of file sharers. Rather, I will focus on the elements of justification that the argumentation draws on—primarily, the idea that file sharing might be bad for some sectors but good for society at large. A critical understanding of this would, in turn, be instrumental when trying to formulate policies that serve to anticipate and respond to this file-sharer argumentation.

It is my aim to explore the particular interests and viewpoints of the agents in the all-too-often inflamed copyfight debate, trying to maintain a neutral view regarding the often vested interests of such agents. By noting not only the technical particularities underpinning the phenomenon but also the sociocultural inclinations that unmitigated file sharing appears to satisfy, this conflict can be much better understood. One of the central insights here is the fact that any one actor passing judgment in this debate only does so from what will inevitably be a restricted view of the media landscape—me included.

3.2 FILE SHARING AS A CRITIQUE OF CAPITALISM?

File sharing and piracy should not be read as monolithical concepts; they play out within a larger context of a highly variegated capitalism. Piracy as a general concept will be further examined and reveals a heterogeneous range of practices. What many of these practices—at least those pertaining to digital piracy—have in common, however, is that they help expose previous Fordist and even post-Fordist models of cultural industry to various forms of legitimacy tests, much as Boltanski and Chiapello (2007: 30–35; 493) acknowledge how the established notion of capitalism was exposed to a number of tests during the period after 1968.

The notion of a test pertains to two degrees of complexity. First, a test of strength, the attribution of which "defines a state of affairs without any moral implications" (p. 31). Secondly, however, Boltanski and Chiapello emphasize that the "strength of the strong" is, however, diminished in a society where a large number of tests "are subject to conditions defining what is a legitimate test" (ibid.). The strictness of this latter test means that brute force is not enough. This is also where Boltanski and Thévenot's (2006) idea of "regimes of justification" becomes easier to understand, as the areas of contestation—areas that are, in my view, largely synonymous with Bourdieu's (1984) concept of the field—stipulate that tests for legitimacy must be between entities that are commensurate: For example, one cannot pay literary critics and be recognized as an inspired, great writer, or become principal private secretary just because one is the minister's cousin (Boltanski & Chiapello 2007: 31).

According to Boltanski and Chiapello (pp. 32–33), critique can act to reveal the nature of these tests and their bearing on justice. *Corrective critique* takes the original criteria for the test seriously. It serves to require tests to be stricter, thereby improving their justice and refining them, potentially without end. An example, relating to file sharing, would be the test of the economic feasibility of unregulated file sharing for publishers and artists; here, the role of critique would serve to take even stricter adherence to the record industry business models and revenue streams, noting that file sharing has helped usher in a new way of conducting business, where for example ticket sales for live performances can be seen to have increased, as the live performance itself cannot be pirated although pirated songs act to advertise this live touring.

Radical critique, on the other hand, does not end there; it questions the actual validity of the test, serves to suppress the test, and ultimately to replace it with an entirely new test. In some of the file-sharer discourse, this radical critique can be found when, as an interviewer, bringing up the concept of producing culture or making a living off this production. What is noted then, is, first of all, an anthropological definition of culture as something that one cannot just produce, sell or give away and that should be available as part of a commons, which it is a human right to access. Second, the "death of the author" trope is brought up—a deliberate counter-trope to the "myth of individual creativity" (Yar 2008). This mode of critique stipulates that the production of cultural goods is not a matter of individual creativity, effort, and excellence and that there is no moral obligation to recognize or reward the individuals concerned. The creation of culture lies in the aggregated amalgam of cultural impulses essentially between entities. Third, both of these tropes rely on the technical notion of a digital flow, in which the boundaries of cultural objects are no longer entirely clear, and files are always endlessly duplicable. Here, streaming is dismissed as merely a technical configuration that cloaks the fact that all digital communication involves the copying of files: By not storing the file that is copied from the server and cached on the client computer, a false precondition is drawn up.

Interestingly, after what has been called the material turn in science and technology studies (and what could provocatively be stated as its adjacent disciplines: cultural studies and media and communication studies), false consciousness would be seen as directly resultant from false configurations in this way. The ways in which human norms and dispositions play out are seen as direct consequences of the various material configurations of reality.

Hence, if the conflict of what would be deemed as piracy and what its consequences would be could be seen as a battle of conceptions, I argue that a useful point of entry into this battle would be to explore the arguments involved, by way of assessing which conceptions and metaphors these arguments rely on. This can never make for an exhaustive account. Rather, what will be exposed is what avenues that critique can take—that is, critiques of established capitalism, as well as critiques of the new norms and conditions engendered by digital file sharing.

The stronger actor can always revert to displacements (Boltanski & Chiapello 2007: 34), where legitimacy tests are wholly or partially eluded. Subsequently, the actor "can rely on principles of legitimacy employed by another side of the critique" (p. 35). Within the file-sharing world, this cuts both ways—very tangibly so. When exposed to critique, the record industry has, for example, been able to appease a range of arguments made by consumers and citizens by employing new services such as Spotify, which act as displacements that, once employed, the critique has to respond to. Likewise, when criticized by industrial actors and IPR orthodoxy, actors such as TPB make themselves exempt from certain legal claims by similarly tangible displacements, such as when they, for example, decentralized their torrent links (magnet links) and even the hosting of their link index (distributed hosting).

What can be noted is how such displacements also make for new metaphors. As will be shown in Chapter 6, given developments in the file-sharing world toward cyberlockers and (at least from the user point of view) centralized BitTorrent indexes, one could argue for the metaphor of blood donation (in which sharing both generates and becomes operable by way of collective proxies and pools of content) to complement more established sociological notions such as the one of reciprocal gift giving. Similarly, as Section 4.9 will show, actors such as Apple, Facebook, and Spotify are all current examples of the notion of what could be called a *mall Internet* where various "walled garden" configurations are employed to remediate the broadcast model of content distribution on top of the underlying TCP/IP infrastructure, which is not originally premised on a broadcasting diagram.

Pundits such as Shirky have repeatedly argued that Napster constituted a "disruptive" moment in the development of consumerism, content distribution, and equitable business models for the Internet. However, many of the things that Napster was said to disrupt—the album as an art form (2000a), unit pricing of online music (2000b)—have later been recaptured by newer business models such as iTunes and Spotify. Hence, a burning question to ask is whether file-sharing acts to displace business models entirely or merely acts as a conduit for more efficient ways to perform consumerism. Taking an empirical, user-oriented view is one way to more comprehensively answer that question.

3.3 REGIMES OF JUSTIFICATION

To classify or categorize the types of justifications for file sharing, we should begin by noting that acts of justification primarily serve as ex post facto explanations of what has already happened or what has already been done. Boltanski and Thévenot (2006: 27) do not write about file sharing or copying per se but have coined the notion of "regimes of justification," to show how such explanations fall into different categories. They emphasize that reflexivity—imagining oneself as a part of larger systems—is inherent to processes of justification:

> Persons must be capable of distancing themselves from their own particularities in order to reach agreement about external goods that are enumerated and defined in general terms. (ibid.)

In so doing, Boltanski and Thévenot recognize different types of generalities that both underpin respondents' analytical frameworks for understanding the social world and the ways they justify their behavior (p. 9). Statistical evidence, for example, often lends itself to instances in which subjects follow "a form of industrial generality," whereas knowledge based on examples (or anecdotes) is instead valued by "the testimony of trustworthy informants and thus relies on a form of domestic generality" (ibid.).

Boltanski and Thévenot observe six "orders or economies of worth," which are systematic and coherent principles of evaluation that all coexist and overlap, however, with their own criteria for assessment: civic, market, inspired, fame, industrial, and domestic. In Boltanski and Chiapello (2007), a seventh such order (or polity) is introduced: that of the projective, pertaining to project-oriented network rationality and flexibility. We will see how a similar notion of progress could be seen to operate as a justificatory regime among my respondents. It is important to emphasize the situational character of justification as individuals shift in a flexible way "from one mode of adjustment to another, from one measure of worth to another" (Boltanski & Thévenot 2006: 16).

Applying this schema to file sharing, the invocation of technological unstoppability could, for example, be described as belonging to both a notion of progress and adaptation (projective, flexible rationality) and to an engineer or industrial style of reasoning. In contrast, the invocation of privacy and freedom of speech would belong to a civic style of reasoning (also related to journalistic discourse, speaking for the citizens, as if it were). However, no one respondent could be entirely summarized by any one of these styles alone—which is also in concordance with Boltanski and Thévenot's findings that any account would incorporate several such partially overlapping styles.

Further, each regime makes reference to or requires different kinds of entities. These entities belong to different categories and modes of thinking, each with their own internal normative rationale that can sometimes be incommensurable. What I found, in my 2006 study, was that the argumentation tended to invoke various collective processes that operate on the level of society at large:

I. "It's unstoppable." The existing Internet infrastructure ensures that high degrees of freedom, heterogeneity, and low universal oversight cannot be suppressed without severe curtailments of civil liberties. Two related modes of reasoning invoked this global infrastructure: first, the utilitarian/pragmatic appropriation of impossibility of stopping the phenomenon, and second, the civil rights appropriation that totalitarian measures would be required to effectively stop the phenomenon on a global level and that such measures would be disproportionate.

II. "The artists/producers don't suffer" / "Culture in general doesn't suffer." A seemingly undiminished audience interest in cultural products can be noted, as consumption (except for audio CD sales) had remained high throughout the surveyed period (2000–2009). There was little acknowledgement that artistic output would suffer—with the exception of the music sector, where economic incentives for production would be biased more toward live performances and licensing than toward record sales. This mode of reasoning, when sympathizing with professional producers, could be said to fall under a unionist appropriation, where the potential economic harm to professional cultural producers is the main referent. When not sympathizing with producers/artists, it could rather be said to represent an audience appropriation, indifferent to the fate of artists but nevertheless dedicated to the quality of output.

III. "It's democratic." The veritable body politic of the aggregated humans and machines in p2p networks, which is unique in that it is simultaneously an aggregate of topographic machine nodes and of vaguely corresponding human beings, forms something that some of my respondents likened to a people's movement. That is, a nebulous mass that has occasional spokespersons and "strategic sovereigns" (Andersson 2009a) in the form of hubs such as TPB. Among file sharers, a collectivist appropriation can be noted—a notion that culture should be accessible to everyone. This perspective sees communication as a commons or shared resource rather than as discrete units of transmissive content. This notion could be connected to the metaphor of a civic "multitude" (Hardt & Negri 2004; Virno 2003). It also relates to the civil rights appropriation listed under process I. Arguably, the civil rights appropriation pertaining to III is more about the weight of the collective, whereas entity I would be more about the safeguarding of individual rights, such as the right to privacy.

The macroeconomic appropriation of the alleged overall good for society underpins each of these regimes—a value that is arguably pivotal for the Swedish discourses, given the country's conception of national civic unity and unusually high levels of civic trust in the nation state, as Chapter 5 will show.

Each of these registers of justification could thus be argued to lend a generally applicable validation for the habit of file sharing, a way of grasping for an enduring, objective defense of it. Within the social sciences, objectivity is nevertheless a thorny subject, to say the least. A critical account of the personal reflexivity of file sharers needs to include a critique of the claims to objectivity that these subjects tend to make.

Boltanski and Thévenot (2006) become useful when criticizing consumers' arguments rather than simply acclaiming them. Discourses act to legitimize certain behaviors, often against better evidence. Take, for example, the common assumptions that serve either side of a convenient dichotomy: Either, it is stipulated that file sharing would simply replace sales, or it is said that unauthorized sampling actually feeds legal purchases. Although the former assumption can be ruled out by invoking Lessig's simple observation that there are at least four scenarios to everyday downloads of file-shared content, only one of which being clearly harmful to producers (Lessig 2004: 68, 296–297), my own fieldwork acts to problematize this notion. Also my interviews conducted in 2012 came to show that the correlation between high file sharing and high media consumption is not that clear-cut:

> Let's be honest, if you're uploading the latest DVD it impacts on the number of sales it will get. That's not to say everyone who downloads would have bought it. And some people might buy anyway if they like it. But it makes it more difficult for small production companies. That's why I like the rule at [NN][2] where you can't upload a DVD or movie until 12 months after release. It gives the guys bit of breathing space. Though to be honest, you'd probably get it from somewhere else. (DT, m54, UK, 2012)
>
> I certainly never buy what I have on my harddrive. Especially when you can download full DVD images. (YG, m20, USA, 2012)

When deliberately provoking one of the respondents, asking whether there actually is a risk that movies and TV shows acquired through file sharing would not be watched or purchased, once they actually are commercially released—as the fans would already have downloaded them onto their hard drives—he responded:

> I would think so, but statistics don't seem to indicate that. But I would not go to the cinema to watch a movie that I have already downloaded. (CI, m30, Germany)

This illustrates how the (alleged) objectivity of constructed statistical reality "out there" complements the lived, subjective experience that respondents simultaneously make reference to, almost as if using personal experience to make up for the hard facts. CI seemed to admit that the facts would speak for themselves but, at the same time, be rather incongruous with everyday experience. One could call it a domestic mode of reasoning taking precedence over an industrial one. This is clearly problematic. As Mills (1940) once remarked, a person's account of what motivates him should never be taken at face value:

> When an agent vocalizes or imputes motives, he is not trying to *describe* his experienced social action. He is not merely stating "reasons." He is influencing others—and himself. Often he is finding new "reasons" which will mediate action. Thus, we need not treat an action as discrepant from "its" verbalization, for in many cases, the verbalization is a new act. (p. 907)

The questioning of norms is not done by an agent who is merely performing a rational calculation of mind; bodily dispositions, habits, and (largely subconscious) affect would be part of this reasoning too.

3.4 THE WEIGHT OF THE WEB

In my 2006 study, the respondents emphasized individual agency, implying a strong reliance on knowledge and skill. One of the points I want to make in this book, however, is that this competence, in turn, relies on totalized, aggregated networks: The larger and more universalized the network gets, agency and latitude in the p2p setting increases.

It needs to be noted that these interviews were conducted at a time when neither the crackdown on TPB nor the subsequent trial had taken place. I will return to the historical dimension of file sharing and copyright legislation in Sweden. Suffice to say that the rate of file sharing, in absolute terms, has not gone down since 2006. Nevertheless, in relative terms, p2p-based file sharing is now a smaller share of the overall Internet traffic than it was then. In terms of demographic popularity it remains largely unaffected; around 45 percent of Swedish Internet users aged 12 to 35 admit to sometimes file-share (Findahl 2012: 17). The trend even shows a slow increase (p. 32).

The participants in my study tended to justify their sharing by holding that it would have, on the whole, a positive impact on society. The impact of file sharing was, in fact, only seen as negative for certain industries—even positive to society on the whole. Much of the file-sharer discourse served to strike a balance between public collectivism (civic solidarity, public utility) and individual autonomy (personal freedom to maximize pleasure), in as equitable a way as possible for these individuals. It was notable that a high degree of reflexivity was required on behalf of the respondents, not only when attempting to reconcile these concerns but also when pondering on the aptness of IPR legislation at large. This reflexivity extends also to the increased public knowledge about issues of copyright and, more importantly, a seemingly increased awareness of the conditions for cultural production, distribution, and consumption.

As was noted in the previous chapter, intellectual property has been intensively debated during the last decade, entailing not only copyright critique but also the etymology of terms such as piracy, the history of copyright, and discussions on the ontological properties of computer files. Another topic that these public debates have touched on is the disjuncture that file sharing has created between retaining authorial rights and retaining profit from these rights. Among my respondents, such topics were actively reflected on, but they were rarely approached as if offering objective knowledge. Rather, they tended to function as open questions and aspirations to learn more. The notion of the solitary author, however, was sternly opposed by my respondents. They thought of cultural products as increasingly corporate constructs—a view that was echoed at the time also by Piratbyrån.

Much of the sentiment on unmitigated file sharing was that it is practically unstoppable and that it had become the expected mode of exchange online. Some respondents had a refreshingly candid way of looking at it, for example, noting the mutual opportunism that it thrives on. Of course, varied justifications and even internal contradictions were found. One consistency, however, was the way the interviewees always had to posit their own behavior as relational to the superabundance of other users, seemingly doing the same thing as oneself does, on the Internet.

Rather than age being the most determinant factor, exposure to technology (as an indicator of knowledgeability, access, and familiarity) seemed to be important. Those who are more skilled and computer literate not only benefit from being able to make better use of their Internet connection but also reflexively see themselves as better placed to understand the technology in question—and by extension, the direction and scope of societal development. This might be primarily attributable to preexisting differences in knowledge, skill, and material accessibility in society, which might, however, be reinforced by current technology. This would arguably be less obvious in Sweden, where levels of Internet and computer literacy are relatively high and evenly distributed in society (WWWF 2012).

Regarding argumentation in favor of unmitigated file sharing, the primary referent in my own interviews—as well as in a lot of Swedish online discourse at the time—was the existing Internet infrastructure as it stands (Process I). Communication protocols such as TCP/IP, alongside open standards and formats, were invoked as being that which makes unmitigated copying possible, on a global level. Second, the observation that cultural consumption had remained high throughout the surveyed period was also invoked (Process II). While several of the respondents actively downloaded unlawfully copied movies, many of them maintained that few other sectors than the one for recorded music would suffer in artistic output. On the contrary, many of these file sharers seemed to hold audience interest in cultural products had not only remained undiminished but, in many instances, had been made even stronger as a result of liberal, unrestricted sharing. Third, the superabundant aggregate of topographic machine nodes (every "peer" in a peer-to-peer network corresponds to a computer but does not always need to correspond to a person) formed something that in some respondents' eyes resembled a people's movement (Process III). This latter invocation was also invoked in forums or on message boards, in captions such as "one million file-sharers can't be wrong."

The user-driven, social Web makes for a particular material setting, as it makes interactions quantifiable in entirely new ways; actions "leave traces" (Latour 2007) in a very literal way. The aggregated appearance of individual interactions can be thought to act as having a certain normative weight, such as when individual users witness traces of aggregated actions (such as the numeric count of number of downloads for certain films or albums) and take that as evidence for significant masses of other users acting in a certain way and/or being made to act in a certain way. This is concordant with Wellman's (2002) tracing of a process where locally enacted, traditional group solidarities are increasingly replaced with networked individualism (specialized relationships, transcending local barriers and enabling scale-free social networks) and Wittel's (2001) concept of networked sociality, where the informational, instrumental properties of communication takes precedence over its familial, community-making aspects and social ties that are intense but short-lived—strong as one-off experiences but weak as bonds over time. The resulting network appears to be unfettered, all-encompassing, transgressive, partial to weak ties over long distances, breaking down barriers and fostering global integration. The overarching topology of this diagram is one of a civic exchange that transcends locality and thus generates a superimposed megastructure—a totality, which might, however, be largely illusory. It is telling how similar this ideal is to the ideal of a universalized, all-encompassing market.

When my approach was repeated in a quantitative study in 2012—tracing justifications in a larger dataset consisting of a selection of the more than sixty-seven thousand answers to the open question included in the Research Bay survey (Andersson Schwarz & Larsson 2013)—I found that the invocation to a loosely defined market solution was in fact stronger among ordinary downloaders than the more dedicated uploaders. This would confirm the hypothesis that nonactivist users tend to regard file sharing more as an annex of the existing entertainment industry complex than many of the confrontational copyleft accounts would have it.

Peer-to-peer-based file sharing is premised on a behavior of search and acquisition. The intended use requires the user to be active and opportunistic. The individual uses do not just accumulate to literally become the system itself: To rhetorically invoke this accumulated use is a form of acceptance of it (especially when simultaneously arguing that peer-to-peer networking is conditional to the current Internet infrastructure). Configurations, when widely adopted, become normative. Those who file-share know they have the technology on their side and the sensible thing, in terms of regulation, would be not to curtail their freedom from outside. My respondents did not even appear to see this as political, until they were further questioned about it.

Paradoxically, alongside the narrative of progress and unstoppability there was a certain element of nostalgia in some of the answers. They involved a recollection of older applications in comparison to the newer, current ones, often likening the succession of different networks to biological regeneration—a view similar to that of generations of network protocols (Chapter 4). In my early studies, older applications such as SoulSeek and Audiogalaxy were sometimes invoked. Correspondingly, virtually all respondents made explicit distinctions between different network applications. These distinctions were often linked to similar distinctions of what types of content various applications lent themselves to.

While being supportive of unregulated file sharing (for several reasons, listed earlier), I would nevertheless claim that unregulated file sharing, despite being based on a strongly libertarian ethos, contains a technocratic dimension. Following Feenberg (1999), a technocratic system masks its political dimension by assigning roles and functions out of apparent technical rationality. While benefiting distribution networks that are often inclusive and vernacular, contemporary file sharing hinges on this technological rationality. Observing the file-sharer argumentation more closely, what hides beneath the seemingly altruistic slogan "sharing is caring" is in fact a very strong assertion, in thought and action, of what is perceived as a civil right, on the one hand, to take part in culture, and on the other, to personally manage one's own informational flows in autonomous ways.

3.5 A SHARED MORALITY?

Similar to the respondents in previous file-sharing studies, my respondents tended to make a clear difference between copying for noncommercial purposes and for profit. AG (m32), for example, clearly distinguished between what he labeled "pirate copying" (actively selling illegally acquired material) and "private copying." As a cultural producer himself, he strongly approved of the latter, in opposition to the former. The morality here seems to follow from what one makes with the file, something that connects also to the valuation of the file (economy) and how its technical form compares to other technical forms (ontology).

He differentiated between "normal downloading . . . for private screening" and "extreme distribution via large FTP servers." Data hoarding could be seen here as a form of tendency toward pirate copying, which would have more to do with the exchange/commodity value of a file rather than its use value. This notion implies that data hoarding would be a substrate of the file-sharing economy that is so manipulative, maximized, radicalized, and professionalized that it would be more akin to monetary-based commodity exchange than the alleged nonprofitable file sharing, which all of the respondents were very keen to embrace. When asked about possible moral duties that were central among file sharers, PN (m15) referred to the very same thing, not selling copied material for personal gain.

> I only download what I need and share everything that I download. (PN, m15, 2006)

Utterances such as these can be criticized, however, for merely serving to appease the respondent's own conscience—they should not be taken at face value. Indeed, when pressed, some of my respondents managed to confront the duality in morality; the private exceptionalism that resonates with the personal ego, stipulating that oneself can deviate from normative imperatives, as oneself is in control and can reflexively moderate one's own actions. I will return to this conundrum later.

Another definition of a pirate is someone who explicitly disagrees with or deviates from an established system. The term is both positively and negatively charged. One of its principal positive connotations is that of radical autonomy, whereas a more negative connotation would be the deviant or illegal nature of this autonomy. This definition was also shared by several respondents, and there was a considerable degree of distancing from the term apparent in many of their accounts. In the more specific context of file sharing, most respondent accounts came to imply that a pirate is not necessarily someone pirate-copying, but someone who would be seen as actively sharing (most likely, large amounts of) material, who prizes rare material, and whose affective investment in the activity is more than ordinary. LS (f25) held that the pirate identity would actually be a "mismatch" to how many young users feel. As there is a minority of people heralding a self-professed pirate identity (or brand), she saw these as playing the role of (more radicalized) spokesmen for the larger group of people (like herself) who would not stress the overt political dimension, who would not "reflect on whether it is right or wrong," but who might, however, still agree that the music business is "too expensive and commercialized":

> I would . . . say that a pirate is the Robin Hood type who does this as an ideological real endeavor, rather than like me—making up arguments to legitimize my own use. (LS, f25, 2006)

With the distinction between downloading for one's own use and downloading for selling, the users' actions appear to be based on some form of tacit moral supposition—that is, not only on explicit utilitarian rational choice. Although LS saw a difference between downloading for her own use and downloading for selling, she dismissed the (industry) argument that "file sharing is theft" as being too abstract—not in the often assumed sense that the concept of IPR is too complex or that the simple argument of theft would be easier to comprehend. Instead, for her, this alienating abstraction would lie in the way the argument of theft simply becomes disconnected from the experience of those who actually file-share. For the respondents, calling "downloading for own use" theft would simply be too far removed from their own everyday understanding of it. In contrast, downloading for selling would, however, equate something more akin to theft or counterfeiting—granted that an actual purchase would be replaced. Ironically, PN (m15) noted that he used to buy counterfeited copies before beginning to file-share. From this, I noted an interesting twist on the "file sharing replaces a purchase" argument: Nonprofitable file sharing could just as well be seen to replace commercial counterfeiting. This was seen in my 2012 study in which an Indian respondent (EC, m23) emphasized precisely this.

Effective and complete curbing of file sharing would entail an effective and complete curbing of private communication over the Internet; something that all of these respondents would see as a draconian, dystopian development. At the same time, in the management of their own cultural consumption, Internet users are given enormous possibilities to act in harmful ways. Granted this empowerment inherent to p2p networking, the crucible for a responsible media use lies in the users' own hands—a sphere of everyday life that lends itself to discretionary morality rather than policing from above.

Whether social utility is best imposed by collective intermediaries or as an entirely private means of personal discretion would nevertheless still be a political contestation. Here, the role of file-sharing communities is vital, as these, to a certain degree, set normative and cultural parameters; what is notable, as in closed file-sharing communities, such as the cinephile forum probed in my 2012 study, is that despite certain hardwired parameters (such as ratio systems for up- and downloading), most behavior is ruled by rather soft, normative measures. These are only partly specific to the community in question, as they largely correspond also with wider sets of values inherent both to a hacker ethic (Himanen 2001), to a late-modern consumer ethic, to a "perceived equity or fairness of relationships" (García-Álvarez et al. 2009), and to notions of a shared commons.

3.6 DIFFERENT FORMS OF FILE SHARING

One distinction I had noted early on, in some of my very first interviews with file sharers (as early as in 2003),[3] is some users considered certain uses to be of a data hoarding kind, whereas other uses were seen to be more culture oriented. The former category, data hoarding, referred to the behavior of acting to increasing one's upload/download ratio, or building an impressive database, somewhat regardless of what the data actually represents, whereas the latter, culture-oriented category had to do with making valuations based on intrinsic quality rather than quantity.

In fact, all of the respondents in my 2006 study described themselves as being inclined to the former rather than the latter, in the sense that they clearly seemed to value the particular pieces of music or film retrieved more than the actual acquisition of them (both as a process of acquisition and a display of it). One dimension of distinction regarded cultural knowledgeability, in the sense of the selective tradition of knowledge and consumption of particular works of art or entertainment (Williams 1961) rather than the anthropological, more holistic sense of culture-as-life world. The other distinction regarded technical knowledgeability (in the broad sense of knowing the right networks or of the more particular skills involved in warez activity). This was often directly associated with a dedication or preference for quantity of content, a form of tendency toward data hoarding.

Both SZ (m31) and VG (m22) noted how some of the clandestine so-called release groups paradoxically mirror the content industry in "moaning" about their releases "leaking" onto the file-sharing platforms. SZ pointed out that also among more everyday file sharers, complaints about so-called leeching would still be common. Yet, he added, it would nevertheless still be the copyright industry that complains most strongly and indeed formulates the notion of stealing as a continuously negative flipside to sharing. LB (f42) similarly noted: "Sometimes you have to keep from laughing when someone on a file-sharing network gets pissed off because someone has taken 'his' or 'her' idea, picture, rip or whatever it may be." Such complaints would be selfish and emotional rather than analytical reactions, she argued, a "me me me bug."

Virtually all respondents distanced themselves from this alleged scene. The perception of data hoarding among the respondents was thus comparable with the notion of a radicalized, hardcore other—the extremist among the moderates. These perceived others were also seen as having much closer ties and a stronger community ethos than the majority of more mundane, casual file sharers. Several respondents held that among certain users, it is the quantitative amounts (gigabytes and terabytes) of data that beget social status. Many respondents attributed the phenomenon to the ratio systems that are found in many networks (most notably DC++, FTP, and other members-only communities) where huge quantities of data have to be uploaded in exchange for download allowances. Yet, it was pointed out that similar rules were ubiquitous already in the old pre-Internet BBS days. The respondents tended to distance themselves from this, not only because data hoarding as an alleged mode of consumption would be decidedly manipulative but also because ratio systems were perceived as having been more common and more pervasive in the past. At the same time, the cinephile site that I explored in 2012 was entirely based on a ratio system.

Contemporary file sharing, as a totality, was seen as one that is too heterogeneous, instantaneous, and ever-changing to be rigidly defined structurally. The notion of an alleged pyramid of piracy or a tiered hierarchy only describes one aspect of the phenomenon; clandestine, exclusive tiers of content circulation really only have a role to play in the very first phases of dissemination (in the first twenty-four hours or so, of a certain movie, music album, or piece of software leaking) or when noting the continued popularity of secluded interest-driven communities, such as the private torrent tracker that I explored in my 2012 study.

When returning to the field, this time to survey the file-sharing world anew, I interviewed a number of members of a particular, highly selective and extensive BitTorrent tracker that is so exclusive that membership requires a personal invitation. Regarding this particular tracker in question, I had actually come across a thread from 2007 in a Swedish online discussion forum, where one user wondered if it really was the "right" kind of people who sought after invites to it; people who were just in it "for the buzz of exclusivity" were occupying space for "real cinephiles" who would, implicitly, be more deserving. Here, data hoarding serves a purpose—it is a requirement for participation. In addition, most closed BitTorrent trackers stipulate rather particular requirements regarding genre and quality as well, as these sites are highly specialized.

> The ratio system is what makes [NN] going. It's the fuel to the fire which causes it to burn. Yes the ratio system can be of a hindrance to grab good movies. Without the ratio system it would be just like The Pirate bay or Demonoid. The ratio system makes sure that you are honest and you seed as much as you leech. (EC, m23, India, 2012)

Because of the exclusivity and secrecy of this particular cinephile site, I had several hypotheses about its members—not least since I had personal experience, ranging back to 2006, from this tracker, knowing about the highly selective nature of content and strict rules to its setup. All usage on it is built around the common practice of an upload/download ratio, with the added qualitative requirement that far from any content will be allowed. Further, any form of disruptive behavior results in a warning, after which the user will be banned for any offense. To maintain its high-quality, cinephile profile, the site incorporates a content policy that is (in)famous in the file-sharing world, outlining detailed rules for what content is allowed, with rather extensive requirements in terms of file names and other metadata. As the site is an attempt to collectively build one of the world's most comprehensive libraries of cult, classic, documentaries, experimental, non-Anglo-Saxon, art house and rare movies, and encouraging custom creation and translation of subtitles for such movies, my expectation was that the users of such a site would be particularly motivated in this area.

Hence, I expected these users to be culturally knowledgeable and highly discerning and to each have quite extensive amounts of content in collection. Further, I expected they would be skilled in terms of finding content and consider it to be easily found, and they would be more meticulous in regard to content than most other media consumers, and occasionally express pejorative attitudes toward nonmembers. I expected them to appreciate the various auxiliary functions of this website. Additionally, I had the presupposition that they would be rather driven, pragmatic individuals—getting hold of what they want when they can get it, so to speak.

The respondents were all male, and all appeared to have a rather specialized approach to both media consumption and technology. Tellingly, several of them rejected the notion of having specialized knowledge in terms of file sharing, Internet, or computers in general and preferred to see themselves as "technologically literate" or "average." Judging from their answers, a relatively high familiarity with technology and the ecology of online file sharing was manifest; however, their technical skill and knowledge did not appear to be as extreme as that of hackers or software programmers.

Their level of reflexivity seemed rather high. First of all, the response rate was much higher in this forum than in forums related to other, more open trackers/indexes.[4] The respondents were sometimes keen to write very long answers: One of them was himself a media student and referred to concepts such as "outlaw heterotopias"; another one was also a student and referred to Baudrillard in one answer, libertarianism in another one, and later blogged about aspects of our interview. One respondent was an occasional activist, keen to question established notions of culture and property. Another respondent wrote a one-page account of the situation for independent movie distribution in Zagreb, Croatia, where he resided. Most of the respondents were able to critically scrutinize their own behavior and opinions. A shared justificatory trope was the emphasis on unstoppability and—in the case of this forum, even stronger than in previous accounts—an emphasis on improvement in access and hence emancipation (especially for people in poor countries or rural areas). The Indian respondent literally described it as having a blindfold removed.

> If you live out in the middle of nowhere but can communicate with other people who love Jess Franco films or obscure b&w movies from the 1930s, it feels great. (DT, m54, UK, 2012)

Some key differences were found between the users of this tracker and other users interviewed: Not surprisingly, the users of the cinephile tracker were more likely to actually buy and collect films, whereas other file sharers who I have interviewed were less likely to actually pay for films, TV, music, and/or games. These file sharers also tended to invoke things like ease of use and convenience more, whereas the cinephile users tended to emphasize the library metaphor, and the heritage of self-reliance that can be seen both among the driven, knowledgeable consumers, and the activists who build alternative infrastructures for distribution, such as TPB or this cinephile tracker.

Interestingly, both of these concepts—universal libraries and self-reliance—can be found in the Open Source community and its hacker ethic (Himanen 2001; Levy 2001; Wark 2004). The hacker ethic is characterized by an ideal of systemic openness and universal libraries, paralleled by a meritocratic impulse, and an awe of highly functional systems, serving the interest of large, even global communities. One could make the argument that such meritocracy (found both among hackers and in academia) fosters a brokered form of collectivism, societal awareness, and ultimately a sense of duty, mainly by channeling subjective opportunism to more utilitarian ends. Yet, in the particular setting of illegal, semi-hidden file sharing, this emancipation is nevertheless compromised—as the functioning of the system does rather little to ameliorate the fact that you have to rely on yourself and that the world remains a dog-eat-dog place, where adaptable individuals are rewarded.

Of course, the cinephile forum members would subscribe to an ideal where these conditions should be ameliorated, but, tellingly, such functionality—an editorial function that serves to advertise the existence of cultural content, enthuse audiences, and serves to educate those who desire to learn more—is, in the world of torrent trackers, rather secondary to the function of mere distribution. Such auxiliary functions are found on this particular site, but the users interviewed displayed a rather lukewarm opinion of these, as they personally seemed to get by rather well without those particular functions. Nevertheless, of course they relied on auxiliary metadata and advice from other users, but this was attributed to the world outside: the mass media in general and the Web in particular. It is important to note how this extraneous knowledge is in fact attributable to a wider sphere, or field, than the site itself.

Consequentially, both my 2006 and 2012 studies showed that self-regulation of file sharing is socially and culturally situated and that there is a wider need to investigate the political character of the file-sharing movement, because I would argue that it relates to new, hitherto rather unexplored modes of voluntary self-regulation. Ultimately, what this self-regulation turns on is how visible and, second, how attributable (or causally provable) the various outcomes of one's actions would be; the former determining how obvious the repercussions of one's actions are, and the latter determining how likely they appear to be.

In my analysis of the quantitative Research Bay study (Andersson Schwarz & Larsson 2013), some telling differences emerged between those who said they sometimes actively upload material and those who only downloaded.

In this global survey, an open question was included: Please give us your own comments on the topic of file sharing, especially how the situation in your home country looks like and what you think will be the next big thing when it comes to the Internet and/or file sharing. Out of the 75,901 respondents, 67,838 had answered this question. Out of that group of people, 5.3 percent had professed to actively upload "every day or almost every day." The answers of this minority of uploaders were compared to the answers of the 61.4 percent who "never" upload but still admit to occasionally or often download.

The justifications of unstoppability/resilience, opposition to government regulation, and the notion that the market will eventually absorb file sharing were somewhat similarly distributed in both groups. The two groups shared an optimistic approach to file sharing, pragmatism, and the notion of personal resilience regarding regulation/surveillance.

The nonuploaders were, however, more positive toward the industry and the notion that the market will eventually find solutions and/or absorb file sharing. This could be thought of as indicating a belief in a Geist of technology —the notion of a general, nonspecific evolution or progress. Moreover, the sentiments of the uploaders tended to have more clearly defined subjects: the vernacular masses of file sharing on the one hand, and the industry and its producers on the other one. In this sense, their accounts seemed to more clearly follow the dichotomous template of a copyfight. The notion of caring for the producers/artists barely existed among the uploaders, while the notion of corporate greed was more common among them. Seeing file sharing as a popular, vernacular uproar against the entertainment industry also appeared to be more common among them.

Granted, there is nowadays a plethora of discourses that stress the evolutionary nature not only of technology but also of markets and society in general. Hence, it is not surprising that these notions crop up in spontaneous replies such as the ones in the Research Bay survey, as means to explain and predict the future of file sharing. What the differences between the respondent groups seem to signify, nevertheless, is that the more active uploaders tend to be more likely to express discourses that have been noted in previous, more qualitatively oriented discussions and interviews with dedicated file sharers. This both confirms the data from these previous studies and shows the danger of believing that what is valid for these smaller subgroups of activists and fans would be valid also for larger groups of consumers and citizens in society at large.

The notion of community/collectivism was surprisingly absent from the survey answers; this could probably be attributed to research design (Andersson Schwarz & Larsson 2013). The general absence of tropes such as mass influence/clout, civil rights and shared community should serve as a reminder to us researchers, as we tend to overestimate those tropes that are of great significance to us. This miscalculation is further worsened the more common these tropes are in the literature. Another source of error might be that a lot of critical scholarship on the topic of file sharing and piracy is based on more ethnographic accounts, which, by design, tend to have a bias toward more verbose, dedicated, and thereby, arguably, more community- and perhaps activist-oriented respondents.

3.7 THE SELF AS GLORIOUS EXCEPTION

The respondents in my 2012 study generally appeared to be rather active, productive consumers. One of them had experience from subtitling movies, others had participated in activism, amateur music production, and blogging. When I asked about the reasons (besides the obvious, functional ones) for keeping the community so closed, one respondent answered:

> It enhances a sense of community, of togetherness. Also helps to build a sense of snobbishness. Our taste is better than other people's. I kind of mean it in a positive way. (DT, m54, UK, 2012)

When prompted with the notion of extreme behavior, they, however, distanced themselves from this, locating this with other users rather than with themselves. Some respondents pointed out that serious users, individuals who hoard data, in fact serve to benefit the community. One user once again invoked the library metaphor to criticize my reference to "extreme users":

> Not sure what you mean with extraordinary, extreme users. I'm glad that some people are dedicated hoarders (ok, call them collectors) and keep huge amounts of content and share it with me and you. Again, would you say that a public library with many many book [sic] is an extraordinary, extremist institution? (UE, m40, Netherlands, 2012)

> Again, I don't have a problem with elitism as a concept. The entire idea of a private tracker is elitist, but within it, things are as egalitarian as could be. (YG, m20, USA, 2012)

While almost all respondents agreed that one is very grateful at first, when starting out, many of them noted how a more veteran approach seems typical for many specialized file sharers:

> This can lead to different psychological effects, such as the perception that everything artistic is neutral. When nothing becomes hard to get, the value of art decreases substantially. Even more insidious is the perception that because massive archives exist and are accessible at any moment, there is no need to watch anything. (YG, m20, USA, 2012)

Does this experience of having access to superabundance entail a form of exceptionalism, or even a sense of omnipotence? For this user (himself apparently a competent reader of Baudrillard and Bataille) the reflection on such issues seemed to come rather naturally. He admitted to the exceptionalist, yet pragmatist reasoning behind his own behavior—bordering on the cynical:

> Personally, I don't justify my use politically. In many ways I consider myself to be above the law, even though I acknowledge that if everyone were to take the same actions there may be negative consequences for the cultural economy. It is also obvious to me that I occasionally deprive independent publishers of their due. I think of myself as set apart from the masses insofar as I grant myself the freedom to view anything for my own benefit and knowledge. This may be elitist and unjustified, but at least it is honest, and anyone who continually talks about the utopian potential of P2P is partially fooling themselves. (YG, m20, USA, 2012)

Another user similarly described his own use in very confident terms:

> taken these together, there is hardly anything i need that i can not find. or to say it the other way around: if i don't find it there, there is a good chance it does not exist. (CI, m30, Germany, 2012)

To me, this appears as a heuristic in which one sees oneself as the exception, knowingly breaking the law occasionally, in the confidence that one's personal norms proscribes any wider misuse. This is a common psychological heuristic that acts to evoke the ethical aspect of law: the malleability that norms and morals allow, but that law as a binary system of code does not allow for. In a forthcoming article (Andersson Schwarz 2013b) I explore this self-assertive stance further. It reminded me of how the actuality of praxis frequently dispels the myth of law as logos, especially when it comes to file sharing. This aspect of praxis can, for example, be noted in the courts' interpretations of law, such as in the Pirate Bay rulings of where the extent of single purpose was assessed to be significant enough to motivate a guilty verdict. In such examples, the flexible interpretation of law takes precedence over binary categories such as whether any actual copyrighted files are hosted on TPB servers or not.

In my 2006 study, PG (m24) invoked the significant monetary investment in a personal computer as a justification for expecting to use it to the fullest, utilizing all the technical means available. AG (m32) pointed to the relative leveling of opportunity that PCs bring; after having spent your money on a computer (and a complementary Internet connection), "you're on the same level as everyone else," he maintained. You ostensibly have the same basic access as everyone else, and, as with PG, he noted that "it is up to yourself" whether to use the information available. This view presupposes an economically empowered subject, having the relative wealth, time, and knowledge necessary. Given the commonness of computer access in the Swedish demographic, there seemed to be an expectance that all but the most dispossessed would have access to personal computers. PG thus considered the individual as the primary agent to be held to account, morally and cognitively; if you do not have the required knowledge for finding and using these networks, it is your own loss, he maintained. This individualism—self-made, autonomous, modestly bashful yet laconic, strongly self-motivated, productive, however, ultimately enabled by technology largely beyond one's own control—will be further outlined in the following chapters.

> Some make use of today's technology, others don't understand it. [. . .] Not everyone can mend their own car and they have to hand it in for repair while others manage to do it themselves. (PG, m24, 2006)

Agency is seen here as inherently individual and expedient. Technology is seen as enabling certain fertile outcomes, but it is essentially the individual's responsibility to be active and skilled enough to exploit it. Individual, deliberate lawbreaking is welcomed in this case:

> If there are laws that you don't find justifiable, I think you could break those laws in order to make a point. (AG, m32, 2006)

AG maintained that he was "furious" about the 2005 law—which prohibits citizens from what he distinguished as not only the allegedly harmful pirate-copying proper but also the allegedly less harmful instances of private-copying such as previewing films. Hence, he would not tolerate it and plainly kept breaking the current law, without ever feeling the need to explain his choices.

The heart of the controversy seems to lie in the strongly felt right to entirely exercise control over one's own, individually acquired cultural products. This mode of voluntary individual control is, as we will see, attributable also to the infrastructural properties of the Internet in general. The right to freely dispose of cultural products (see Section 2.1) is, in the eyes of these respondents, being directly proscribed by current copyright legislation. This individual right was, in most respondent accounts, seen as so natural that file sharing would not even be primarily considered as breaking any laws. The respondents' own understanding of the nature of file sharing differed remarkably from the mainstream discourse of malevolent copying replacing sales, so that in their view, it was actually the law itself that would break with the naturalness of the individuals' ability to freely dispose of their cultural goods. The actuality of free exchange thus becomes the touchstone to which the legal discourse of crime and delinquency becomes merely secondary. The law itself becomes a deviation from this established techno-economic norm.

3.8 THE NOBILITY OF NONINDUSTRIALISTS?

It can be shown that the file-sharer mode of argumentation—as exemplified by my findings—time and again reverted to probabilistic reasoning around the potential impact of the phenomenon on more established cultural producers. While drawing up normative distinctions between more extreme uses of file sharing (data hoarding, as some respondents called it) and more normal uses (private sharing rather than pirate sharing), this normative distinction suggests that the former (hoarding) approach would be thought of as, in some ways, more detrimental to the exchange of cultural content, as it performs the same operation as the instrumentalist, market model of communication. It thrives on the quantifiable nature of data, treating it as a substance that could be traded in bulk like any other. It should be noted, however, that in practice, the global file-sharing ecosystem relies on this large-scale, semi-industrial ripping of content, often illustrated by the notion of a pyramid of piracy (Chaudhry et al. 2011; MPAA 2006) or a scene of elite uploaders, enabling dispersion of pirated copies; the recent raid on Megaupload can be seen as an indicator of this semiprofessional opportunism as well (Williams 2012).

While generally advocating a typically civic approach to culture, the file sharers in my study thus tended to dismiss industrialism, both within the sphere of established cultural production (where record labels and representatives of the copyright industry were seen as abysmal) and in their own sphere of unestablished, unsanctioned exchange of copyrighted content (where respondents tended to distance themselves from these alleged data hoarders, albeit with more ambivalence than the more strongly avowed dismissal of the previous category). It is therefore plausible that individual file sharers might look on the actions of those who facilitate the sharing with great ambivalence, depending on how considerate the managerial work is seen to be: While "keepers of the archive" are seen by many as heroic actors, either in their rebelliousness or in their service to "stewardship of a knowledge ecology," their actions could equally be dismissed as cynical, short-sighted, or plain greedy—this is also how TPB, Megaupload, and other hubs have been portrayed in a lot of pro-copyright industry discourse.

Interestingly, the same would go for more established industrial actors. While multinational corporations tend to be dismissed for similar reasons as mentioned, struggling independent labels could be lauded for their labor of love and can even harness fans to work for them, for free, if the right levels of fan affection are nurtured (Baym & Burnett 2009). For upcoming, non-established ventures dealing with the problem of distribution, whether they are met with love or hate can seem arbitrary. Consider, for example, the dismissal of Grooveshark and unequivocal embrace of Spotify by music industry insider Lindvall (2011a), which is notable given that Spotify, as we will see, also began its life as a rogue index of non-authorized mp3 files.

What would this entail for policy or regulatory concerns? I have argued that these civic viewpoints would be more partial to struggling artists than to faceless corporate rights holders (Andersson 2012b). This should prompt transparent systems in which remuneration would preferably go to song writers and artists and not to excessive management and intermediaries. Industrialists would have much to gain in terms of civic assessment, if being able to prove how remuneration means something for cultural creators—emphasizing those instances where citizens (cultural creators) become enabled to take their amateur production to a professional level, thanks to record labels and other intermediaries taking the monetary risk. Recent austerity policies among major record labels have made such subsidies a rare privilege; nevertheless, there are signs of a sea change (see Section 8.1).

Imagining the Internet in a systemic and complex way is essential for any researcher of digitally embedded consumption—not least, since every Internet user him/herself would have a similarly imaginary view of the way the Internet works, interacting with these systems on a regular basis yet never being able to fully see or overlook the entire arrangement. Hence, as I will elaborate on in Section 6.3, all attempts at imagining the way the Internet is structured, and the potential ways it would impact the rest of society, are based on estimations and probabilities.

The file sharers recurrently emphasized that the systemic properties of the Internet are very expedient to mass-scale, unmitigated copying and that any attempt at a comprehensive, universal crackdown would be both futile and require totalitarian measures.

Conversely, the notion of a free-for-all, premised on the diagrams of networked individualism and networked accumulation, might risk reinforcing a simplified view of the cultural economy, ignoring necessary zones of inertia and disconnection that are required for developing originality, and nurturing those practices that are not automatically expedient to universal market logics. To argue for file sharing to be entirely unrestricted is very much to argue for borderless competition—laissez-faire economics.

Further, this chapter has touched on many of the dilemmas in a situation where users are endowed with such reproductive powers as they are in the current digital landscape: If regulation from above can never be total, self-regulation is always bound to be viewpoint dependent. This might lead commentators to argue against self-regulation, as individual discretion has a bias towards personal gain. Another conclusion from this chapter would also be that users would benefit from a wider range of perspectives, so that a mutual understanding between consumers and industry can be sought. Framing industrial concerns differently, with a clearer eye to a consumer—or even better, civic—mode of understanding would be a great start.

Intermezzo
Two Gatherings

2009

Her friend was well connected in the Stockholm hipster netherworld. He had had an early beta user account for Spotify, and he raved about it every time they talked about it; that was last year. Now, she had also made sure to get a trial version user account for Spotify, after they had opened up the invites process, and for this particular event she had even bought a twenty-four-hour period of paid access: No one wants to hear those annoying ads when blasting party tunes on loud volume, even less so when also having friends over.

The moving-in party was in full effect. People were filling the rooms of the 1940s vintage co-op, drinks were being poured, the gradually increasing buzz of babbling voices had her turn up the volume even more, so that sock-clad feet would begin tapping and moving over the crisp wooden parquet floor. The Very Best's "Warm Heart of Africa" was filling out the room, and a small group of people was congregating around the MacBook, enthusiastically chatting about what to fill the playlist queue with. "Yah, but those dubstep tunes are not on Spotify," one of them murmured. "You have to find it on YouTube."

Before Spotify, it was a cumbersome task to fill up playlists on one's own computer with stuff that you thought your guests would like. Most of the time, it all ended with people loading up Soulseek and trying to type in the particular songs they required to hear at that very instant. The alcohol rarely made these types of queries particularly easy.

Now, in 2009 in a place like Sweden, every party is effectively a Spotify party. In fact, parties can begin long before the actual event, by creating open, collaborative playlists where people can add whatever songs they want to hear—in advance. The playlists, all presented through the smooth, dark user interface of the Spotify client, allow songs to be cued while another song is playing, and those who feel like hearing, let's say, Boy George or the Bangles but can't find these artists in the computer's local music folders can easily search and find them on Spotify.

Even better, you can browse for serendipity. Through loading up some of your friends' playlists, you get exposed to new stuff that you might not even have heard of beforehand.

This is great, she thought, because at the first party she threw after having installed Spotify for the first time—when neither she nor her guests were in the habit of making pre-loaded playlists—she had stumbled into a genuine enigma: the empty search box where you are expected to type in what you want to hear. Her brain had been completely blank.

But that was *so* last year.

1999

The tinny quality of a 128 kbps mp3 file fills the student dorm pretty solidly, after all. It's probably the third time that Komeda's "Boogie Woogie/Rock'n Roll" is played this evening, and it's not even ten o'clock. Bodies are set in motion; some guys sway spontaneously and make silly moves synchronizing with the equally silly song. The sparse furnishing of the room is counteracted by its limited floor space to begin with; not even twenty people are gathered here, but the cramped nature of these lodgings make them a small crowd, absorbing both sound and drips of cheap beer.

We are in Linköping, home of the Swedish military-technological complex; a university town where cadres of engineers have been educated. Here, fleece-clad young men sing the joy electric as they tinker away—playfully unaware that in less than a year, in early 2000, the stock market will plunge and many of the currently budding tech start-ups (some of the more well-known Swedish ones being Boo.com, Framfab, and Icon Medialab) will be memories past.

Linköping is also home to one of the first student-run computer societies in Sweden, Lysator, founded in 1973. In the small borough of Ryd, Lysator members have built Europe's first residential computer network: RydNet. The construction of this local area network (LAN) was initiated in 1991, and it was inaugurated in September 1994. At most, 350 computers were connected. In 1996 the local borough built a larger network, SUBnet, and during the same year, RydNet's Internet connection was improved through establishing a 100 Mbps fiber link rather than, as previously, a 512 kbps radio link. RydNet was closed exactly five years after it was inaugurated, as SUBnet superseded it. By that time, in 1999, most of the student apartments in Sweden were connected to the Internet.

In late 1997, Per Rylander had moved into a dorm room in Ryd. He soon became aware of SUBnet. A few hundred computers were connected at the time, and around fifty of them made their music folders available. It was possible—but cumbersome—to manually go into each connected computer and see if the sought after musical snippet was there. He created a small program that scanned the remote computer and listed its music files in a text file. In early 1998, he released Perry's Mp3get (Reldin 2002).

Mp3get did not work like Napster that came after it. First, it was limited to SUBnet; second, it was in many ways much simpler, and it was more like

Direct Connect (DC) in that everyone made their own folders available and focused on what their friends put up on offer. Because the sharing was only between friends, it was considered legal at the time. One person who was around at the time puts it this way:

> Mp3get was very simple and democratic. Everyone could download, without requirements that you would share something yourself. Napster was also very simple but when it disappeared and DC became the standard, I could no longer be bothered. If I remember correctly, most DC hubs demanded that you personally offered lots of material in order to get access. It became far too much of a 1337 warez scene—if you didn't make it your full-time job to trade stuff, you were not allowed in.

Now, in 1999 in a place such as Linköping, every party is effectively a LAN party. Still, Napster hasn't even begun to make any leeway yet. Playlists gleam in the smooth, dark user interface of WinAMP, and songs can be cued while another song is playing. Those who feel like hearing, let's say, Boy George or the Bangles but can't find these artists in the computer's local music folders can easily browse other student's folders via Mp3get.

Even better, you can browse for serendipity. Through logging on to the local network and browsing through your friends' folders, you get exposed to new stuff that you might not even have heard of beforehand.

This is great, compared to those old days when you had to bring out all your CDs and load up whatever you thought your friends would like. The CDs would all get scratched and end up in the wrong jewel cases, and you wouldn't even find anything reasonable to listen to anyway.

Now, this is something else—so much more convenient, so much more choice. It feels like the future is here.

4 Material Complexities / The Nested Historiography of Digitization

> Optical fiber networks. People will be hooked to an information channel that can be used for any medium—for the first time in history, or for its end. Once movies and music, phone calls and texts reach households via optical fiber cables, the formerly distinct media of television, radio, telephone, and mail converge, standardized by transmission frequencies and bit format. (Kittler 1999: 1)

The current situation of computer end users sharing copyrighted material with impunity—en masse, anonymously, and with full discretion—is often depicted as a crisis of control: the spiraling by-product of the convergence of computer, audiovisual, and telecommunication media making it possible to convert any textual product to instantly duplicable data. This convergence is also said to imply the interconnection and blurring of roles between users, distributors, and producers, as well as "narrowcasting" (see Hirsch 1998; Jenkins 2006). The technological "monster" of file sharing was spawned largely as a result of the consistent digitization of cultural products brought about by the content industry itself, through its dedicated conversion to formats such as CD and DVD throughout the 1990s. Thanks to increased broadband connectivity and the implicit potential of extensive sharing, it was apparent, already in 1999 with the soaring wildfire popularity of Napster, that the situation seemed—at least in terms of its widespread adoption—irreversible.

Ironically, the praise of free flows of information, which has been so vital to the historiography and futurology of the Internet, suddenly became problematic when it was realized to what extent old media forms would be remediated by new ones. File sharing, which in its early days was more or less synonymous with Napster, thus came to prompt an extensive system of prohibition of information exchange through laws and technical implementations: Literally thousands of civil lawsuits have been issued by the entertainment industry in their worldwide clampdown on illegal file sharing. Perversely, this tendency toward the constriction of civil liberties on purely commercial grounds seemed to coincide with the aftermath of a world-changing event, which came to inhibit civic communicative exchange in much more sinister ways: 9/11.

A series of protocols that allow for unrestricted data exchange—in other words, the various networks that comprise the Internet—were used in ways that were in part expected, as digitization (the encoding of cultural artifacts as pure data) and the subsequent exchange of this data had been prefigured as a fictional imaginary in a variety of discourses ranging from cyberpunk to neoliberal, celebratory accounts of the Internet as an "information superhighway." What was wholly unexpected was how quickly this infrastructural transformation came about and how monumental its impact was on certain economic institutions, most notably the entertainment industry. File sharing thus moved the compass of informational capitalism in a direction that directly contradicted "the carefully mapped-out plans drawn by some large corporate and government players" (Oram 2001: 395). As we have seen, the copyfight metaphor suggests that there would be a tug-of-war going on, between two views of how to use technology and information. The totalizing, binary aspects of digital infrastructures appear to force each side of the debate to adopt a stance that asks for all or nothing: either giving consumers and users the maximum amount of control over the application of technology and information or maintaining that the providers of information or technology should be able control all uses of it. If any slippage is allowed, each strategy is thought to fail.

While still constituting a vast part of the overall data traffic on the Internet, in sheer volume BitTorrent traffic is currently being paralleled and even superseded by streamed video and cyberlockers. Regarding the recently documented raid on one particularly well-known such site, Megaupload, and the closure of private file-sharing hubs such as Library.nu, it should be noted that the landscape of private torrent trackers operating outside of the public limelight is still largely unaffected by these public crackdowns. File sharing on the Internet could, so far, be compared to a multi-headed hydra (Maxwell 2007) in the sense that it constantly evolves and mutates, in reaction to regulatory measures but also in precautionary moves, anticipating interventions from the legislative establishment by strengthening the resilience, (relative) anonymity, and the inability to oversee the file-sharing infrastructures.

If there is one lesson to be learned from the Pirate Bay trial, it is that the infrastructures tend to outlive even their progenitors; the founders of the site are now expecting prison sentences, while the site lives on and has become even more resilient than before, being mirrored on several different servers and seeing numerous caching services offering access to it even in countries where the internet protocol (IP) address of the site would be filtered or blocked. When writing about TPB in 2009, it made sense to talk about this site in terms of establishing a resilient hub or, as I called it, a "strategic sovereign" (Andersson 2009a). Now, however, while the site still remains more popular than ever, some new developments are discernible that should be troubling to whoever runs it.

To begin with, we should note the growing tendency among national jurisdictions of filtering access to services such as TPB. These blockages can, however, be quite easily circumvented through the use of proxies and mirror sites. A more troubling threat, in the short run, would be court injunctions against ISPs who host or offer access to the site. Since the infamous trial in 2009, the management of TPB is unclear in terms of who actually runs the site. One thing is for sure: Between May 2010 and February 2013, the Swedish Pirate Party (SPP) offered server space, hosting the front page of the site. The actual torrent orchestration, it should be noted, was, however, separate from that operation (and was dispensed with in 2012, as TPB resorted to exclusively use so-called magnet links). The party offered this support when Cyberbunker, the German ISP that was hosting TPB's front page at the time, was the target of a court injunction. This would arguably have made it harder to close down TPB, because it could now be seen that doing so would be akin to political censorship. Nevertheless, one should recall that the original raid on TPB in 2006 involved a sweep of the entire server hall where the site was hosted, taking down political websites as part of this crackdown. Later, it emerged that this raid might have been the result of secret diplomatic bartering between the US and Swedish governments, but that allegation remains unconfirmed. Recently, in February 2013, the Swedish antipiracy group, Swedish Rights Alliance, threatened the SPP with legal action unless they would not dispense with this hosting. The hosting was then taken over by the Catalan and Norwegian Pirate parties, and more lately TPB seems to have shifted server routing on a regular, cat-and-mouse basis.

Authorities in a number of countries have recently been winning injunctions against TPB. In December 2012, a proxy of the website run by the Pirate Party UK was shut down, following a threat of legal action by the British Phonographic Industry (BPI). These events should teach us that affiliating one's strategic hub with political entities does not guarantee immunity; as we will see also in the next chapter, constant efforts have been made to make the sharing even less tied to central hubs or singular ISPs.

What is more troubling, however, is that a shift in regulation seems to be under way in which the concerted focus on hindering illicit media consumption is increasingly understood to be enabled through surveillance practices. Through monitoring, tracking, identifying, and enumerating both users, hubs, and even the actual cultural artifacts in circulation, the ambition is to nip file sharing in the bud through a combination of two tendencies: data mining and its subsequent extraction of patterns and prediction of future movement and the establishment of governmentality, in that users who expect to be surveyed change their behavior accordingly, beginning to police their own behavior. The move toward policing ISPs and hubs instead of individual end users is both easier to implement and less problematic to argue for, when compared to draconian lawsuits and the outright prohibition of information exchange. With the establishment of new, proprietary platforms for social networking (Facebook, Twitter, Google+) and for media consumption (Spotify, Hulu, Netflix), extensive data collection and analysis can take place in the back end, allowing for this more strategic corporate anticipation of popular behaviors. Further, by letting everyday civic activity play out on entirely commercial, privately owned platforms, the distinction between private and public can be more thoroughly policed than previously.

4.1 THE NESTED HISTORIOGRAPHY OF FILE SHARING

Throughout the last decade, most file-sharing applications have been fairly rudimentary in that even those applications that involved a central server for keeping track of the files circulating (Napster) or those applications that rely on links indexed on ordinary Web servers (BitTorrent) still require users to actively seek out the material they are after and to personally signpost the material they want to upload and spread. Most, if not all of the current file-sharing applications are configured to beget engagement and tinkering in that they reward individual user skills: The infrastructures involved are far from self-explanatory, and those users who know their way around are rewarded. To instigate one's acquisition of content is a decidedly active operation, whereas the speed of the actual download, once it has begun, depends more on the overall network. The ease of finding a particular file is a function of the amount of users offering that particular file at the time, combined with the way the design of the application allows for easy availability in terms of editorial selection and search. If a file is inaccurately named or labeled, it matters little if hundreds of users are simultaneously offering it—it will still be next to impossible to find it by means of a pure, unaided search function. The role of an index of links, such as TPB, is thus to simplify the users' search for content, as such indexes provide metadata about the files actually circulating. As we will see, the hyperlinked nature of the Web is able to provide further deepening and improved editorial functions, systemically extraneous to the actual exchange itself. In terms of legality, under the DMCA such extraneous functions are allowed if they provide a considerable range of non-infringing uses. An index that is, in the court's opinion, exclusively geared toward torrent exchange of copyrighted material (e.g., TPB) would in this view be much more problematic than one that provides a range of parallel uses, most of which are legal (e.g., Google).

I would argue that this emphasis on individual activity can be associated to at least four images of the archetypal media user:

1. The "interpretative resistance" of the *active audience* thesis in 1980s and 1990s Anglo-American cultural studies, typified by authors such as Ang (1991), Morley (1992; 1993), Fiske (1989), Livingstone (1990), and Lull (1995).
2. The *hacker ethic* outlined by Himanen (2001), Raymond (1999), Wark (2004), and others, whose emphasis lies on the freedom to tinker and to improve technological systems in evolutionary ways, through concepts such as crowdsourcing and participative infrastructures.

3. The visible productivity of what has been called "prosumers" (Toffler 1980), "pro-ams" (Leadbeater & Miller 2004), or "produsers" (Bruns 2008), nowadays broadly typified by the concept of mostly *amateur-based contribution* of user-generated content in Web 2.0 and social networking.
4. The entrepreneurial, futuristic *techno-entrepreneurialism* mentioned earlier, typified by Silicon Valley startups, Harvard and Stanford alumni, publications such as *TechCrunch* and *Wired Magazine,* and authors such as Kevin Kelly, emphasizing new platforms or services. This ethos has recently been criticized by Morozov (2013) as a form of "solutionism."

The difference can be expressed as that between participation in media production (active engagement) and interaction with media content (passive engagement); Carpentier (2011) expands on this in his critique of user-generated content. Ironically, the audience as an object invented by media institutions and corporations, as criticized by Ang (1996), returns through the reification of audience numbers that digitization makes possible. Further, the often hyperbolic claims and assertions of the fourth group of commentators often involves a dismissal of the first wave of audience participation. One example would be the acerbic dismissal of television articulated by Shirky (2010), where the entire medium of television is casually written off as a sedative—a black hole where media audiences' time is consumed in unproductive ways. The sophisticated reconceptualization of the entire notion of "couch potatoes" articulated through the turn to media anthropology by the abovementioned authors in the 1980s and 1990s is largely dismissed. Lunenfeld (2011) seems to make a similar move, in pejoratively characterizing television as inducing a "diabetes of the mind."

The cognitive value that television has for its audiences—the ways they interpret, answer back, and negotiate with it—apparently all falls short when compared to the allegedly more productive use of time among Wikipedia editors (to revisit Shirky's example). The TV audience activity is not accounted for in terms of leaving any tracks—data trails—that, in turn, could be harnessed and transformed into monetary capital.

I hope this example helps show how the present notion of audience activity has an uncanny mirror image, in that—due to the nature of digital infrastructures—the vastly expanded possibilities for creativity, interaction, and choice simultaneously engender "data doubles"—subjects for surveillance, monitoring, and tracking. In this sense, the possibility to tinker, to cloak one's activity, and to avoid interception are features that could be said to typify unregulated file sharing; this is what distinguishes the phenomenon from pacified media uses. I would argue that this is what separates media consumption through file sharing from those modes of consumption that are more willingly submissive to corporate infrastructures of monitoring and metering. The differences appear more starkly here than when looking at the actual content circulating, since both file-sharing infrastructures and legal infrastructures allow for a long tail to thrive, while in many ways remaining partial to mainstream content. The ability to maximize both extremes of the long tail diagram is, as we have seen, a function of distributive capacities (which are strong, both in legal and illegal models). At the same time, the ability to highlight the middle section of it is, instead, a function of an editorial capacity (which still remains to be improved after the huge leap forward in distributive capacities thanks to digitization). Equally, when looking at the subjectivities engendered by file sharing, many similarities seem to exist between ordinary cultural consumers and file sharers. Whether this is a result of ordinary consumers in fact being file sharers, I cannot say, but when looking at the younger segment of the population in a country such as Sweden, that seems to be a largely verifiable observation. Similarly, when examining the self-reflexive attitudes among file sharers—most notably, dispositions toward the nature of culture and assessments of what actually counts in terms of cognitive labor—these attitudes largely resemble those found among active audiences of the second kind (hackers) and third kind (techno-libertarians).

These latter two dispositions share a range of features, but what could be said to separate them is their attitude to legality; whereas a hacker creates an entirely new infrastructure through interfering with existing ones, devil may care, a techno-libertarian entrepreneur makes sure to pursue and ultimately secure the legality of his/her intervention, aligning it with the monetary system to be able to scale it and potentially reap the fruits of it.

All of these personas—the active, hard-won, inquisitive audience exerting a tactical resistance of the mind; the inquisitive interloper claiming negative liberty and the freedom to tinker; the entrepreneurial innovator claiming positive liberty, demanding an audience for him-/herself—relate to each other and can all be found, in different degrees, in any mode of media activism (floppy disk- and BBS-based warez cultures of the 1980s and 1990s, fanzine cultures, cassette cultures, radio activism in the vein of Bertolt Brecht in the 1920s, or video activism in the vein of 1970s grouping Radical Software). The file-sharer image is often charged with the connotations of these more radical examples, because these radical outlets—fulfilling all three propensities—tend to become the most visible instantiations of processes that shape or re-format the media ecology.

One example of explicitly activist usages of the current BitTorrent infrastructure as a technical protocol for self-published audiovisual content would be Adnan Hadzi's Deptford.TV project, aiming at building collective infrastructures for grassroots documentary filmmaking, involving collective archiving, editing, and dissemination (Deptford.TV 2006; 2008). A predecessor was Torrentocracy, a now-defunct project launched by Gary Lerhaupt (graduate student in computer science at Stanford University), which aimed at combining RSS flows and BitTorrent with ordinary TVs to potentially create a two-way model of broadcasting, integrated seamlessly with the conventional domestic context. More conventional BitTorrent search engines for explicitly alternative or noncommercial content include indytorrents.org and legaltorrents.com. These nested instantiations of media activity can, in turn, be historicized by turning to the concept of nested historical cycles of peer-to-peer distribution.

The structural diagram of person-to-person distribution—vernacular dissemination enabling exchange also between those nodes placed at the very periphery, or collectively between subgroup and subgroup—can be said to have its own genealogy. Since the surfacing of Napster and similar computer-based p2p applications around the year 2000, several waves of p2p protocols and applications have been seen, all belonging to what can be labeled the most recent historical cycle of file sharing. However, this most recent cycle of p2p distribution is in fact embedded within two larger historical cycles, namely the historical cycle of file sharing as foundational to the Internet, since practically all data networking that we know of relies on the free and unrestricted copying of files, and—far more generally—the potentially ancient historical precondition of sharing where copying or, at least, imperfect duplication can be seen as the principal mover of culture (Boon 2010, drawing on Tarde 1903).

4.2 DIFFERENT GENERATIONS OF SHARING?

Structural shifts and changes in the very ordering of the Internet should not be historicized as decisive, clear shifts. The development of the Internet is facilitated by the gradual adoption of new protocols (software applications) that are augmented by material upgrades in Internet connections, processing speeds, and demographic factors such as adoption of broadband. While the practice of file sharing is popularly established, policy makers and lawyers representing the interests of industries affected by this disruption have argued for an uprooting of the currently open, communal nature of the Internet infrastructure, replacing it with sanctioned, proprietary networks. These concerns have been addressed in the US debate on network neutrality (Wu 2003) but underpin the debate in Europe as well, especially with regard to the introduction of directives such as the IPR Enforcement Directive (IPRED), the Telecoms Reform Package, and agreements like the Anti-Counterfeiting Trade Agreement (ACTA).

Napster, Gnutella, Freenet, and the abovementioned Mp3get can be grouped and labeled a first generation of p2p networking. When launched in 2000, Gnutella was a fundamentally novel application, but compared to more currently popular networks it is, by today's standards, fairly crude. Gnutella's popularity coalesced with the second generation of networks, emerging in the shadows of Napster. This second phase of file sharing is principally defined by the FastTrack network. What defined the newer networks was a better efficiency in the balancing between centralizing and decentralizing elements and the ability to download from different peers simultaneously. In terms of popularity, it was FastTrack and Direct Connect (alongside the short-lived Audiogalaxy application) that emerged after the demise of Napster. Because of its reliance on visible hubs, Direct Connect is more amenable to monitoring and policing; most of the file-sharing lawsuits against private individuals in Sweden stem from their use of this application in the mid-2000s.

BitTorrent, developed by Bram Cohen in 2003, can be said to represent a third wave of p2p-based sharing, as it blurs the distinction between up- and downloaders and is specifically adapted for high-bandwidth connections and gigabyte-size video and software files. Its mesh topology makes for a radical decentralization, constantly shifting, making the actual data flow much less overseeable in its entirety. Arguably the exchange is impossible to track in any detail, unless the peer computers involved are directly monitored. The fragmented way in which the content is "swarmed" means that it is hard to accuse one single user of sharing a copyrighted file in its entirety—unless his/hers is the only node sharing this file, or the entire downloading session is recorded at the receiving end. The stable elements in the BitTorrent architecture are the trackers, links, and indexes that orchestrate the exchange. This might help explain the move, during the later part of the last decade, toward policing the hubs and ISPs.

Because of the parallel existence of so many different protocols, the contemporary file-sharing environment is fragmented, with a varying mix of current and emerging p2p applications dominating in different regions. FastTrack applications like Kazaa and Grokster were, for example, more popular in the United States, while eDonkey has been very popular in the United Kingdom, Germany, and Israel.

The pace of technological change has been fast, and migratory shifts from one network to another have often come about as responses to regulatory measures, such as when the alleged demise of file sharing that resulted from the downfall of Napster was in fact only based on the downfall of one singular network among many others. Some of the file-sharing sites or networks that have been litigated against and/or shut down since Napster are Grokster, eDonkey, TPB, Oink.cd, Demonoid, TV-Links, and more recently, Megaupload and Library.nu.

However, it has not always been external crackdowns that have led to the adoption of new applications and protocols. Certain early file-sharing protocols, such as Gnutella, rapidly fell out of popularity even before the advent of BitTorrent-based sharing—arguably as a result of being technically outmoded, not as a result of policing. Gnutella still exists; it is extremely decentralized, very hard to shut down, impervious to external measures, and thus overlooked by the policing authorities.

Alongside BitTorrent, Web-based cyberlockers—most notably, Rapidshare and Mediafire, in addition to countless other sites and services—represent what seems to be a current trend within file sharing. I would not, however, call this a fourth generation of p2p-based sharing, as they break with the p2p diagram and instead work as a continuation of server-based storage, more akin to FTP than to Napster.

Superficially, it seems like these newer models would offer a smaller variety of files, because they all have to be seeded, allocated publicly available links, and announced via Web-based forums. But in reality, the mobility, accessibility, and ease of Web-published file directories seem to have contributed to a plethora of content searchable and available via an ordinary Web browser.

Reasonably severe attempts have been made at closing down the cyberlockers infrastructure, such as the globally coordinated raid on Megaupload, led by the FBI and aided by New Zealand police forces (Williams 2012). Also here, national jurisdictions seem to safeguard relative autonomy: In late 2011, the Swiss government reported that their comparatively liberal Internet regulation would be sustained (Lee 2011), effectively allowing services such as Rapidshare to remain operational. Some infamous unauthorized indexes of copyrighted literature, such as Library.nu, Aaaaarg, and Avaxhome, similarly operate by having an index placed on Web servers, where links are found that point to material located elsewhere—most often on cyberlockers.

Several protocols interrelate; the Internet could be seen as layers upon layers of complexity, made possible by the underlying protocols. Spotify may seem centralized and unidirectional but nevertheless features p2p "under the hood." Web 2.0 and cloud computing may seem decentralized and bi-directional, but these phenomena are only made possible by the employment of huge server farms, constantly dependent on a constant flow of cheap electricity and hardware—and thus dependent on the geopolitical conditions.

New, safer services geared toward a client-server or producer-consumer diagram are making inroads. Later in this book I will discuss this as a process of "spotification". Whereas p2p-based file sharing is expected to have grown by 16 percent from 2009 to 2014, other means of file sharing, such as cyberlockers, are expected to have grown by 47 percent. Despite this growth, p2p as a percentage of consumer Internet traffic is expected to have dropped to 17 percent of consumer Internet traffic by 2014, down from 39 percent at the end of 2009 (Cisco 2010). Besides pointing to how the legislation and execution of copyright laws have hardened and ultimately come to serve multinational corporations, cyberliberties activists also point to the appeasement of civic demands by means of such mall-like outlets. Meanwhile, the nebulous economy of the file-sharing world and other illicit distribution networks continues to thrive, arguably growing. This underworld is next to impossible to fully survey or even oversee, for various reasons that we will return to.

4.3 COMPLEX ASSEMBLAGES REQUIRE UNDERLYING UNIFORMITY

The Internet can be said to be sequestered vertically, in terms of access to its various applications: Think of it as layered according to the network stack, with the physical layer at the bottom, followed by various protocol layers, some of which literally comprise applications, requiring specific means of access. Without access to the Skype software, one cannot, for example, use that particular voice-over-IP (VOIP) application. It can also be seen to be sequestered horizontally, in terms of linguistic and geographical borders. Further, the vastly heterogeneous and ambiguous nature of the digital media ecology—its wide range of content circulating and communities generated—all rely on a paradox: Complexity of expression requires a high degree of uniformity of language/protocol, even totalizing aspects.

Like human language in general, all digital communication relies on a shared code. The difference, however, between machine-based communication and human communication is that whereas humans have the capacity to parse ambiguous, often contradictory and circular thought, our current machines cannot allow for any ambiguity or uncertainty of language/protocol. This dynamic between totalizing, determining aspects and heterogeneous, decentralized ones is vital for understanding digitization. As many authors have pointed out (e.g., Lessig 1999; Galloway 2004; Galloway & Thacker 2007) one needs a grasp of complexity—the understanding that systems can be rigidly determinist on one level, while highly malleable on another—to avoid falling into the traps of crude determinism.

A historiography of the Internet needs to take into careful consideration the underlying infrastructural conditions—primarily, the Internet protocol stack, where the Internet Protocol Suite (known as the TCP/IP model) and the Domain Name System (DNS) are the central constituents—and the spatio-temporal durability of the various establishments that harness these underlying infrastructural conditions in different ways. The Internet contains, within it, a range of heterogeneous applications and practices; some with a long life, some already forgotten. The IP number system, for example, is particularly durable (however, addresses are running out and the new IPv6 system is being gradually implemented). Applications such as e-mail are extremely durable, as are protocols and applications such as Gnutella, Soulseek, and BitTorrent, whereas particular instantiations that make use of these established protocols—such as the Kazaa client used to access content shared through the FastTrack protocol or the µTorrent client used for accessing content shared through the BitTorrent protocol—are much more susceptible to discontinuation. The history of the Internet is full of sites and services that were discontinued without disrupting the underlying phenomenon of which these hubs served as instantiations: GeoCities was abandoned while the personal homepage lived on; MySpace fell out of fashion despite the trend of social networking; Audiogalaxy was outlawed despite the popularity of exchange of mp3 files. Just as one must not conflate the epiphenomenon with the primary phenomenon, one must not conflate the instantiation of a wider phenomenon with the phenomenon itself.

Instead of trying to devise a singular history of the Internet, rather we should embrace its complexity while heeding its totalizing aspects, observing it as an amalgam of various network applications, which all harness the preexisting conditions in various ways. In the case of p2p-based file sharing, my argument is that the applications and protocols should be read as precisely this; various forms of exploits (Galloway & Thacker 2007) of the preexisting comparatively open architecture. When examining BitTorrent, it is apparent how surprisingly durable and parallel to the operability of the underlying IP these exploits can be.

Second, it is important to recognize the mutual interplay between online operability and off-line. As Franklin (2009: 224) has pointed out, "the Internet and its constitutive practices and structures need to be construed not just as-a-technology but also as-an-idea." As online phenomena become normalized over time—becoming recurring, naturalized elements constituting everyday life—they can be argued to bring about new ontologies of the world. This is essentially an irreversible process; once people learn the concept of unregulated copying (at least in the particular ways this is instantiated by p2p-based file sharing), it is put into circulation and arguably only undoable through forgetting. Various authors have elaborated on different aspects of this.

Lakoff and Johnson (1980; 1999) have described how abstract thinking is dependent on metaphor; they note that metaphors express conceptual conditions, as opposed to a more traditional view in which metaphor is seen as mere embellishment in language. Larsson (2011; 2012a; 2012b; Larsson & Hydén 2010) has applied his theory to the phenomenon of file sharing, highlighting the heavy-handed ways in which the law tries to anticipate behaviors enabled by new, digital media while established metaphors (theft, interference, and so on) are razed or renegotiated (Larsson 2012d). Von Busch and Palmås (2006) have expanded on the Deleuzian concept of abstract machines, where processes or phenomena taking place in society are likened to machines or apparatuses (Barry 2001: 4–5), and these signs become resilient memes (Dawkins 1976) that can spread as if by contagion (Thrift 2009). See Sampson (2011) for a further discussion.

4.4 COMMUNICATIONS PROTOCOLS

The communications protocols that govern the shape of the Internet are the TCP/IP model and the DNS, and, for the Web, hypertext transfer protocol (HTTP). Taking these protocols in earnest, one will see that they set the framework for how the Internet has evolved and how it works on a global level. Some of the more significant books that explore this dynamic are Post (2009), Wu (2010), and Zittrain (2008). While the TCP/IP infrastructure makes for radical decentralization (akin to a fishnet structure where all nodes are essentially equal), hierarchical network standards such as the DNS are also vital (akin to a spiderweb structure, where some nodes are more central than others). These protocols look like they do for functional reasons, where a highly decentralized solution was required, not least regarding the problem of creating an infinitely scalable network without losing track of addressees and thus making the data un-transferable. The DNS is vulnerable to censorship as it can be unilaterally filtered, but such filtering is not exhaustive, as it is quite like erasing an entry in the phone book while letting the telephone number still exist.

TCP/IP preceded and has made possible today's file-sharing networks. Above all, this is due to so-called end-to-end design, where the underlying communication is designed to conserve resources in the best way—that is, by simply transferring ones and zeros, regardless of what those bits represent. When the information is piecemeal, broken up into small packages, it often becomes impossible for an outside observer to know what greater whole each individual part is meant to be part of. That discernment is not made at the point of transmission, but only when the packages are taken apart at one end and reassembled at the other. The only truly open network is, in this sense, a stupid network. The only thing it does is to shift data packets to the correct IP address. It does not care about what is inside the packages, or what they are meant to represent. No intelligence can be said to exist in the network—only at its endpoints. Smart features, such as encryption, content filtering, and quality of service, is handled by the computers that connect to the network rather than by the actual network itself. Post (2009) makes an analogy with telephony: The logic of the Internet can be said to be based on a stupid network with smart clients at each end, while telephony has always been based on dumb clients but a very centralized, intelligent network consisting of switchboards, relays and connecting stations. Telephony and the postal service might appear to be p2p, but actually only create the illusion of it, from a user point of view, as the underlying structure is centralized, rigid, and not very scalable. This logic is, ironically, attributable also to some of the file-sharing networks; they enable free exchange among users thanks to a centralized structure. Napster, for example, relied on a central server to connect the individual peers.

The Internet's own postal addresses are the IP numbers that become assigned to each machine that enters the network. The system, DNS, that converts those IP numbers to linguistic Web addresses was rolled out in 1983. What is special with the DNS is that it is based on a hierarchy, which can be likened to branches or pyramids. At the same time, these are not based on a central server but are also distributed, much like the TCP/IP suite. What is really remarkable is that the DNS is entirely administered by a private organization, the Internet Corporation for Assigned Names and

Numbers (ICANN), based in California and founded in 1998 to resolve the issue of how to coordinate the network without all too totalitarian control. Abbate (1999) has accounted for how this nonprofit company came to emerge and how it handles requests for Web addresses—with the power to refuse certain domain names.

The recent debacle over global Internet regulation reveals some of the vagaries of global regulation, as seen at the World Conference on International Telecommunications (WCIT) summit in December 2012. The regulatory landscape of the new millennium can be characterized as "a complex ecology of interdependent structures" with "a vast array of formal and informal mechanisms working across a multiplicity of sites" (Raboy 2002: 6–7). Spatial and geographical complexity has increased; the local is enmeshed with the global, as supranational legislation and global protocols and standards govern the uses of technological infrastructures.

> Global summits such as WSIS and the Internet Governance Forum (IGF), and regulatory bodies such as the Internet Corporation for Assigned Names and Numbers (ICANN), have experimented with new forms of multi-stakeholder collaboration that move beyond the exclusivity of intergovernmental relations. (Hintz 2013)

ICANN is one of the most visible incarnations of how protocol-based regulation can work on the Internet. The real civic input of actors such as ICANN is more likely to lie in their bottom-up—often latent and informal, but nevertheless effective—ways of shaping policy, for example through setting technical standards (Hintz 2013: 286).

Mitchell (1995: 112) stipulated that computer code becomes law on the Web, something that Lessig (2006) and others have subsequently pointed out. Unlike the workings of common law—with actors who are granted the power to punish you physically if you do not follow it—the rules for how to use the Internet are literally embedded in its hardware and software. Thus, there is less room for misinterpretation; in that respect, the use of digital infrastructures is ruled by binary logic. Either you can do certain things, or you cannot. Certain behaviors are given precedence in the system design and become built-in. The irony with file sharing is that the suggested behaviors that have been locked into the IPs in fact give the individual a lot of latitude, as these original protocols were introduced to maximize flexibility, anonymity, and scalability. Thus, another paradox emerges: The binary logic is—after all—found to reside with the law, rather than with the technology's way of functioning, since what this particular technology's latent lock-in effects actually enforce is not a tethering of the user but, instead, increased degrees of freedom.

Communication protocols can be seen as structural operators that provide both opportunities and limits. Taking a historical perspective, it is also clear that the newer, protocol-based communication technologies, such as p2p, streaming, and VOIP have added new layers of functionality to the Internet infrastructure. Through these architectural structures, various innovations have been consolidated; expected uses and behaviors are in this sense ossified, rigidity introduced.

Still, one should not conflate the nature of the underlying protocols with the actual social structures generated. Although these are related, there is nothing to say that the social networks seen on, for example, Facebook are more akin to either fishnets or spiderwebs, respectively. Rather, what is typical for social networks—similar to the familial human bonds in a village or between members of a global online community—is their ability to take the shape of so-called small-world networks, exhibiting both centralizing and decentralizing characteristics. What makes a small-world network so useful is its tendency to require very few "jumps" for a message to reach its intended recipient. These networks are found everywhere, both in nature and society, and are similar to so-called scale-free networks—complex networks, where most nodes have very few connections, and a small minority have many connections. As we saw in Section 2.8, scale-free networks can be said to be emblematic for free, unregulated markets marked by unequal distribution, and contemporary society seems to be increasingly characterized by such power-law diagrams.

On the other hand, the centralized diagrammatical structure—referred to earlier as the spiderweb—is the foundation for how we envisage almost all mass media: TV, radio, and newspapers. Historically, these mass media are closely aligned with the history of the modern nation state (Anderson 1991; Cardiff & Scannell 1987), and they can be attributed to a disciplinarian, panoptic approach to regulation, often assuming a Gaussian, normal distribution in the shape of a bell curve. The active node in the middle is thought to broadcast material to thousands of passive recipients: content that is culturally encoded (Hall 1980) in anticipation of a viable glut of viewers that is centered around and above the median-income household.

4.5 LAYERS UPON LAYERS

Post (2009), Oram (2001), and Wu (2003) present what I would call a mainstream technologist view of the Internet: a network-of-networks, originally devised as consisting of machines that were assumed to be always on, always connected, and with a permanent IP address. According to this view, the Internet should be seen primarily as an assembly of millions of local networks, joined together by means of an open protocol, systemically "blind" to what gets communicated, enabling messages to be re-routed independently of missing nodes. However, as Shirky (2001) maintains, with the invention of the Mosaic Web browser, what began to spread was instead a client-server model. Personal computers were not always connected and therefore did not have fixed IP addresses—they were only assigned a temporary IP address when dialing up their Internet Service Provider (ISP). This prevented PC users from hosting any data or net-facing applications locally, and instead servers were designated as powerful machines always connected and with a fixed IP address, while PCs were used only as passive clients for occasional Web browsing.

In 1996, with the onset of ICQ (the first PC-based chat system), machine-specific IP addresses became even less relevant, because the ICQ protocol made the individual users addressable, regardless of what machine they were using.

> This is analogous to the change in telephony brought about by mobile phones. In the same way that a phone number is no longer tied to a particular physical location but is dynamically mapped to the location of the phone's owner, an AIM [AOL Instant Messenger] address is mapped to you, not to a machine, no matter where you are. (Shirky 2001: 31)

However, with this disconnectedness and relativity of network addressing, PCs were able to virtually take on functions that had previously been restricted to servers alone. This was made all the more obvious with the rise of Napster and other file-sharing networks overriding the problem of non-permanent IP addresses to let the end nodes of the Internet communicate directly with each other. As hardware and software improved, treating PCs only as clients became less and less tenable. In a similar spirit, Oram saw the development of p2p and file sharing in many ways as teleological: "The continuation of a theme that has always characterized Internet evolution: loosening the virtual from the physical" (2001: x).

This appears to contradict what Hayles (1999) has concluded about virtuality—that virtual data is always carrier bound—yet, one can nevertheless note that in terms of practical functionality, increased machinic performance allows for functions (such as the ability to act as a server) to be assigned to locations where they were not initially intended. Regardless of the implied direction of technological development in such a statement, the recognition that permanent IP addressing and rigid client-server structuration has become radically transformed by p2p is important.

Around the turn of the millennium, the concept of peer to peer emerged into the public conversation:

> At that point in history, it looked like the Internet had fallen into predictable patterns. Retail outlets had turned the Web into the newest mail order channel, while entertainment firms used it to rally fans of pop culture. Portals and search engines presented a small slice of Internet offerings in the desperate struggle to win eyes for banner ads. The average user, stuck behind a firewall at work or burdened with usage restrictions on a home connection, settled down to sending email and passive viewing. (Oram 2001: vii–viii)

Oram continues by noting that the computer field then became "awakened by a number of shocks" (p. ix). A number of technologies, not fundamentally new in themselves, he asserts, were discovered by the users and came to have wide social impact—not only Napster, but also SETI@home, a project that distributes real-time computation across millions of online personal computers through making use of idle time, and the completely decentralized (still existing) Freenet and Gnutella networks. The client-server model of the past came to appear as surpassed. Instead, according to Oram, the significant communication takes place among cooperating users at the "tiny endpoints on the Internet." On a p2p file-sharing network, any computer acts as a client when searching and downloading files from another computer and acts as a server when it provides files to other computers on the network.

This may seem to contradict the ways in which code and protocols set the limits for use, but once again we should note that for the Internet, these frames are unusually wide, although specific. Any new feature can be built on top of the underlying infrastructure, as long as it does not violate the basic principles of it. These new features can be very complex, which is demonstrated both by IP telephony and by BitTorrent. As noted, among hackers there is an ambition to find gaps in the underlying communications layers that can be exploited in various ways, most often to the benefit of certain actors—and to the detriment of others.

What Oram and many others represent is thus a historiography of the Net, portraying a shift from p2p to server-client, then back to p2p again. The very first TCP/IP applications were of course a form of p2p networks, because the relatively few computers that were connected were of similar status and therefore did act as both transmitters and receivers. The commercial expansion that the Web went through in the 1990s came to arrange the Internet according to a server-client diagram, not least because the modem connections of this era usually entailed fast download speeds but limited uploading possibilities. This, Oram notes, degraded Internet use to a kind of second-rate passive surfing. What the developments during the last decade would have meant, according to this historiography, is essentially a return to the p2p functionality—albeit at a technologically higher, more complex level. Above all, this has been achieved through imaginative software solutions, partly in the development of Web 2.0, partly within the realm of distribution of data-heavy media content. In many ways, what we are witnessing at the moment is yet another layer of complexity, perhaps even a fourth step in this historiography, as yet another reversion might be taking place. We are seeing new updates to the server-client diagram—where the broadcasting structures are making use of the new, more sophisticated techniques developed in recent years.

Taking the historicity of file sharing into account, it becomes obvious that history is not linear, but that the network's diagrammatic structures are constantly reused. Older media forms affect the newer ones—while the new media forms also affect the old (as Bolter & Grusin famously argued in 1999). Herein lies a certain irony to digitization. With file sharing garnering popularity during the first decade of this century, it was, surprisingly, possible to remediate old audio-visual media forms in a distributed, granular, fishnet-like way, without the possibility of totalizing control or overview. Products, designed for centralized broadcast, began to circulate in a decentralized manner. The basic way to transfer information on the Internet—chopped into packets—is currently better suited to the fragmented, asynchronous file sharing of BitTorrent, compared to synchronous, real-time video streaming. Therefore, p2p is in many ways a more efficient use of network infrastructure.

However, the enthusiasm for p2p has led to many careless statements about its technical superiority. In fact, p2p is inappropriate for many applications. Most search engines work best by using a central database rather than a kind of secondhand guessing of circulating content. Electronic marketplaces have to provide an overview of supply and demand in one location, at one time, to set a clear price. With regard to transparency—that everyone should know all the relevant data at once—p2p is therefore not particularly suitable. Real-time searching requires centralization in one way or another. This can actually be seen in file-sharing protocols: Napster used a centralized server, FastTrack uses supernodes that store temporary information about other nodes, while a central component to the worldwide BitTorrent ecosystem would be the centralized, searchable indexes that are published on the Web, parallel to the actual file sharing.

Similar to the ways DNS is imposed onto the underlying basic structure, different centralizing elements are thus inserted into the p2p diagram. At the same time, p2p is such an efficient way to exploit the underlying structure, that many services which might appear unidirectional or centralized in fact involve p2p-based technologies. In the networks for cloud computing that Google and Apple have recently developed, for example, clusters of distributed machines working together along the periphery of the Net are utilized to speed up user access to the cloud. Meanwhile, the BBC and other stakeholders have collaborated in a consortium, P2P-Next, which has examined the uses of the BitTorrent protocol for streamlining commercial video distribution over the Internet. For a long time—until December 2008 when they switched to a HTTP-based protocol—the BBC's media streaming software iPlayer utilized a p2p-based distribution system, Kontiki.

4.6 BITTORRENT AS A PROTOCOL AND A SERVICE

With BitTorrent, files are made public through a process in which submitters upload an initial first copy of a file to the network (a process referred to as "seeding"). In sync with this, a static log file with the extension .torrent is published on an ordinary Web server. This file contains information about the file: length, name, identity, and tracker URL. Trackers are software agents that enable downloaders to find each other. As the torrent file is deposited on the Web, conventionally in large, searchable directories such as TPB, it is easily available and reachable with traditional search engines such as Google.

In November 2009, TPB discontinued its tracker and in February 2012 replaced the use of torrent files with an even more decentralized way of orchestrating the sharing, utilizing so-called magnet links. No copyrighted material is ever physically hosted on the trackers or in the indexes. Still, BitTorrent indexes and trackers provide means to receive and send copyrighted data between users. Legally, if the servers are deemed to have this coordination as their main purpose, while having few or any other purposes, the server owners can be judged as directly aiding and abetting copyright infringement on a large scale.

This visibility and potential traceability of the individual seeders prompted BitTorrent's founder, Bram Cohen, to wrongly predict that BitTorrent would not be optimized for widespread illegal distribution (Hellweg 2004). However, in almost a decade, BitTorrent has been regarded as the prime application for legal and illegal transfer of large video, audio, or software files. BitTorrent is, nevertheless, not at all suited for real-time video distribution (streaming) and was, until 2007, only very rarely used for commercial purposes.

Trackers can be either public or private. The addresses to public trackers can be added to any .torrent file, allowing the tracker to be accessed by anyone who wishes to participate in collective file sharing. Before it was disabled, the Pirate Bay tracker was arguably the world's most famous and extensively used public tracker; the Pirate Bay website now only remains as a torrent index.

A private tracker, on the other hand, is a BitTorrent tracker with restricted access, in that users are required to be registered with a website or community to use it. Most often, registration works by a user-invite process in which users have to be invited by other users to access the site and share digital files via the tracker. One reason for this secrecy is to minimize the risk that antipiracy groups would infiltrate communities and instigate legal crackdowns, but another reason is that many communities want to maintain certain standards concerning spamming and misconduct. Private trackers tend to implement rather strict rules, to maintain stability and reliability, and are often specialized in terms of genre and types of content. Despite being accessible by means of invite only and remaining very elusive in terms of public presence on the Web, many of these closed file-sharing communities comprise thousands of users.

In debates on file sharing, these p2p-based technologies are usually invoked as aggregated totalities, embodying altruism, community, or even resistance. When seen this way, individual user intention arguably only plays a parenthetical role. What appear to play a more central role, however, are the infrastructural particularities of the network architecture.

Take, for example, the default BitTorrent setting that makes each user share each fragment of the file as soon as it has been downloaded, hence reinforcing the protocol's particular logic of sharing from the very outset, improving the resilience of the network while discouraging leeching behavior. Or, likewise, take the negative aspect of the very same protocol: the problem of file death as peer interest trickles off, and no more seeders are available (Pouwelse 2004).

It is important to distinguish between BitTorrent as a company and the Internet protocol itself. As an open specification, the BT protocol does not belong to anybody; any developer can write a BT client. Project Chrysalis was a newer version of the BitTorrent engine, designed by the BitTorrent company, that was marketed toward commercial users. Although the underlying engine remained the same, its interface was designed to be simpler and more graphical, allowing for personalized, private sharing among individuals and e-commerce initiatives on behalf of corporate users (Thomson 2011). Also, in 2013 the SoShare service, a file-transfer service for particularly huge files (up to 1TB in size), was launched. It remains to be seen how popular such attempts will be, as previous attempts to commercialize the file-sharing experience have had mixed results. Further, a lot of commercial Internet operations rely on p2p operability: Both Facebook and Twitter employ the BitTorrent protocol to transfer huge code updates within their internal infrastructures, across servers. "The internal Facebook swarm turns every server into a peer that helps in distributing the new code, which gets it updated as quickly as possible. Without BitTorrent this process could take several hours to complete" (Renkema 2010).

4.7 LEGAL CLAMPDOWNS AND THE EMERGENCE OF ISP LIABILITY

Since 2001, when a US federal court required Napster to close down, numerous legal clampdowns on file sharing have been enacted throughout the world. In 2003, several lawsuits were launched by the RIAA against a large number of file-sharers worldwide, particularly in the United States. In 2004, the British entertainment industry began prosecuting civilians, and end users were prosecuted also in Austria, Denmark, France, Germany, and Italy. A similar strategy also took place in 2005 in Sweden, as well as in the Netherlands, Finland, Ireland, Iceland, and Japan. A strategy of attacking p2p network providers to shut down entire services and to seize customer information had also emerged during these years: In February 2006, for example, authorities from Belgium and Switzerland shut down one of the key servers for the eDonkey p2p network. Three months later, German police seized on 3,500 file sharers.

A parallel strategy is to go after the hubs. In 2005, Swedish ISP Bahnhof was raided by police on the suspicion that their servers were facilitating file sharing. In May 2006, PRQ was raided—twice. In 2009, the Pirate Bay founders were subsequently prosecuted, alongside national implementation of the EU Intellectual Property Rights Enforcement Directive (IPRED). This law marks the introduction of yet another strategy: forcing the ISPs to block access to file-sharing hubs.

IPRED was implemented in Sweden after a long delay, embraced by a wide political majority including both social democrat and center-right parties. It grants powers to the entertainment industry to enforce copyright policies more indiscriminately, at the expense of private individuals and ISPs. We will later see that it was paralleled by discussions of a broadband levy, a proposal that was embraced by various actors at the time but died in the water.

In combating file sharing, IFPI (2005) and other actors have conceded that they mainly target ISPs, as these are considered critical links in the general debate on Internet regulation. By forcing ISPs to block certain domain names, regulatory actors can discourage end users from accessing sites, such as when Danish ISPs were forced to block the thepiratebay.org address in 2008. However, what happened in that particular instance, as in many other instances of DNS blockage, was that re-routing and alternative DNS entries were quickly set up. Users were encouraged to access the site by using proxies, for example, bypassing Danish ISPs. As several countries have more recently tried similar blocking, numerous Pirate Bay proxies have mushroomed,[1] bypassing local filters. After all, DNS is only a shell on top of the underlying IP registry, assigning alphabetical names to the numerical IP addresses.

Also, a pattern had been apparent already with the seizure of servers at Bahnhof: Directly after this clampdown, only a brief decrease in Internet traffic was observed, and soon the graphs of traffic statistics were back on the same levels as earlier. The publicity resulting from the Bahnhof raid had only prompted a very brief interruption in end-user behavior, which soon went back to normal. This pattern was replicated in the raid on TPB in 2006 and, more universally, by the IPRED implementation in April 2009.

The Data Retention Directive (2006/24/EC) was adopted in 2006 and implemented by most European countries in 2009, requiring telecommunications operators and ISPs to store their customers' connection data for up to two years and to make it available to the authorities on request, allowing for preemptive surveillance of entire populations. However, the Telecoms Package in 2009 would apply more directly to file sharing: In the negotiations that led to it, the IPR industry lobbied for so-called graduated response measures (i.e., that citizens who infringe on IPR see their Internet access cut off, without fair trial). The proposed amendment 138 that outlaws such measures was nevertheless pushed through the legislative process and ultimately was adopted in compromised form, resulting in at least some degree of civic protection (Horten 2012).

To remedy IPR efforts at closing down hubs and stifling user access, it must also be mentioned that all online hubs that make possible an exchange between individuals do enjoy some legal protection under the E-commerce Directive (2000/31/EC), implemented in Sweden in 2002; a lot of discourse on the legality or illegality of TPB invokes this law. Further, in EU copyright law, as implemented by the InfoSoc Directive (2001/29/EC), those member countries that allow for a certain degree of private copying must also provide a compensation system so that authors be compensated for the alleged income losses that private copying entails. Hence, a private copying levy (also known as blank media tax) exists in many countries as a form of collectivization, a solution in which one industry (the storage media manufacturers) subsidizes another one (the copyright industry). This subsidization is somewhat ambiguous, however, in that (following the so-called Padawan ruling) only products aimed for private end users shall be subject to levies for private copying (via the product price). Hence, also here the law makes a distinction between storage hardware aimed for professional and private use.

Digitization enables multifunctional devices that can be used for both private and business purposes. Further, although all digital communication builds on copying, many of the end-user functions are not related to copying content in any practical sense; the user may potentially never take advantage of this copying functionality. Further, private copying remuneration is actually not intended to cover piracy—that is, illegal file sharing—although this is a common misunderstanding.

In Sweden, a levy was introduced in 1998, then called a *kassettersättning* (cassette tape retribution), later renamed *privatkopieringsersättning* (private copy retribution). Following a ruling in October 2010 arising from the dispute between SGAE (a Spanish collecting society for song writers and music publishers) and Padawan (a company that markets CD-R, DVD-R, and MP3 devices), the European Court of Justice (ECJ) made it clear that the sheer possibility of being able to use a storage medium for private copying would justify that private copying remuneration be applied also to that medium. In 2011 and 2012, the Swedish levy, similar to many similar European counterparts, was therefore expanded to include also USB flash drives and external hard drives.

The levy is handled by Copyswede, an umbrella organization for collection societies in Sweden. Although the levy enjoys broad parliamentary support, surveys indicate that the recent expansion lacks public support. In 2011, only 14 percent were in favor of the new levy for these products, while more than half were against it, and over a third had no opinion at all (Zirn 2011).

As the levy is not intended to cover alleged losses made from file sharing, proposals have been made—throughout welfarist countries—for some kind of compensation system or cultural flatrate. This discourse has a history that almost parallels that of p2p-based file sharing itself. Already in 2004, a *Berlin Declaration on Collectively Managed Online Rights: Compensation without Control* was presented at the Wizards of OS conference, a proposal very much in the vein of collectivist, social-democrat compromise. At the same time, the American cyberliberties organization EFF presented a similar proposal, as did Attac and other leftist organizations (Fleischer 2004; 2008a). In Sweden, the proposals for a third way of cultural compensation reached an apex that coincided with the raid on TPB in 2006.

In late 2008, Swedish collecting society STIM (representing song writers) proposed a broadband levy, a collaboration with ISPs in which broadband users would be suggested to pay an additional monthly fee and then be allowed to share freely. They, however, gave up the idea in late 2010, partly as a result of the decrease in file-shared music in Sweden: Spotify was thought to have made the proposal redundant. However, it emerged that the STIM version of the idea was more or less indistinguishable from the licensing proposition that Spotify was making at the time; the emergence of Spotify therefore preempted all kinds of proposals for new forms of blanket levies or fees in Sweden.

What is interesting is that both this broadband levy proposal and IPRED rely on tendencies toward state corporatism: the first one in a leftist, economically redistributive way, not directly authoritarian, operated by executive branches of the state or organizations operating under remit; the second one in a much more authoritarian way in which actual judiciary powers are entitled to private entities. Some degree of state corporatism has always been inherent to social democracy, as this political legacy has historically fluctuated between these two ideologically quite different forms of state intervention and state-sanctioned monopolies. Fleischer (2012a: 255–258) discusses corporatism and the establishment of institutions monopolizing the representation of certain trades or guilds (such as IFPI) in 1930s Europe, emphasizing that only when such representation is monopolized, we should label them corporatist, such as in Mussolini's Italy or Salazar's Portugal.

I propose that the political appropriation of unauthorized file sharing can be devised along a similar scale between authoritarianism (or vanguardism) as one extreme and corporatism (social democracy) as another (see Section 5.2). Since both the traditional left and the traditional right contain both of these tendencies, a left-right divide seems to exist—but diagonally rather than horizontally across the traditional political spectrum. The Swedish center-right parties, for example, contain opponents as well as proponents to the EU-wide authoritarian policies such as IPRED, ACTA, and data retention. The same goes for the parties on the left.

As part of the new EU-wide regulatory landscape, IPRED allows organizations representing the copyright industry to retain IP addresses from ISPs to litigate directly against potential copyright abusers. When it was implemented on April 1, 2009—prior to the guilty verdict, later the same month, of the Pirate Bay founders aiding and abetting copyright infringement—surveys showed that this "generally did not affect the Swedes' attitudes about illegal downloading of motion pictures" (MMS 2009). The percentage who equaled downloading copyrighted material from the Internet with theft had even decreased in that particular study. Other findings have been made that suggest that IPRED has not significantly altered the extent of illegal file sharing or, to any significant extent, the social norms that it rests on (Svensson & Larsson 2012). Another report (Findahl 2009) showed that file sharing only marginally declined in 2009 (with just a single percentage point, later to be continually resumed to levels higher than previous years). The hopes raised by the copyright lobby—that file sharing would be declining and that the creation of a legal Internet would be imminent—appeared rather unfounded, at least in Sweden.

The copyright industry seeks to benefit from a media image that portrays unregulated file sharing as being on the decline, and the introduction of IPRED (which happened almost at the same time as the conviction of the men behind TPB) was put in such a narrative in the national media, along with the projection that traffic would be anonymized (Gustafsson 2009). However, some figures indicated that file sharing regained popularity in the year after the IPRED implementation, which was also reported in the media (Olsson 2009). As with previous lawsuits against file-sharers in Sweden (Gustafsson 2008), the implementation of the IPRED law did not lead to many legal cases being instigated—yet some changes in norms appear to have ensued, as research indicates greater caution among active file-sharers (Svensson & Larsson 2012).

Those threats to privacy that are overt and spectacular—the proposals contained within the SOPA and PIPA spring to mind—are well documented and often invoked by cyberliberties activists. Perhaps less discussed, and more opaque, is the surveillance state currently under construction. A distinguishing feature of current EU-wide legal proposals such as ACTA and IPRED has been the implementation of state surveillance by proxy—that is, its new reliance on ISPs and private investigators to both detect and punish purported file-sharers through active, mass surveillance of Internet connections and through implementation of graduated response or three strikes policies for cutting access to infringing users. An early mover in this direction was the French national surveillance entrusted to Trident Media Guard, a private firm charged with collecting data for graduated response warnings under HADOPI. Currently, the United States faces a similar six strikes policy adopted by voluntary agreement of major ISPs.

Under the new regime, ISPs' protected status as a neutral carrier would be reclassified; ISPs would share responsibilities for user infringements and, by order of the state, must actively police the network on behalf of private rights holders. Government surveillance is potentially moving to the transport layer of Internet access in response to pressures to step up the social response to file sharing. ISPs are increasingly being treated as gatekeepers with greater responsibility for digital rights management. The old legal tradition that treated ISPs as neutral conduits for customer communications extended the legal indemnification of carriers for infringing content passing through the network (DeBeer & Clemmer 2009).

In August 2006, Cecilia Renfors (former director of the Swedish Broadcasting Commission) was commissioned to look into the issue of file sharing and copyright. Her study was published on September, 3, 2007, arguing for three strikes-type obligations also for Swedish ISPs. These findings were severely criticized by the Swedish Competition Authority and several other institutions and commentators, prompting the government to shelve the report. In September 2011, a new task force was established in Sweden to handle the backlog of lawsuits filed by Antipiratbyrån and the IFPI, including cases against file-sharing civilians. A National Coordinator on IPR-related investigations (Nationella gruppen mot immaterialrättsbrott) was founded in 2008 but intensified litigation during 2011 (Söderling 2011).

The end of ISP neutrality has been accompanied by impressive efforts to propagandize and reeducate citizens of their responsibilities to abide by maximalist copyright laws and by regular news reporting on litigation campaigns waged against suspected file-sharers and their hacktivist enablers such as TPB and Megaupload. The campaigns to inculcate fear, suspicion, uncertainty, and doubts about infringing activities online are deliberate and documented strategies of the content industries and their trade associations. The response of many net-savvy Internet users to the IPRED, the Data Retention Directive, and ACTA was to initiate new privacy protection routines using cloaking and encryption (Larsson & Svensson 2010; Larsson et al. 2012a; 2012b).

4.8 FORCED DISTRIBUTION AND RENTIER CAPITALISM

In my conclusive chapter, I will turn to Serres' (2007) notion of the *parasite*, a term that in his context must be read in a non-pejorative sense. Rentier capitalism can be described as a mode of profit making that is essentially parasitical. What is interesting is that this accusation can be pitched toward many of the institutional actors that crop up in the file-sharing debate.

File-sharers tend to criticize entertainment companies for being rentier capitalists in terms of the overly long protection schemes now enjoyed by rights holders. A patent or a copyright is a limited-time, state-sanctioned monopoly that acts to bolster the capitalist utilization of the work in question for the private rights holder.

Although recent research shows that the patents system lends itself to rent seeking (Boldrin & Levine 2013), the crux of the matter is whether the monopoly granted for entirely new works or for generic, otherwise accessible resources. This is why copyright stipulates a minimum degree of originality and does not allow for protection of ideas; there must be a high enough barrier to discourage rent seeking (Landes & Posner 1989). However, from this perspective, the extension of copyright terms can be argued to be rent-seeking behavior that acts to the detriment of the public domain: These are works that have already been granted protection.

Now, among the more radical opponents to copyright, the argument would be that all cultural creativity is derivative—essentially, imitation—but that argument is fallacious in that it stipulates a binarism: It does not allow for the variegated, shifting uniqueness of works. Some works are more innovative than others. Seen in this view, the binarism of the current system—automatically granting protection by default—is after all less problematic than a system that rids the author of any protection whatsoever; the current protection can be signed away by the author. The current binarism serves the author at the expense of the collective, while the radical copyright critique stipulates a binarism that serves the collective at the expense of the author. In this sense, radical copyright critique entails a communist dimension, whereas the original copyright paradigm is based in liberalism.

A less confrontational approach would be that of the right of free disposal of one's rented artifacts (as explored in Section 2.1).

> Say, I live in a [rented] house . . ., I'd still consider "my house", since I'm the one who lives in it. I may have a contract . . . within which I pay rent, . . . but I do not see why that also should give [the housing corporation] the right to suddenly decide that the rent should go up, or that I have to leave, and in many countries there are laws that protect renters against such an extremist idea of "property." (UE, m40, Netherlands, 2012)

Arguably, this, however, only goes to justify sharing artifacts that one has acquired legally to begin with. At the same time, the entertainment industry has began not only accusing the pirate sites for being rentier capitalists but also point to those legal companies within the openness industry that extract profit from the circulation of pirated material. Similarly, it can be argued that what the pirate sites in effect do is to enact forced distribution, against the will of the rights holders or other societal actors. Lindvall (2011b) gives an insight into how Grooveshark has made this their business model. According to her, they use forced distribution and the user data generated as a form of extortion:

> We use a label's songs until till we get 100m uniques [sic], by which time we can tell the labels who is listening to their music, and then turn around and charge them for the very data we got from them, ensuring that what we may them [sic] in total for streaming is less than what they pay us for data-mining. (Grooveshark investor Sina Simantob, in Lindvall 2011b)

Recently, a twofold action program has therefore been proposed among entertainment industry representatives to stifle attempts at monetizing flows of pirated material: (1) Introduce a mandatory fine for every time a business advertises on a known pirate site. Cutting off advertising, it is said, has, for example, killed off offshore pirate radio in the past. If advertisers do not want to be fined, the burden would be on them to make sure their ad funding does not go to pirates; (2) Remove safe harbor protection from search engines that continue to show search results for known pirate sites. This latter proposal is clearly problematic in that it would have to impose a prescreening of what material is allowed to appear in search results; this is the opposite of the retroactive approach inherent to current US and EU legislation.

Regardless of the efficacy or practicality of these proposals, the phenomenon of ad funding is extremely interesting, as it prompts us to question the line between legitimate and illegitimate online ventures. As we will see in Section 5.7, the case of TPB directly prompts such questions. Further, it would be elucidative to investigate why the ads on these pirate sites are so poor and often demeaning toward women.

The online market for low-end ad space is vastly complex, and there is a lot of slippage. Space is leased to providers in bulk, often on a rotating basis, and these often lack oversight because filling space is done by automated scripts. There exists a great number of companies serving the hidden Web in this way, providing ad networks and so-called behavioral targeting. In 2008, TPB was caught displaying Google AdSense ads in inline frames, probably because of the ability to "tap" AdSense ads that were supposed to only appear on a different site, by slotting these ads through an advertising server that rotates several ads. As this constituted a violation of Google's use policy, this practice soon came to a halt. But exploits go both ways; TPB would not have had much control over what ads were shown either.

To the pirates' defense it should be added that they most often run a very low budget operation; the idea of a staffed ad sales department would be out of the question. (Similarly, many low-budget, open-source ventures tend to resort to poor quality, automated ad networks, despite being fully legal and even able to attract more legit advertisers.) In any event, it would most likely be very hard to attract established brands to associate themselves with criminal sites; this effect is of course further accentuated by the already poor quality of surrounding ads, creating a negative spiral. What is more, if pirate sites were to serve legit brand ads (e.g., Nike, Starbucks, etc.) those companies would imminently receive legal threats from the MPAA and RIAA anyway, as part of the copyright industry's overall strategy.

An alternative to ad-based solutions would be systems based on donations. However, the current donation infrastructures tend to involve ties that are trackable. Totally anonymous donations are increasingly becoming outlawed as part of Data Retention politics, and because TPB relies on user anonymity, they do not want users potentially seeing their names tied to TPB and to get in trouble because of that. Similarly, TPB administrators would be worried about their own identities. Even if they were to use multiple conduits to launder the money, they would still risk a paper trail. Even Bitcoin, an online currency that has low traceability in its virtual state, requires identification when real money is to be exchanged into Bitcoins.

Adding to the complexity of this ecology, many skilled users have installed browser plug-ins that block interstitials, pop-ups, and scripts (e.g., AdBlock) and thus avoid the ads. As with nonpaying users on Spotify, only those users who are new to the operation (relatively unskilled)—or simply unwilling to pay for "freemium" access—would become subjected to advertising. Equally, they might not be bothered, unwilling to sacrifice time and effort into blocking the ads.

4.9 RETREATING INTO THE CLOUD: SOCIAL NETWORKING SITES AND "WALLED GARDENS" AS FORMS OF ENCLOSURE

After noting the teleological accounts that surrounded p2p by the beginning of the century, we will now turn to the expedience by which p2p as a technological protocol, in fact, has come to serve commercial ends and has become one tool among many in the design of a safer, more centralized—but arguably also less free, more tethered Internet, akin to cable TV (Zittrain 2008). The term *spotification* will be introduced, as it pithily summarizes these trends by connecting them to the tendency among commercial operators to harness the once unbridled user agency and force it into walled gardens governed by cloud computing, made possible by massive data centers.

The term *Web 2.0* flourished around the same time as p2p entered the public imagination. Before the year 2000, hardly any of the services labeled Web 2.0 even existed: Wikipedia, photo-sharing sites such as Flickr, video-sharing sites such as YouTube, blogs, and social networking sites. What distinguishes Web 2.0 is that users themselves are involved in the creation and distribution of content. As with file sharing, this is enabled by innovative software solutions, which make it possible to increase the horizontal information exchange, for example, by allowing users to comment, quote, and recommend. At the same time, Web 2.0 is made possible by massive, centralized data centers. In that sense, it is not a product of p2p, but rather a further development of the server-client diagram; essentially, it is client-server at the root, however, with new features added on top, enabling a higher degree of user feedback. The current platforms for social networking make for a specialized subcategory of Web 2.0 functionality; they stipulate very rigid parameters for user behavior and any comparison between these, and the modular, programmable hyperlinked nature of the underlying Web substrate should be made with extreme caution. On these newer, corporate platforms, the freedom to tinker is severely restricted.

In March 2010, Google's position as the most visited start page in the United States was surpassed by Facebook (Dougherty 2010). It seems to be a general trend that Internet users are spending increasing amounts of time within enclosed spaces such as Facebook, the Apple iTunes Store, and Spotify, which all are structurally separated from the general, noncommercial Web. These platforms require the user to have a verified user account—often with a direct link between the user details on record and a credit card. Hence, users can also be expected to act in a less anonymous way. Even the Web surfing that currently takes place outside of those walled gardens becomes filtered through Google's operating system, browser, and various network services. Currently, this type of surfing does not show signs to subside, despite anecdotal evidence of user migration from some platforms to other ones.

Users might agonize over the ways Terms of Use documents are spelled out on Facebook and Instagram and vote with their feet, but the resilience of the Facebook platform might be reconsidered when noting that the "Like" button is in fact a device that allows for surveillance of user Web browsing outside of the Facebook ecosystem (as it plants a so-called cookie in the user's Web browser for each such page, regardless of whether the button is actually clicked or not). Services such as Facebook Connect and Facebook Apps allow users to log in using their Facebook username on a plethora of other sites and services, strengthening the role of Facebook as an infrastructural resource on the open Web. Without having to gather the information themselves, newspapers can, for example, implement Facebook Connect and—by the very instant the user consents to it—get access to information on users' status, age, gender, interests, education, and so on.

Further, companies such as MySpace and Facebook have reshaped hyperlinking to suit their own purposes. In early 2007, MySpace added a function that redirected all the links from its users' MySpace pages to outside pages, so that all links were diverted to the domain msplinks.com, after which the user would be automatically forwarded to the linked site as originally intended. This was a direct response to spammers who were abusing MySpace to link to illegitimate sites and thereby cheating the Google PageRank feature. By cluttering a MySpace page with comments that would link to external sites, this would falsely indicate popularity. The introduction of the msplinks.com domain as a filter meant this scam was rendered impossible, and it was claimed that this reduced the prevalence of spam. However, the introduction of these kinds of proxies was in all likelihood not only a concession to Google. Revamped links of this kind are also a way for companies such as MySpace and Facebook to monitor exactly what types of connections are made by each user. It provides unprecedented opportunities to measure traffic and to see who makes linkages and to what. This increased traceability is introduced with the argument that it protects users and the overall quality of service.

In September 2011, Spotify launched Facebook integration, so that Facebook users would be able to listen to music recommended by their friends or listen to music by pressing a play button inside Facebook, without logging in to Spotify. Usage is made more convenient but totally trackable as well.

In these ways, the Web is becoming increasingly de-anonymized and adapted to target groups. If only the users begin to act under their real names, supporters of this system tend to argue, nasty comments, hateful behavior, and proliferation of morally questionable content will decrease—while the potential for targeted advertising, niche services, and recommendations will increase. The idea is that users would accept this partial invasion of privacy, thanks to the increased convenience and security. Harmful user behavior is taken as a pretext for increased control. The Swedish debate during the aftermath of the Pirate Bay trial accentuated the authoritarian undercurrent to these arguments: Whereas those who advocated external control seemed to hold a Hobbesian view characterized by distrust in the general populace, the activists loosely aligned with Piratbyrån invoked Spinoza and his trust in the multitude (Andersson 2009c). Later (Section 7.8), it will be shown how cyberliberties activism also owes a lot more to Hume than to Hobbes.

Moreover, platforms are increasingly integrated with entertainment outlets, much in the same vein as the Spotify-Facebook collaboration discussed earlier. Google owns YouTube, and both Google and Apple have announced strategies of making cloud computing a more integral part of the online experience. Both of these types of services require reliability and proximity to servers. In Sweden, one of the main ISPs, Telia, has openly cooperated with Spotify since 2010; its subscriptions are bundled with Spotify subscriptions, and one can only suspect that traffic carrying Spotify data is prioritized over other types of network traffic.

In the United States, the issue of network neutrality had been heavily debated in recent years—a discussion that never really gained traction in Sweden in the same way. This is a pity, as most people ought to be wary of a situation in which direct competitive advantages are built into the infrastructure, benefiting certain types of services and content. Dominant, market-leading software can, after all, be abandoned by users overnight, if a better option pops up, whereas the dominance that is embedded directly in the hardware is much harder to break up or opt out of. Arrangements of this type may prove to be a quick way to undermine the freedom and independence that the Internet has previously stood for, in which innovative players gained popularity simply by offering services that were quickly embraced by users.

Unfortunately, several tendencies indicate that such a development is precisely what could be expected during the coming years, especially as an increasing share of traffic is consisting of entertainment material such as video on demand and online video gaming, often streamed through appliances that are more closely related to television than to PCs. These new devices—smartphones and tablets—only allow software that has been approved by the manufacturer, and they cannot be altered or changed by users in the same way PCs can. Under many contracts and jurisdictions, jailbreaking or unlocking a smartphone is even a criminal offense. Although these appliances might be extremely innovative in terms of convenience and the fuzzy concept of user experience (Snickars & Vonderau 2012), they are not generative, but tethered in the same sense as television sets or telephones (Zittrain 2008). They are stupid terminals designed for intelligent networks. Parallel to this there is a movement in which the service provider-owned physical infrastructure is increasingly moving toward so-called hosted services: software that is not even stored on your machine but in the cloud. Further, the current transition from the old system of IP addresses (IPv4) to the new system of IP addresses (IPv6) might potentially allow for any object—even mobile phones, vehicles, clothing, and buildings—to be connected to the Internet and given a unique address. This would hinder anonymity in a much more radical way.

Commentators have argued that all of these developments amount to deliberate interventions to sanction commercial, harmless surfing over the allegedly feral, anonymous behavior that unregulated file sharing would stand for. The price of this safer Web experience would be a significantly narrower range of content, compared with the de facto unlimited offerings that file sharing would provide for. Several trends seem to be converging toward this more institutionally sanctioned, regulated, recaptured Internet where surfing is de-anonymized, linked to the user's true identity and credit card; growing parts of the physical infrastructure are owned or controlled by service- and/or content providers; an increasing share of traffic is consisting of streamed audiovisual content such as video and online games; machines are equipped with unique addresses and are locked in terms of user tinkering or reprogramming, as neither source code nor execution takes place in the local machine, but in the data cloud.

The term spotification is in many ways illustrative. This concept emerged in the Swedish blogosphere during the winter of 2009–2010 and outlines a business model of enclosure in the era of the long tail (Anderson 2006). It was coined in February 2009 by Fredrik Edin—one of the original Piratbyrån supporters who has been most critical toward the ways in which Piratbyrån did not fully manage to widen the debate on ownership and civil rights and the ways in which the administrators of TPB took the pragmatic decision to allow for ads and pornography. In order to spotify something, a commercial service provider has to take something which is free (that which previously constituted some sort of common"), chop off its tail (that is, curtailing the supply and minimizing the technical quality), encode it (that is, setting up rules for how it can be used) and, lastly, impose a fee for using it (either through an advertising model or through a subscription model).

Tellingly, the bitter logic outlined in this model is the same one that drives the invasion of public space by shopping malls; it is a universal model of enclosure. A similar term for this dialectical process is found in the writings of Deleuze and Guattari: *re-territorialization.*

In the light of this, the Facebook-Spotify integration mentioned above could in fact be read as a form of double spotification: Spotify links are embedded inside Spotify's Facebook app. To play songs from a playlist linked through Facebook, one would have to install a Spotify app particular to the Facebook platform to play the music; this is a form of nested architecture that is antithetical to the open Web.

5 Geographical Conditions / Sweden as a Case Study

The Pirate Bay and Spotify

> The goal was never to get big, but to get copied. (Fleischer, in Reddit 2013a)

The file-sharer discourse that I analyzed did not take place in a vacuum. In my interviews, emphasis was placed on representation, agency, justification, and morality, as well as on technical, economic, historical, demographic, and geographical conditions—all in all, invocations to generalities. Similar invocations could also be found in blogs, newspapers, debates, and Web-based comments.

One such generality is the presupposition of individual subjects who are highly knowledgeable and highly discerning, while simultaneously being, on the one hand, caught between solidarity and public collectivism and, on the other, a predisposition toward individual autonomy and the freedom to maximize pleasure.

Two rather extensive research programs on p2p-based file sharing in Sweden have run parallel to my own research: MusicLessons (active in 2005) and the more recent Lund University research program Cybernorms (instigated in 2009). The explicit focus of MusicLessons was "to deepen the understanding of how p2p technology will support new business models and to evaluate and compare threats and opportunities, providing a better basis for policy-making" (Findahl & Selg 2005), while the latter is still ongoing, providing insights regarding the contrast between actual law and legal norms. I have been able to collaborate and analyze some of the results from the Cybernorms project (Andersson Schwarz & Larsson 2013). Further, since 2007 Findahl conducts a yearly survey on Internet usage in Sweden. My own research is intended to complement quantitative data of this kind. Similarly, my research has gained from some of the insights provided from Cybernormer. Also, Linde and Lindgren (2007) have confirmed some of my findings, in that they argue that Swedish cyberliberties activism turns primarily on the individual rather than the (traditional) collective. The invocation to collectivism among the activists only takes place through second-order reasoning, where the benefit to the collective is thought chiefly as a by-product of the individual benefit. The users interviewed in Linde and Lindgren (2007) also emphasized how important it is to be in control of one's own media distribution, something that resonates with my own research and the notion of great personal latitude by means of harnessing network effects as an economy of scale. In the following, I will expand on two questions: Why file sharing become so popular in Sweden, and how this country makes for an interesting case study.

5.1 SWEDEN'S INFRASTRUCTURAL AND DEMOGRAPHIC ADVANTAGE

The Swedish file-sharing demographic is characterized by an already widespread access to Internet technologies, both in terms of knowledge/skill and wealth. Especially for the younger generations, access to computers, smart phones, and broadband are part of the quotidian. Sweden is a very rich country, at the same time characterized by relatively small gaps in income distribution, enabling extensive access to technology and material consumption. In recognizing this, one should not presume class or gender as primary determinants—although ever so important—but instead highlight the question of what kinds of subjectivity the activity of file sharing engenders. The defining feature seems to be one of inclination and reflexive choice; a typically post-Fordist, late modern attitude, made possible by reliance on those greater collectives and infrastructures facilitating that choice, something that is not unique to Sweden but to the increasingly reflexive individualization of Western societies; a tendency outlined by many contemporary sociologists. Additionally, this tendency is arguably bolstered by the common invocation to technological efficiency; as we will see, engineering has a special place in Swedish modernity.

There are varying statistical figures, but a general assessment would be that around 20 percent of the adult population (approximately 1 to 1.3 million) have been estimated to be regular users of p2p-based file-sharing networks (out of a national population of 9 million). Blomqvist et al. (2005) point to a European survey indicating that digitization has practically made the computer the main storage of music for every two out of three Internet users. Based on statistical surveys in 2007 from the SOM Institute (Göteborg University), 75 percent of all Swedish fifteen- to nineteen-year-olds had "downloaded" music, and 50 percent had downloaded films. The figures for twenty- to twenty-nine-year-olds were 63 percent and 45 percent. Approximately 70 percent of all men and 32 percent of all women aged fifteen to twenty-nine had downloaded films (Antoni 2007). In the age span of fifteen to twenty-nine, only 25 percent said that they did *not* download, and among students—usually being within the same age span—only one in five (21 percent) did not download (Ghersetti 2009). The validity of these reports can, however, be questioned, since they use the imprecise term "downloading."

Antoni (2007) concludes that such downloaders of film and music are active music consumers and cinemagoers as well.

Historically, Sweden had a very early establishment of fiber-based broadband—in which both upload- and download speeds are high—compared to, for example, ADSL/dial-up connections, which are more common in Britain and the US. Ilshammar (2010; Ilshammar & Larsmo 2005) has noted this rapid broadband development and generally high infrastructural standards, something that Strandh (2009) connects with Sweden's uniquely strong secularism. This secularism has fostered strong individualism and a reflexive questioning of normative ideologies, Strandh argues. He also adds the particularly strong libertarian ethos among the geeks who have had a key role in establishing online companies and services. To this, we should also note the strong heritage of engineering, and a largely technocratic official culture, characterized by not only a high Internet penetration but also a situation in which online connectivity has a vital role for citizenship, political and economic participation, and public life.

Even RIAA's own policy guidelines, where they argue for an ISP enforcement program to deter p2p infringement, advocate a consideration of "essential services":

> ISPs are not required to impose any mitigation measure that could disable a subscriber's essential services, such as telephone service, email, or security or health service. (Sheckler 2012: 13)

The question is, then, where to draw the line for essential Internet connectivity in a country where things like banking, tax queries, and national insurance are rapidly becoming almost exclusively dependent on Internet access. Early on in their history, Piratbyrån had a slogan that, in a perhaps exaggerated way, centered on this: "Welfare begins at 100 megabit."

Recently, Sweden was ranked as number one in the global Web Index, which is a composite of factors indicating the role of the Internet to citizenship (WWWF 2012). While Sweden is world-leading regarding communications and institutional infrastructure, as well as political, economic, and social impact scores, the researchers conclude that in terms of the use and breadth of the Web—categories such as usage and content—Sweden has definite room for improvement, taking the twelfth spot on the global list. "While roughly 91% of Sweden's population uses the Web, the information available to them is surprisingly low compared with other top-ranking nations" (WWWF 2012: 9). Taking a macroview, perhaps this relative lack of content services can help explain the remarkably rapid breakthrough of p2p-based sharing in Sweden during the last decade; the infrastructure and the civic disposition were in place long before legal content providers were able to catch up.

Sweden's strong secularism is closely correlated with a reflexive self-image of efficiency, engineering, and optimization of societal functionality.

Of course Sweden shares these features with many late-modern economies, but given the importance of export, R&D and engineering to the Swedish GDP, technical competence, and modernization are central concepts—the national self-image is in this sense likely to be more similar to, for example, Germany than to Greece. Educational levels are high, as is the general grasp of the English language; as a small nation highly reliant on innovation and export, there is an element of looking up to more culturally resonant countries, such as the United States. For many people, technical competence is conditional to everyday life. This might help to explain the currency that the argument of technological inevitability had among my respondents, as well as in the publicly mediated Swedish file-sharing debate. Of all the modes of justification that my respondents used to defend the phenomenon, the notion that it is—at least on a global level—unstoppable appears to be the most principal one.

Not only are high degrees of technical competence common among the general population. Typical modern values, such as secular belief in rationality and self-fulfillment, are more extreme in Sweden than in virtually any other country (Inglehart & Welzel 2005; Zuckerman 2008). Sweden ranks extremely high in surveys of so-called postmaterialist values (e.g., public concern for issues such as political participation, freedom of speech, and environmental protection) compared to older, materialist values reflecting greater existential insecurity (e.g., public concern for issues such as economic endurance, rising food prices, and crime rates). The more widespread postmaterialist values are, the more the citizenry tends to value personal autonomy (relative to income) as a source of subjective well-being. Further, according to some scholars, such values beget reflexivity.

The notion of "institutionalized individualism" (Beck & Beck-Gernsheim 2002) means that collective belonging is often established by means of mute, depersonalized agglomeration, akin to what sociologists label *Gesellschaft*; a term that was introduced in 1887 by Ferdinand Tönnies to characterize forms of social organization with few close relationships and responsibilities and low degrees of group loyalty, and where individuals act mainly out of rational, instrumental self-interest. This is concurrent with the modes of social order in developed, increasingly postindustrial societies, outlined by sociologists such as Beck, Bauman, Castells, and Giddens: more complex everyday relations, seemingly characterized more and more by choice (for good and for bad) and arrangements of personal management of one's own identity and social relations.

Here, the reflexive capacity of seeing oneself in other people becomes paramount. Newer, more active forms of individualism try to make up for the potentially egoistic or opportunist attitudes of an individualistic way of life by striving for a "reflexive autonomy," meaning "a behavior that respects and even highly esteems the different opinions and interests of other citizens and that voluntarily searches for civil contract with others. In this way, an independent individual should take care of social integration"

(Braun & Giraud 2001: 4). In this mode of citizenship, the role of the state is to moderate and supervise the autonomous interactions of citizens. A citizen's individual development in terms of career, education, and the like is understood to be one's own responsibility but is enabled by existing welfare systems. Hence, empowerment, self-esteem, and entrepreneurial attitudes are paralleled with two propensities that might appear contradictory. The first one is the individual impulse toward charity and community-making, as citizens recognize the mutual nature of precarity and exposure. The second one would be the recognition that the social welfare state—nevertheless increasingly eroded—is still there to catch you if you fall; a relative security makes for a relative latitude in terms of life choices. This, I would argue, is what signifies a postsocial-democratic legacy, in that the onus shifts toward the individual, exposed to globalization and neoliberalism, while the social-democrat welfare state still exists in the background.

The older scarcity values were rooted in a generational, collective experience of poverty and war, with industry, wage work, nation state, and class affiliation as its constitutive elements. Inglehart's original observation (1971) has later been moderated and amended (see Abramson 2011 for an overview), as postmaterialism has, for example, been adjoined by wider recognition of domestic work and feminized consumption (see Giddens 1998). Ironically, these austerity values are now making a return—throughout Europe—with neo-nationalist parties such as Sverigedemokraterna (who entered the Swedish parliament in the election of 2010, notably ranking far higher than the SPP). However, according to the individualization thesis, such parties would be more indicative of a nostalgic, retrograde, peripheral reaction to late-modern development, rather than representing any new sets of values with widespread appeal.

5.2 A SWEDISH (POST-) SOCIAL DEMOCRAT ETHOS

What will be presented is a social-democratic theory of freedom, in which individual agency is (paradoxically it might seem) increased by the size, strength, comprehensiveness, and durability—in short, the universality—of the collective. This is concomitant with the macroeconomic idea of network effects, or welfare gains. Still, a shift has been under way during the last decades, enabled through the welfarism of a "third way" (Giddens 1998) and, later, the turn to a form of center-right governance that adapts the state individualism thesis and couches it in a more neoliberal context of privatization and a clearer focus on economic rationality, GDP growth, and maximization of utility.

The term *digital politics* is intended to refer to movements that strive to safeguard civil liberties on the Internet by addressing the actual regulation of the Internet (e.g., the Electronic Frontier Foundation (EFF), Knowledge Ecology International (KEI), Telecomix, La Quadrature du Net). Terms such as cyberliberties (Burkart 2010) and Net activism (*Netzpolitik* in German, or *nätpolitik* in Swedish) would be synonymous to this. These terms should, however, not be conflated with the concept of "cyber-activism" (Bennett 2003; 2008) in which the Internet is used as a medium through which activism is performed, nor should they be limited only to refer to (parliamentary) politics (Barry 2001: 7). When compared to the traditionalist, national bias of the established polity, digital politics are characterized by a transnational, globalized, and highly technophiliac exchange. The popularity of file sharing and the prevalence of activist hubs such as TPB can be seen as indicative of a wider shift in late-modern societies that is not unique to Sweden, although Sweden will be seen as a particularly acute example of this development, illustrating a wider shift in politics toward a late-modern ethic characterized by "networked individualism" (Wellman 2002) or "network sociality" (Wittel 2001). As the category of the political is wider than those instantiations of politics that are channeled through parties and nongovernmental organizations (NGOs), I will focus on the larger framework, where utilitarianism, nationalism, individual autonomy, and collectivism have to be balanced on a daily basis. Mass-scale file sharing can thus be connected to the secular, late-modern organization of contemporary technological society, where personal freedom is made possible thanks to a universalizing, overarching collective.

In fact, Swedish reflexive modernity should be seen as an example of how the tendencies of individualization and reflexive modernity have excelled thanks to, rather than despite, the country's documented historical concerns with solidarity and collectivism. Historically, the nation state has been anticipated by most Swedes as something beneficial, empowering citizens rather than restraining them. Sweden was the first nation to establish a nationwide register over its population (in 1631), yet its twentieth-century history is, arguably, less characterized by intrusive examples of state surveillance than many other European countries.

Increasingly, however, various political strands have come to emphasize ways of life and subcultural affiliations that point to a way out of statist, nationalist modernity—instead emphasizing global-local connections, individual latitude, Pareto distributions instead of Gaussian normalcy, voluntary self-regulation instead of authoritarian, centralized control, and, by extension, the formation of bulwarks against state control; quasi-civil societies serving as strategic sovereigns in the justificatory discourse. I use the prefix *quasi*, as more often than not in the Internet era, such hubs take the form of online communities that are highly noncompulsory and permissive. This antiauthoritarian, antistatist impulse is visible not only in pirate politics but in the identity politics of feminist and environmentalist parties and movements as well (Burkart 2013).

> Like other social movements, pirate politics is conflicted between communalism aspiring to the attainment of a creative commons such as the

> public domain, and individualism consistent with liberal and anarchistic ideals. The communitarian perspective valorizes the public goods characteristics of digital cultures and the natural (i.e., untampered) Internet as providing online agora. (Burkart 2013: n.p.)

At the same time, the aggregated, mute character of huge, anonymous collectives seems to be instrumental for individual autonomy, in that these agglomerates become large enough to drastically lessen the dependence on personal (friendly or familial) bonds. Collectives of this scale—on a national scale, encompassing all citizens—become institutionalized and bureaucratic: a well-known narrative of modernity. The idea of the common good is seen to hinge on them, but at the same time, the collective becomes rarified to be experienced more as a mute, abstract, totalizing structure. The civic interaction with it is impersonal, semi-anonymous, bureaucratic, ultimately *Gesellschaft*-like. Tellingly, many of the newer structures engendered according to the mentioned reflexive-individualist schema are also highly *Gesellschaft*-like, rather than *Gemeinschaft*-like, close-knit communities. I will elaborate on these concepts.

The singular most helpful book that this argument rests on would be Berggren and Trägårdh (2006). This book examines the historical continuity of what is defined as a typically Swedish notion of personal independence: True affiliation can only flourish between people who are economically independent of each other, and this personal autonomy is granted by means of a uniform, all-encompassing state dependence. A key example would be the establishment of subsidies, national insurance, or student loans of a decidedly individualized kind—not, as in some countries, extending to family units. Thanks to institutionalized welfare of this kind, the individual can afford to take chances and become empowered. This directly harks back to Rousseau's definition of autonomous individualism facilitated by an abstract, evenly distributed dependence on the state as a legal safeguard against all interpersonal dependence (Berggren & Trägårdh 2006: 44–50; Karlsson & Rider 2006; Trägårdh 2007). One example is the postwar implementation of personal ID numbers in 1947; an infrastructural innovation that eases virtually all semi-institutionalized social transactions but simultaneously becomes extremely prescriptive and normative: This recourse to personal numbers is, in effect, a requirement to enjoy citizenship. Further, its operation requires an absolute trust in the state system.

The Swedish ideal is therefore different from traditional continental liberalism, which places emphasis on secondary instances of power, acting as intermediaries against overly dominating state interference or monopoly (either by way of local communities, churches, corporations, or by constitutional safeguards). In fact, the constitutional structure of Sweden can be criticized for its lack of jurisdictional intermediaries, jeopardizing the legal security net for individuals in quandary with state authorities. Lawyers, priests, doctors, and social workers are generally appointed by the state, and it is not possible to take one's case to the Supreme Court by appeal to any notion of constitutionally protected, fundamental human rights. Civil rights, as they are expressed in Swedish law, are generally defined as "social rights" fit for the people in general, often declared as responsibilities of the state instead of acknowledging rights as demandable by individuals. This structural deficiency in the Swedish system is reminiscent of the bleak Platonic ideal of expert rule and has led some commentators to criticize Swedish government as a form of "parliamentary dictatorship" (Berggren & Trägårdh 2006: 373). What is telling, for our ends and purposes here, is that this structural deficiency could actually be seen in the ways the Pirate Bay trial was thought to politicize the legal process, both regarding the question of intent among the accused and regarding the alleged bias of judge, jurors, and investigators.

What also struck me, during my work on understanding p2p-based file sharing, is that Swedish modernity also hinges on a far-reaching effectuation of the ontological process of separation that Latour's modernity hinges on (Chapter 2). What is more, the notion that individuals are determined to maximize personal gratification and convenience (as well as societal and personal efficiency) through the all-encompassing system are tendencies that are also found in the technically mediated collectivity of p2p. In a typical p2p system, the scope of choice for the individual node is a direct function of the size of the aggregated totality: The more nodes that are interconnected, the wider the availability, durability, and reliance of the entire network, for everyone involved.

Further, as the regulatory system lays claims to be as totalizing as possible, instilling social control into its citizens, there is also a rich tradition of sidestepping the system among cunning individuals. Sweden has a long tradition of private imports of goods, home brewing, and tax evasion; it needs to be underscored that we are dealing with a country that only very recently made the transition to full-scale capitalism. Until 1989, Sweden was, to a significant extent, a semi-capitalist country, in many ways akin to East Germany or Poland in its reliance on central planning and state regulation. Perhaps, it was in some aspects even more statist than most Eastern Bloc countries as a result of its homogeneous population and language and the trust that citizens invest in the state.

Much of this has changed. After a severe economic crisis in 1992, Sweden made a transition toward more neoliberal governance: deregulation of markets, privatization, and a social democracy of the middle way. In September 2006, Sweden changed to a center-right government, and in 2012 the leading center-right party Moderaterna adopted Berggren and Trägårdh's state individualism to lay at the conceptual heart of their political program.

What is clear is that the core concept of state individualism—shunning old *Gemeinschaftlich* structures of dependence such as the family, in favor of a *Gesellschaftlich* structure of interdependence between state and individual—makes it an ambiguous concept: Socialists use it to talk about individualism and equality instead of class; liberals use it to couch their more radical individualism in more welfarist terms instead of merely talking about economic growth. Hence, we could devise a postsocial-democrat ethos that appropriates the state individualism thesis but emphasizes the ways individuals can utilize the collective structures to their own benefit. This discussion will be expanded by turning to McKenzie Wark's discussion on social democracy and social topology in Section 7.8.

Further, noting the proposals for cultural flat rate or the more radically leftist idea of a guaranteed income (Sections 4.7 and 7.8), one difference between general welfare of this kind and selective, contingent welfare is that the former contains an odd, volatile aspect in that it actually opens up for a right-wing, neoliberal claim that everyone would be granted the same life prospects. Through its emphasis on individualism, state individualism is by its nature uncharitable; it can easily slip into atomistic individualism.

5.3 AT THE PERIPHERY OF THE CENTER

Another relational condition unifies the Nordic countries. As cultural studies scholar Mikko Lehtonen once pointed out to me, these countries share the collective experience of being "at the periphery of the center." Countries such as Sweden and Finland are, in many aspects, world leading in terms of developmental standards, but at the same time small enough and peripheral enough never to be fully recognized as truly influential actors. What is more, the small size and relative homogeneity of countries such as Finland and Sweden makes them easier to conclusively describe as I do in this chapter; of course there is a lot of internal complexity and contradictory elements, but on the whole it is actually possible to distinguish a typically Swedish social contract—as long as we make sure to clearly stay away from essentialist notions of ethnicity, culture, or language, as I hope I manage to do here.

In the context of file sharing—and the diplomatic pressures on behalf of US trade and intellectual property organizations that will be noted in this book—both the current center-right government and the preceding social democrat government showed signs of acquiescence. As we have already noted, in the realms of cognitive capitalism—I would place both the copyright-dependent entertainment industry and the more pragmatic openness industry under this banner; the United States is still in the business of cultural imperialism, the rest of the world largely an annex to its operations. The overall US export in cultural commodities instills gratitude and awe in places such as Sweden; at the same time, it is a cumbersome process for Swedish citizens to get hold of more obscure material, such as early releases of television episodes that have not yet been aired in Europe. This prompts a pragmatic situation, similar to junkies who are ready to do anything to get their fix and who genuinely both love and hate their drug of choice.

In the pirate ethic, an element of ambivalence is required toward this US-dominated techno-industrial complex. As we will see, to "maintain hardline Kopimi" as the Pirate Bay spokespersons would do, one has to distance oneself from the entertainment industry, staunchly asserting that US jurisdiction does not extend to Swedish soil. The more pronounced one's pirate stance is, it would seem, the more it is characterized by the outward appearance of a process of Othering. At the same time, this process has to take place in the vicinity of the empire to gain relevance and efficacy: If we are to use the language of parasites and viruses, the exploit hinges on being able to tap the host while subverting its operation by, so to speak, using the same language. In the digital realm, nearness can be defined as primarily a matter of time (Virilio 1997)—and having the means to redistribute content with infinitesimal latency is a function of both technical capacity and geographical location. It is not a trivial fact that the main language used on TPB is English: This is the language of the global entertainment industry, and it is also the language of international trade and managerial efficacy.

The concept of "people's movements"—or, as was also noted among my interviewees, "folk sports"—appeared to me as a way of establishing not only a populist resonance, but also the notion of an intermediary against both anarchy and the potential totalitarianism of a strong state apparatus (Berggren & Trägårdh 2006: 104). However, in Sweden, the latter role of such intermediaries has been obscured and subsumed by the strong historical impetus of national progress and the state as a benevolent entity, prompting a politicization of movements to act in the utilitarian interest of benefiting national society at large, rather than acting as interest groups in their own right. According to Berggren and Trägårdh, the Swedish labor movement bred a romanticized image of its people's movements, as such images also tend to play on the patriotic notion of a small country performing well in sports, industry, technology, and the like. Hence, underpinning phenomena such as TPB is a dimension of nationalist sovereignty; something that helps explain the die-hard approach that the owners of this site projected against the demands of the US copyright lobby.

When asked whether file sharing in Sweden could be said to constitute a people's movement, some respondents initially found this a rather alien label. However, VT (m21) referred to file sharing as a "national sport"—at least in sheer numerical terms: "There is no [other] activity that has more users." PN (m15) agreed on the label, because "everybody file-shares," while VG (m22) noted that "'everyone' likes film, music and computer games." Meanwhile, LB (f42) thought the label applicable not only to the sheer demographic numbers but primarily to the increasingly visible groups of "conscious file sharers—who are finding ideologies around the phenomenon," maintaining that file sharing would never have been intended as a "national people's movement" but has come to appear so, owing chiefly to its massive popularity.

AG (m32) disagreed, contending that the phenomenon is not homogeneous enough to warrant such a label as its participants do not express a coherent, unified opinion: “It would be like saying that buying goods, reading books, or watching musicals would constitute people’s movements.” He noted that “people’s movement” is a positively charged expression and therefore might be strategically employed by pro-file-sharing interests: “The Pirate Party wants to call it a ‘national people’s movement,’ but that’s only because they want to gain from this rhetoric.” VG (m22) refuted this; he saw file sharing as more than mere consumption because of its highly organized character: “File sharing is, however loosely, organized! To shop for goods, read books and watch musicals is pure consumption. File sharing is much more than that!” He also emphasized the highly active nature of the phenomenon and the crumbling distinctions between consumers and producers that follow from it. This concurs with Lindgren’s notion of Swedish file sharing as akin to a social movement (Lindgren 2009; Linde & Lindgren 2007).

5.4 PIRATBYRÅN: THE EMERGENCE OF THE POST-PIRATICAL

Piratbyrån was a loose collective that coalesced during 2003, mainly on the IRC channel #hack.se. Piratbyrån came to serve as a propaganda institute, a think tank and an alternative news agency for the pro-file-sharing movement in Sweden. Its website, active between 2003 and 2010, served both as a practical how-to guide/Web reference to file sharing, as an alternative news agency, a message board, an opinion-making organization, a portal (similar to Zeropaid in the United States), and as a think tank facilitating a platform for more academic/intellectual discourse around the phenomenon. The organization was founded in 2003 as a reaction to Antipiratbyrån (Anti-Piracy Bureau), a similarly ad hoc, nongovernmental antipiracy organization, sponsored by the Swedish entertainment industry (still operative under the name Swedish Rights Alliance). In June 2010, coinciding with the death of Ibrahim Botani, a prominent member and co-founder of the group, Piratbyrån announced that they had disbanded.

Piratbyrån was small in terms of how many people were involved. Its operation was restricted to the Swedish language, and they had no offices or money. It was led by a handful of spokespersons, formulating a critique of issues pertaining to copyright and file sharing. In an interview, Marcus Kaarto compared their activities to a gas: “You can’t get a hold on us” (Quinn 2006b). Its motley crew of affiliates[1] tended to formulate a more academically informed critique than, for example, the Pirate Party or sites such as TorrentFreak or Zeropaid, drawing strongly on contemporary critical philosophy. For more insight into their mode of reasoning, see their publication *POwr, ❑ ❑ ❑ ❑, Broccoli and KOPIMI* [sic] (Piratbyrån 2009) and the rationales outlined in the recent interview (Reddit 2013a) with a few of the participants. Part of the hazy nature of Piratbyrån was that they avoided making formal decisions, instead organizing in real time on IRC.

In fact, Piratbyrån should not be thought of as an organization at all; it had no membership list or any predefined structure. All of its visible infrastructure was the website, while a lot of the ongoing discussions between its affiliates took place in IRC channels. Besides this, the people involved participated in various pranks and art events: In 2008, Piratbyrån refurbished an old bus, which they took through Europe as a performance of both art and activism. In Sweden, the collective is also intermingled with the planka.nu network, advocating free commuter infrastructures and hacking the urban environment, through things such as a collective insurance scheme, allowing to reimburse participants if and when they are fined for free riding public transport.

Piratbyrån can be described as a gateway as much as it was a thought virus. It was explicitly designated not to represent each and every file sharer, yet it became a handy tool not only for learning about the technology but also for rallying support, executing pranks, and facilitating the social exchange that goes with file sharing—emphasizing human, relationally acquired word-of-mouth knowledge.

> Piratbyrån (The Bureau of Piracy) is not an organization, at least not primarily. First and foremost, Piratbyrån is since its beginning in 2003 an ongoing conversation. We are reflection [sic] over questions regarding copying, information infrastructure and digital culture. Within the group, using our own different experiences and skills, as in our daily encounters with other people. These conversations often bring about different kinds of activities. (Piratbyrån 2008)
>
> They stirred up interest and started getting people to call stuff into question. Before Piratbyrån was founded, in 2002, no-one spoke of file sharing in the open; it was something you did secretly. (VT, m21, 2006)

Although its message boards allowed users to share expertise, even the more factual discourse used implied a stance that was doubtlessly pro-file sharing, and on some of its message boards, both users and administrators could vent very partisan views. The Piratbyrån website was like a mix of an ideologically instigated pamphleteering organ and a semi-public sphere.

Piratbyrån deliberately chose not to be anti anything, but emphasized instead how the file-sharing movement was for all forms of digital copying. This was a strategic decision. Despite being founded in opposition to an alleged Other, Piratbyrån was based on positive affirmation; they intended to anticipate rather than to react to the copyright industry, avoiding a defensive position. They continuously had to prove their seriousness to not to appear as a consumer revolt by teenagers wanting everything for free (Linde & Lindgren 2007). They sought to avoid a reactive tendency in which the enemy is construed as a monolithic, catch-all nemesis (as in the leftist movements of the past, invoking "the man" or "the system"). This, however, meant that the Piratbyrån affiliates were perhaps seen as more ambivalent in their standing than members of traditional political movements: They were undoubtedly leftist, especially in their anticorporate stance and with their close affiliations to anarchism and antiracist, antisexist activism. Yet—although they would never admit to this—the libertarian side of the file-sharing argument can make for unlikely bedfellows. The pragmatism that helps explain the efficacy and popularity of TPB also allowed right-wing entrepreneur Carl Lundström to give financial support to the site, and it is somewhat peculiar to see pornographic advertisements appear next to articles about the artsy progressivism of Piratbyrån. The markedly different ideological backgrounds of TPB founders Sunde and Svartholm Warg also indicates that the file-sharing cause is somewhat distinct from the traditional left-right spectrum.

Because of their near-ubiquitous presence in the Swedish mass media discourse around file sharing, reaching an apex when TPB was brought to trial in April 2009, it could be argued that Piratbyrån and TPB were thought, at least among Swedes, to be representative of all file sharers. Although this was refuted by many of my respondents' accounts, this allegedly ubiquitous role needs to be taken into consideration: Although Piratbyrån might not deliberately have strived to represent the larger sphere of file sharing, its mediating role made it a force that was continuously present—materially, socially, and discursively. This strategic action could, in the context of the file sharers who I interviewed, be summarized as "maintaining doing what they are doing" in the face of harshening legal frameworks and public disapproval. It comprised a reinforcement of the sovereignty of material networks, communities, and applications for a sharing that remained largely uncontrollable by legal/corporate authorities, essentially by continually pointing to the ceaseless continuation of the activities already being routinely performed:

> The best strategy is to keep file sharing, sampling, deriving, copying, getting better broadband connections/"mp3-players" so that we become even more dependent on these phenomena and our actions make copyright so washed out that it is no longer needed. Since in practice, it is already non-existent on certain levels. (sign. "Blenda" commenting Fleischer 2006, my translation)

It remained in the interest of TPB and Piratbyrån to emphasize the growing ubiquity of file sharing, user-generated content, and media usage premised on a p2p logic, because the more consolidated such media uses were becoming, the more out of sync the current legal system would appear. When being accused for advocating "technological determinism," Eriksson (2009a) invoked Kittler, coolly arguing that the radicalism of p2p-based sharing only becomes radical in relation to the preceding historical context—which can itself be shown to be of a very specific nature: The established modern media ecology of unidirectional mass media is in itself deterministic. It was when the corporatism of the RIAA, the MPAA, and IFPI began to reveal its tendency toward primitive accumulation on a worldwide scale that the activist reply would be to support the counterprocess of primitive, borderless accumulation outside of the established monetary economy—hence the focus on simply keeping doing what one is doing.

As file sharing has been characterized by so much conflict, one way of seeing these formations would be to define them as partisan and countercultural. However, since they come to represent such large populations of Internet users, they can equally be seen as expressions of popular opinion—hence the tendency to label file sharing a people's movement or consumer rebellion. What is clear is that the significance of these entities cannot be explained by market logics or the communitarianism of the hacker ethos alone.

The invocation to totalities—"The whole Internet works in this way!" "The whole population is involved in this!"—begets utilitarian rationales. The tendency to formulate cyberliberties activism in such utilitarian terms could be attributable either to technical efficiency (What is best for the network?) or nationalism (What is best for Sweden?). Whereas these modes of reasoning are crucial to the Swedish pro-file-sharing argumentation, they are of course not exclusive to the Scandinavian context. But the modest size of these countries means that formations such as Piratbyrån and TPB tend to enter into the national debate more easily—where tropes are not only debated in mass media that have national reach (such as debates on public service television) but also invoked by reference to the good of (national) society as well. One case in point would be when Sunde appeared on national Swedish television in September 2008 defending the decision to host even the most offensive material such as court documents from murder cases.

After 2009, things changed. The activist focus was shifted toward issues pertaining to data retention, surveillance, and the ACTA reforms package—many of these issues transcending national borders and instead being enacted in pan-European collectives such as Telecomix and La Quadrature du Net. The Swedish mass media also shifted its focus, and references to pirates began appearing few and far between.

Gustavsson (2012) recounts how some of the early Piratbyrån affiliates have now hovered toward the academy and public life. She quotes teenagers who are currently active in documenting court cases and staging protests. Many of these younger activists started by hanging out in Piratbyrån IRC channels, sometimes at the early age of twelve. Some of them are full of admiration, almost reverence, toward the original Piratbyrån activists:

> –They allowed us to participate and learn.
> –Fleischer and the gang. They were already there during the Napster era.
> –But they are becoming part of the establishment now, they are all soon professors. It feels like they are disappearing.

–I texted Marcin about a trial, but he needed to babysit his children. (Gustavsson 2012, my translation)

Web campaigns such as the deliberately faceless Kopimi movement seem to have outlived the activities of Piratbyrån. The Kopimi concept and logo were created by Ibrahim Botani in 2005. It is somewhat similar to alternative copyright licenses such as Creative Commons, but should really be seen as an anti-license or non-license. Instead of functioning as an extension of copyright, a Kopimi notice specifically encourages that the work be copied—for any purpose, commercial or noncommercial. Kopimi is therefore similar to the CC0 license created by Creative Commons, which is a waiver of all of one's copyrights and related or neighboring rights, but instead of merely allowing for copying, Kopimi adds a positive imperative, urging others to copy. Piratbyrån published most of its work under this alternative license, and several pranks and reappropriations of Kopimi have emerged, not least since Piratbyrån actively encouraged people to do so. Thus, Kopimi can be read as a condensed version of Piratbyrån's legacy of positive, rather than merely negative, liberty.

As a continuation of the merry prankster ethos that suffused Piratbyrån, in 2010 the then nineteen-year-old philosophy student Isak Gerson and twenty-two-year old Pirate Party chairman Gustav Nipe founded the Missionary Church of Kopimism *(Missionerande Kopimistsamfundet),* a congregation of file sharers who believe that copying information is a sacred virtue. Gerson was active in the SPP's youth movement as well as the Christian Student Movement (KRISS), and the Church of Kopimi was an attempt to combine these ideologies. On January 5, 2012, Kopimism was—after three application attempts—accepted as a legitimate religious community in Sweden. This is a clever move in that religious discourse is a form of communication that enjoys better protection than secular communication; for example, Article 9 of the European Convention on Human Rights (ECHR) stipulates freedom of thought, conscience, and religion, while Article 14 prohibits discrimination based on matters such as religion. The EU Directive on protection of personal data (95/46/EC) stipulates that things such as ethnic origin, political opinions, or religious beliefs are to be regarded as special categories of personal data.

Moreover, in the context of this book, it is important to read the Church of Kopimism as an enactment of quasi-religious aspects that actually underpin a lot of technocultural progressivism: the notion—part inspired by the Deleuzian-Spinozan concept of "dividuals" (popularized in Sweden by Bard & Söderqvist 2009), part inspired by the Californian techno-utopianism of Kelly (1995)—that, practically speaking, we are all interconnected and that there is no border between the Internet and the human brain. Further, this notion can be successfully integrated with the notion that duplication and imitation are not only found at the heart of social life (Tarde 1903) but also found throughout the natural universe.

5.5 THE PIRATE BAY: LOOSENING THE VIRTUAL FROM THE PHYSICAL

The Pirate Bay, the world's largest archive of BitTorrent links, has enjoyed continued, massive popularity despite lawsuits and industry threats—quite possibly because of its very location in Sweden, out of reach of US jurisdiction. By 2008, the site had reached over 25 million unique peers and over 3 million registered users. By the end of 2009 it had over 4 million registered users, and in May 2011 it sported over 5 million users.

The site can be seen as an assemblage of many things: an ad-financed website; a brand; several data servers; a BitTorrent tracker; and a Web-based index of BitTorrent links, constantly entangled with temporary collectives of individuals (Fleischer 2010c). The site labels itself "the world's largest BitTorrent tracker," alternatively "the galaxy's most resilient bittorrent site," and its primary function, as these labels indicate, is to track and index torrent files. The site was started in November 2003 by Svartholm Warg, "anakata," and Neij, "TiAMO"; later, Sunde, "brokep," also joined. They all were affiliated to Piratbyrån; their involvement in TPB was mainly attributable to them being the most technically skilled programmers (Svanell 2013). In fact, the original tagline was "Piratbyrån's own torrent tracker," and Piratbyrån has jokingly labeled TPB "a long-running project of performance art." In October 2004, TPB nevertheless became a separate organization. Since then, two key steps were taken to further implement the tendency of loosening the virtual from the physical (Oram 2001: x). In November 2009, TPB shut off its tracker service permanently, instead making use of entirely decentralized ways for peers to find each other and the desired content, by the use of so-called distributed hash tables (DHT), peer exchange (PEX), and magnet links. In the original design of the BitTorrent file-sharing protocol, peers (users) in a swarm relied on a central computer server (a tracker) to find each other and to maintain the swarm. PEX greatly reduces the reliance of peers on a tracker by allowing each peer to directly update others in the swarm as to which peers are currently in the swarm. Since March 1, 2012, TPB does not even offer torrent files anymore—it only offers magnet links. In addition, the index hence became much smaller; the entire listing of all its titles and magnet links can be fitted on a CD-R or a USB stick.

As we will see, these aims were announced even before 2009, and it seems like a desired development from the beginning—a more thorough decentralization of this kind makes the site even less prone to takedowns. The nimble size of its index attests to the ease of mirroring the site across different servers. Sites such as mirrorbay.net maintain listings of URLs that can be used to bypass local filtering. Around the world, several auxiliary services exist that offer access to the site by proxy, for users in jurisdictions where the original Pirate Bay Web address is blocked. Moreover, the actual Pirate Bay front page is, as we saw in the introduction to Chapter 4, currently hosted by pirate parties. This process of radical decentralization was also expressed in more whimsical forms through assertions such as in 2007, when TPB tried to purchase Sealand, a military platform off the coast of England, and to place servers there, enjoying diplomatic immunity, or in 2012 when TPB jokingly announced that it would put servers on aerial drones.

What really gave the site its infamous status was by publishing the so-called legal correspondence submitted to it from various media companies and collecting societies that threatened it with legal action, only to be met by a deliberately provocative stance from the site's administrators. TPB became known not only for its prankster-like exploits but also for its die-hard dedication to hosting all sorts of material, even in the face of controversy. However, international legal pressure led to the famous raid against the service in May 2006, when fifty police officers confiscated not only TPB's and Piratbyrån's servers, but also a hundred other servers belonging to the hosting company PRQ's customers, leading some commentators to label the operation politically charged—and arguably even constitutionally illegal. Three days later, TPB was back up, while the legal machinery had begun to grind, while considerable interest had been gaining momentum in the mainstream media. Paradoxically, the clampdown had generated even more publicity and traffic to the site. This type of backlash seems like a common occurrence for TPB and similar actors; the mass media coverage ensuing from various types of crackdowns and blocks sparks a public interest and leads to users flocking to the site.

The presence of entities such TPB and Piratbyrån has been vital to how mainstream media has framed file sharing, in Sweden and abroad. In the months following the highly publicized police raid, not only did the Swedish mainstream media interview the representatives of TPB, but overseas publications such as *Vanity Fair* and *Wired* gave coverage to what was rendered a phenomenon of global interest (Daly 2007; Quinn 2006a; 2006b). Swedish public service television covered the phenomenon in several news reports, alleging that the raid was executed as a result of US coercion, while the largest national newspaper *Aftonbladet* interviewed key managers of TPB, alleging that "the [Swedish] people stood behind them" (Nilsson 2006). Various national newspaper ran minisites entirely dedicated to the topic.

TPB stands out as a leading example of charismatic authority in the file-sharing world, especially during the phase (2003–2009) when its administrators staunchly opposed any legal reprimand with crass language—something that its current administrators (whose identities are unknown) occasionally try to emulate, but not with as much gusto and success. Examples of this correspondence can be found on the infamous Web page at http://thepiratebay.org/legal. This, alongside merchandise and film documentaries in the visual style of punk and nonconformism, helped shape a profile of the site's administrators as assertive hardliners. Despite the original founders having been forcefully removed from managing the site (as an effect of the recent Swedish court orders), TPB still appears to maintain a high reputation and credibility in the file-sharing world—perhaps even more so, after the highly publicized trial that actually led to prison sentences for the four defendants.

> Normally the people who ran file-sharing sites decided to close down when the entertainment industry appeared with their legal threats. They tended to be 18–19 year-old guys who got frightened and thought that the letters' claims were true. Other sites try to be silent and act in secrecy. They're afraid of the industry. We don't think file-sharing is in any way wrong, and it shouldn't be banished as something one does in secret. (Sunde, in Kuprijanko 2008, my translation)

The fame held by TPB is indeed so strong, that fake sites such as torrent diamond.com have begun stealing the graphic design of the site to falsely appear to be legit among unassuming file sharers, even sporting false user comments. In 2013, it emerged that a Finnish antipiracy organization (CIAPC) had similarly copied the site's design to build a fake sharing site that would convince users to go to legal alternatives instead.

Already in 2007, TPB's spokespeople lamented the lack of competition from other trackers or torrent link indexes (Maxwell 2007). In a private conversation that I had with Sunde in 2008, he hinted at making the index more decentralized. That the file-sharing world would benefit from a wider variety of competing actors is a belief that he has continued to repeatedly argue for. In a public chat session he recently argued that it was about time for TPB to be replaced:

> TPB should die (I've said this for a few years) so that something good will replace it. Come on, it's 8 years old website [sic] with essentially no updates. There must be something better . . . (Sunde, in Reddit 2013b)

As with large parts of the Internet ecosystem, there exists a kind of echo-chamber effect in the torrent ecosystem as various meta services rehash and re-index data that originally comes from influential sites such as TPB. According to Sunde, most of the original data that the meta torrent search engines scrape has been coming from TPB, isoHunt, and Mininova. Of these latter two indexes, isoHunt was partially based on TPB's torrents, and both isoHunt and Mininova used to rely on TPB's tracker.

The more recent trend toward a proliferation of cyberlockers alongside an unruly underground ecology of private torrent trackers could be summarized as a form of "cloudification" also apparent within the realm of illegal file sharing; a veritable piracy-on-demand where people stream movies and music from third-party storage facilities, often to mobile devices and TVs. Some of these cloud-based websites allow people to set up automatic downloads of new shows the moment they are uploaded to piracy sites. Through using so-called seedboxes, users rent space on a remote server and instruct this server to file-share for them: This is another aspect of the de facto virtualization of file sharing.

5.6 TRANSNATIONAL DIPLOMATIC PRESSURES

PRQ, or PeReQuito (meaning both "parakeet" and "cocaine" in Spanish), is a Stockholm-based Web hosting company, formed in 2004 by Svartholm and Neij. It is now owned by Mikael Viborg, who took over the company in 2008. The company was famously raided in 2006, alongside Carl Lundström's hosting company Rix Port80, as part of the crackdown on TPB.

The business model of PRQ is also to allow for the most offensive or inconvenient material to be hosted. The company places great emphasis on an anonymity promise that they never disclose customer information to third parties. In June 2007, PRQ was criticized for its controversial decision to provide hosting for Web pages that promote pedophilia, such as the North American Man/Boy Love Association (NAMBLA), a pedophile advocacy organization. Svartholm and PRQ distanced themselves from the content but held that the company complied with Swedish law and that freedom of speech also applies to controversial groups. PRQ also provides hosting for the French far-right blog Fdesouche.

It is not widely known that the servers of Chechen news portal Kavkaz Center, hosted by PRQ, were seized in a raid on May 6, 2006, following an accusation from the Russian Embassy that the news portal incited terrorism. The prosecutor in charge was Håkan Roswall, the same prosecutor who a few weeks later authorized the notorious crackdown on TPB.

As no publisher was appointed, it was doubtful whether the news portal enjoyed constitutional protection under the Press Act. The district court, where the seizure was appealed, made the assessment that the material on the Kavkaz Center would not be protected by the Constitution as the news portal did not publish a paper edition. In an article about the case (Fria Tidningen 2006) Viborg points to the absurdity of a media-specific interpretation of constitutional law. Further, news agencies such as TT and AP enjoy constitutional protection despite not having paper editions.

When the police arrived at PRQ later the same month, this time to carry out the raid against TPB, a publisher was, however, appointed, and Kavkaz Center could enjoy constitutional protection. Further, the seditious texts had been deleted by now. Fredrik Neij, then the co-owner of PRQ, informed the police about this, and they forwarded the query to Roswall, whose response was to take down the servers anyway.

In 2006 it also transpired that the perseverance of TPB—and the fact that Swedish authorities could do little by way of forcibly closing it down—had prompted Americans to lobby the Swedish government on the ministerial level. According to the Swedish public service broadcaster SVT, this was the initial cause for the May 2006 police raid on the site. This indicates to what degree the site was considered a threat to US IP regimes. SVT revealed that a delegation of representatives of the Swedish Ministry of Justice and the Swedish police had traveled to Washington, DC, to meet representatives for US authorities and organizations (JO 2007). Prior to this visit, the MPAA had contacted the Swedish Ministry of Justice several times, beginning in July 2005.

SVT claims that the Ministry of Justice had asked police and prosecutors to act. The Ministry of Justice, however, denied any such unilateral pressures (SVT 2006a). However, three weeks later, the day after SVT's investigatory documentary, the minister of justice at the time, Thomas Bodström, publicly admitted that the US Embassy had threatened Sweden with blacklisting, but he denied accusations of having ordered police or prosecutors, as that would be a constitutional crime in Sweden (SVT 2006b). The US Embassy in Sweden also confirmed, in sweeping terms, that TPB had been mentioned during negotiations (SVT 2006c). When SVT made a Freedom of Information request to see 947 e-mails pertaining to the case, only 210 were disclosed. SVT appealed this decision to the government, but the decision was sustained, not deemed to be public information (SVT 2006d). Numerous complaints were made to the Parliamentary Committee on the Constitution (KU) and to the Parliamentary Ombudsmen (JO), but in 2007 the case was shelved by the latter (JO 2007).

In an odd turn of events, three years later the Wikileaks "cablegate" release of US Embassy communications with the State Department—which disclosed persistent and aggressive efforts to influence EU member states to adopt the strictest possible versions of national legislation to harmonize up to EU Directives on copyright—revealed that strong lobbying pressures were brought to bear on the EU and EU Member States by the United States during the period of reforms, beginning around 2006. The Wikileaks release in 2010 uncovered sensitive communications from the US Embassy outlining cumulative efforts by the US diplomatic post on behalf of the International Intellectual Property Alliance (IIPA) and the Pharmaceutical Manufacturing and Research Association (PhRMA) to influence Swedish politics and law to benefit those trade groups, following IIPA and PhRMA pressures on the Office of the US Trade Representative (USTR) to place Sweden on the Special 301 Watch List, a blacklist intended to name and shame US trade partners.[2]

As Falkvinge (2011) has pointed out, there was a checklist of US demands on the Swedish government; many of these demands standing in stark contrast to either EU directives (e.g., requirements regarding ISPs rights to safeguard customer data—which contrasts with the USTR's proposition that rights holders be permitted to obtain the identity of suspected infringers from ISPs in civil cases) or to the Swedish constitution (the diplomatic demands revealed in the cables were to "prosecute to the fullest extent" the owners of TPB, but letting the executive branch interfere with the judiciary is illegal in Sweden). Further, Falkvinge argues, these demands would open up for data retention and a removal of ISP carrier neutrality.

The IIPA works as a private agency assisting the USTR on various 301 projects. They designate geographical areas of concern annually on the 301 timetables and gradually have expanded their lists of countries of concern to practically all countries in the world. "Internet piracy specifically, was labeled a 'significant concern' in Brazil, Canada, China, India, Italy, Russia, Spain and Ukraine" in 2010 (ECA 2010). IIPA recommended that Sweden make watch lists in 2008 and 2009, indicating active monitoring and an aggressive posture for the first time.

In March 2009, prior to the Swedish implementation of the EU IPR Enforcement Directive (IPRED), the US Embassy noted that the Swedish Justice Ministry was "fully on board" and that "it would be counter-productive to watch list Sweden at this point" (US State Department 2009). Sweden had the commission presidency at this time, and many of its discussions with the United States, hence, had to serve the double purpose of expressing national views or acting as spokesperson for various members in the EU.

In August 2009, the Swedish ISP Black Internet, hosting TPB at the time, was forced by court order to prevent access to a specific list of movies and TV shows. The district court ruling came after a civil lawsuit from a group of multinational corporations including Columbia, Disney, and Sony. For technical reasons, the entire site would have had to shut down to prevent these titles from being shared. Also in the Court of Appeal, the Black Internet verdict was sustained.

On October 1, 2012, PRQ was once again raided by Swedish police. As a result, several file-sharing sites were taken down, some of them later resumed services but the main target—the torrent site Tankafetast—was permanently discontinued. The days after this raid, the SPP once again saw a boost in memberships.

Wikileaks found a haven in Sweden for its operations prior to the arrest of its founder, Julian Assange, on suspicion of sexual assault. Until August 2010, Wikileaks was hosted by PRQ, but when it emerged that Wikileaks was targeted for disruption by police and threatened with disconnection, the SPP announced that they would be hosting and managing Wikileaks servers. The site is currently hosted mainly by Swedish ISP Bahnhof in the Pionen facility, a former nuclear bunker in central Stockholm. According to more recent statements by Assange, Switzerland and Iceland would, however, be the only countries where WikiLeaks would be safe to operate.

The move by the SPP to offer Wikileaks server location is a similarly clever move, as the constitutional protection enjoyed by political parties is exceptional in Sweden. The SPP has never had any formal ties to Piratbyrån or TPB but has repeatedly expressed support for their business—and the move to host TPB's front page also came with a populist benefit. Just as the party can point to its soaring membership every time a service provider such as PRQ is raided, it can point to its active affiliation with manifestly popular services such as TPB.

A fascinating paradox inherent to this tendency of using hosting providers as strategic hubs would be the way this form of politics mirrors neoliberal speculative financial capitalism: To guarantee the technical feasibility of such a hub, encryption, secrecy, and closure is needed—much in the way bank secrecy, server vaults, and reliable, durable rerouting measures make sure to uphold the resilience of the global financial economy. Hintz (2013) focuses on the example of the Icelandic Modern Media Initiative (IMMI), and he shows that to be effective, also grassroots civic activism has to take a transnational route, striking strategic alliances with fellow groupings around the globe, as well as pragmatically drawing from best practices observed. Further, a common way for these alternative groupings to become operational is to altogether disregard or bypass regulatory obstacles, practically dismissing institutionalized multistakeholder governance.

5.7 "SPECTRIAL" AND A FOILED COMMERCIALIZATION OF THE BAY

In May 2007, prosecutor Håkan Roswall announced the indictment of the founders of TPB, also including Web entrepreneur Carl Lundström. In January 2008 they were charged for preparing and abetting copyright infringement—a criminal case with civil damages. The trial against TPB in February 2009 was extensively covered by Swedish and international media. It is noteworthy that similar cases of abetting copyright infringement had never previously been tried by Swedish courts (Ebadi & Johansson 2009). TPB's representatives repeatedly asserted that they had not breached any Swedish law, as they merely provided access to works on their website and were not hosting any of the actual works on their servers. The prosecutors argued that the database of torrent links that they provided—placed in categories and directly searchable—thus constituted a more dedicated service than the general ones that companies such as Google provide.

More interestingly, in the context of this book, the founders of TPB were accused not only of financing and maintaining the website (thereby abetting copyright infringements) but of actively supporting and encouraging what could be seen as an ontological dismissal of copyright and, in effect, a boycott against the entertainment industry. In this sense, the trial—albeit perhaps not a political trial per se—definitely had political undercurrents and/or repercussions. This can be debated, since, of course, the definition of what is political lies in the eye of the beholder. Adding to the claim that the verdict was political, it transpired in the aftermath of the trial that the judge and several of the prosecutors had been members of pro-copyright organizations. They were tested for partiality, but the investigator found that mere membership in organizations aiming for the development of copyright would not be enough to warrant retrial. Further, the lead interrogator Jim Keyzer was employed by Warner Brothers Entertainment just after the investigation was finished—something that was explicitly criticized by both Sunde and Fleischer at the time. In September 2007, TPB had reported

MediaDefender—a company that specialized in sabotage and pollution of illicit p2p networks—to the Swedish police following the leak of e-mails showing that the US-based company had set up "honeypot" file-sharing services designated to lure users and plant spyware on their computers; TPB accused the media corporations that had been affiliated with MediaDefender for data intrusion. That investigation was, however, written off by Keyzer.

The trial was mocked by Internet activists as a kind of spectacle—a "spectrial," For example, file-sharing activists questioned the nature of the evidence used in trials such as this one. In 2008, Piratbyrån compiled an evidence machine (*Bevismaskinen* in Swedish): a piece of software designated to show how anyone could fabricate screen captures with user names, file names, and IP numbers as evidence of infringements.

After several weeks of hearings at the Stockholm District Court, all four defendants were convicted for aiding copyright infringement. They were each sentenced to one year in prison and a total of €3 million in damages. The verdict was, however, instantly appealed to the Swedish Crown Court, leading the case to be revisited. In November 2010, a Swedish Appeals Court sustained the verdict, decreasing the original prison terms but increasing the fine to 46 million SEK. Currently, it is unclear who runs the site; however, since 2010 the SPP has offered bandwidth to the service.

The verdict puts the question of the agency of file sharing at center stage: No one was in fact found guilty of the actual crime, since the actual sharing was enacted by the site's active users, ranging in the hundreds of thousands. The four defendants were found guilty of aiding copyright infringement. Further, in terms of the SPP hosting the site, commentators such as Fleischer (2013) have noted that this would constitute a nested agency: "aiding the aiding of aiding . . . " The shift of technology since 2006—magnet links and distributed hashing—would also mean that we would now be talking about a different type of site than the one found guilty in 2009. Hence, the commentators mean that the question of whether TPB in its current form aids sharing would have to be reinvestigated.

Further, in October 2009, a district court ruling—parallel to the much more famous spectrial—forced Neij and Svartholm to abstain from managing the website and its tracker. It could be a matter of interpretation, however, as to whether a literal reading of the ruling would mean that they would only be barred from running the service from the thepiratebay.org URL and from running torrent trackers (as the site switched to torrent-less sharing a month later).

Svartholm was never present at the appeals court, as he had fled to Cambodia and claimed absence because of illness. In June 2012, he was, however, charged with hacking Swedish IT firm Logica (service provider to the Swedish tax office), having repeatedly extracted sensitive personal records over a time span of two years. In September 2012 he was deported to Sweden and is currently in prison. Neij is allegedly in exile in Laos and has had his passport revoked, whereas Sunde's situation—being exiled from Sweden while running his new, legit Internet enterprise Flattr—has been documented by Svanell (2013). Flattr, founded by Sunde in 2010 after he left TPB in August 2009, is an online payment system that allows users to make micropayments to cultural creators they want to support; users pay a bulk sum of money that they can choose to allot by clicking on the pages of affiliated cultural creators.

In the context of this book, highlighting the overlapping nature of media activism and entrepreneurialism, another turn of events is of specific interest. During the summer of 2009 it was suddenly announced that TPB would be sold. By being purchased by software company Global Gaming Factory X, TPB would become a subscription service. The price was set to €6 million of which half would be paid in shares and the remaining €3 million in cash—that is, the same amount as the damages incurred in court. However, what was sold was in fact only the Pirate Bay brand, and the deal was seen as suspect by many commentators: "There is something fishy about the Pirate Bay deal from the beginning. . . . The fog of lies, empty words, debt, questionable business ethics, and defecting companions lies thick" (Sundberg 2009, my translation). The owner of Global Gaming Factory X, Hans Pandeya, turned out to have large tax debts, and soon the deal failed. Still, this affair had cast a shadow of a doubt on TPB as a noncommercial social networking site and on the possible intentions of its founders. Intensive discussions took place in the blogosphere, as the potential business deal seemed to greatly undermine the devoted support the site had long enjoyed.

In 2010, another actor offered to take over one of the most central elements of the complex Pirate Bay assemblage: its servers and Internet connection. As the abovementioned founders had been banned by court order from running the site in any way whatsoever, the SPP took it on themselves to give bandwidth to the site. Soon, the Pirate Bay front page was plastered with Pirate Party campaign material; something that would have been alien to the originators of the service, as they have never openly affiliated themselves with said party. Tellingly, this move to SPP hosting had followed after pressures by US trade interests: Sven Olaf Kamphuis, the operative Director of Cyberbunker, was threatened with severe fines and possible imprisonment as long as he kept hosting TPB. The injunction against him was issued by the Hamburg District Court, following a complaint by the MPAA. In February 2012, the Swedish Supreme Court refused to hear an appeal in the case, prompting the site to change its official domain name to thepiratebay.se from thepiratebay.org. This move was claimed to prevent susceptibility to US legislation and a more robust DNS compatibility.

This shows that a service such as TPB is ontologically "sticky"; the abundance of connections and interrelating actions acts like glue and ties venture capitalism, party politics, partisanship, and even the idea of into its vortex. TPB was never simply one thing; it can be seen as a conservator of a mainstream cultural supply, as well as a radical opponent to the big media corporations, as a harbinger of free media distribution, or conversely, as a hedonist absorption of mere self-gratification—having commercial capacities (as shown by the Pandeya offer) as well as political clout (as manifested in the Pirate Party affiliation).

In the light of this, the way TPP is ad-financed is highly problematic. To begin with, outspoken Internet entrepreneurs such as Caldwell (in Morrissey 2012) have complained about the poor level of advertising inventory throughout the openness industry: SNSs such as MySpace and Facebook seem to be characterized by great ambivalence in that they are platforms (utilities) at the same time as they are entertainment hubs (supposed to generate money from page views and clickable ads, hence creating incentives for users to stay on the sites). The problem is that this latter model is inherently distorted by the poor value of such page views or clicks. Historically, the model has so far lent itself to generic advertising of the most base kind, Caldwell argues: gambling, porn, scams, novelties, ring tones. Spotify could be said to suffer from a similar problem, although perhaps not as pronounced. However, whether this is simply a case of market maturation remains to be seen.

What would be altogether more troubling is the rife pornography on TPB and the often demeaning or outright fraudulent advertising that funds the site. It is not insignificant that the known administrators of TPB have all been male and the whole ethos and discourse of the site having been geared toward the archetypal masculine tinkerer. Piracy here becomes synonymous with prowess, self-determination, two fingers put up against one's adversaries.

The commonly occurring pornography shared on the site was discussed on Piratbyrån and socialism.nu message boards as early as 2003–2004, at the incipient phase of TPB. Those defending the pornography pointed out that the site includes a function to filter out such material, and Svartholm professed a steadfast attitude from the start: Anything that the users deemed worth uploading would be hosted on the site, unless a court order demanded the content to be taken down.

> **anakata (2003–11–24 | 01:37)** As an admin (I admin everything from the server to the computer to the Net line), I have this to say: I do not act as torrent police, nor do I plan to. The only rule is that the things have to be what they are claimed to be, but I don't keep any form of active check on this. If a torrent meets these criteria, there has to be a court order for me to remove it. (Piratbyrån 2003a, my translation)
>
> **cato (2003–12–10 | 01:36)** People download and seed whatever they want. That which people don't crave will disappear automatically from the tracker. In other words, the people decides what should be there or not. Can it be more democratic than that? (Piratbyrån 2003b, my translation)

In fact, the sexism—an issue that was intertwined with the highly permissive approach toward the funding of the site—was one of the main catalysts for deepening the split between Piratbyrån (arguably more concurrent with the positions expressed on socialism.nu) and TPB (arguably more concurrent with the positions of the SPP) over the subsequent years. The quarrel is, in a way, a typical case of whether pragmatism should trump idealism: It could be compared discussions among socialists whether alcohol sales should fund a concert venue or whether the private company is suitable as organizational form. As should be clear from the recent documentary *TPB AFK* (2013), Sunde is an avid vegan and socialist, while Svartholm is an anarcho-liberal proponent of drugs and pornography, while Neij remains rather politically uninvolved. Despite this, the three were able to collaborate mainly through their devotion toward pragmatism.

For most of the site's existence, ad space was leased to third-party companies, which offered bandwidth in return or funneled money from ad revenues; the link to Israeli entrepreneur Oded Daniel was brought up during the trial. Since 1999, Daniel holds a patent for a Web-based ad-serving system. Sunde and Svartholm had conferred with Daniel in 2005 and 2006 about advertising arrangements. Daniel, a self-professed tax dodger ("only losers pay tax"; Thors 2008), had two companies, Transworld Advertising and Random Media—the former being registered in Independence, Montana, and connected to the porn sites Empornium and PureTNA (and, in addition in some way connected to a company called TargetPoint and an ad aggregator/server called clicktorrent.info), and the latter being registered in the British Virgin Islands and similarly opaque. Its postal address was a PO box held by the tax-planning and estate-management company Geneva Management Group (GMG) in Switzerland. Until August 2006, the company Eastpoint Media also ran the ad sales for the Scandinavian market (Löwenfeldt 2006), allegedly seeing a turnover of $95,000 per month through TPB (Olsson 2006). The correspondence between Daniel and the defendants never proved that they were making profits but did indicate that considerable profit streams were coming from advertising. The defendants nevertheless held that these gains only covered the costs of running the site.

This all goes back to the notion of rentier capitalism (Section 4.8) in which companies charge fees or extract ad revenue to let users download content uploaded by other users—an operation that requires little risk and little prior investment. It begs the question whether an old paradigm of expropriation is replaced by a new one, this time characterized by power-law distributions, as discussed earlier, trailing the low end of the attention spectrum with ads to match. How can an actor such as TPB claim innocence or nonaffiliation to the tax-dodging, transnational corporate finance world when arrangements such as this were in place? TPB was, in this sense, part of the same international financial cabal that activists worldwide disassociated themselves from—Daniel and company being part of "the 1 percent" of rentier capitalists, arguably leeching profit without contributing to the real economy.

This question was once again prompted by the legal threats against the SPP in February 2013. How ethical is it of a political party to make business dealings that contribute to an ad-financed service whose profit to a considerable extent comes from pornography and whose owners remain opaque, most likely based in tax havens such as the Virgin Islands—a service that, in key aspects, remains almost identical to its forerunner that rendered prison sentences for its owners? Further, will it be possible to claim significant other uses, in line with the Safe Harbor provisions in the DMCA and European law, when the service asserts a clear pirate identity, something that was asserted also in speeches and rhetorical declarations?

Still, before one can attest that profits have been made, calculations need to be shown that the revenue has exceeded the costs by a large margin. No such evidence has been produced in the Pirate Bay case.

Further, that only the law would set the limit for what to host, as Svartholm asserts, could be seen as an odd reliance: Holding that the law is the only arbiter would arguably be to reinforce it, reifying its binary logic. However, the quote makes sense if we consider the Pirate Bay administrators' devotion to maximalism, or, perhaps more correctly, accelerationism, of pushing until system boundaries are reached—either the technological boundaries or the legal ones.

5.8 THE SWEDISH PIRATE PARTY: ATROPHY OR RENEWAL OF POLITICS?

Piratpartiet (the Swedish Pirate Party; SPP) is a Swedish political party, founded in January 2006, claiming to stand outside of the traditional left-right scale and focusing exclusively on issues of Internet privacy and reform of Swedish intellectual property law. Imminently after the foundation of the SPP, European organizations representing the entertainment industry warned of "the danger that Sweden, normally considered to be a strong upholder of EU standards and a promoter of culture, should instead be seen as the haven for a cult of copyright infringement that has achieved global reach" (IFPI 2008: 22). The SPP is considered to be the world's first Pirate Party, inspiring people to establish pirate parties in a number of countries and US states (Pirate Parties International was founded in April 2010). Some of these national branches have won local council seats, and the German Pirate Party (GPP) has seats in the Berlin state legislature.

Also the SPP began as a website. In 2006, Rickard Falkvinge established the piratpartiet.se website, garnering momentum and within twenty-four hours collecting the 1,500 names required to register a political party in Sweden. Early on, the party garnered a lot of publicity, but only managed to assemble 0.63 percent of the overall votes in the September 2006 election for Parliament. In the 2009 European Parliament elections, however, they assembled 7.13 percent of the votes and gained one seat in the European Parliament (later expanded to two seats as part of EU parliamentary reform). Despite this success, the 2010 general election once again saw a weak turnout for the party, with only 0.65 percent of the votes (however, still being the biggest party outside of Parliament).

The relative failure in the 2010 election could partially be attributed to a clumsy statement by Falkvinge in August 2010 regarding the possession of child pornography. He held that mere possession should be not be criminal and that the party wanted to reform current legislation on child pornography. Although the Swedish association for journalists and press freedom gave support for the proposal—because an all-too-sweeping law would waste police resources on things such as Japanese manga comics—the statement led to internal conflicts and was later retracted. On January 1, 2011, Falkvinge departed, and Anna Troberg became acting party leader. The party was originally only stating a position on matters of personal integrity, free culture, and IPR law reform but, in 2012, began to consciously diversify into other policy areas.

The SPP has had its strongest electoral support among men born in the 1980s. Only around 10 to 15 percent of its members are female. Party membership rose sharply in the police raid against PRQ in 2006 and even more markedly during the Pirate Bay trial and implementation of IPRED in 2009, making their youth organization, Ung Pirat, Sweden's largest political youth organization in April 2009. In October 2012 the membership had, however, dwindled, making them the third largest youth organization, tailing those of the two largest established parties. However, it has emerged that SPP membership cannot be compared with other political parties, as it is done on the Web for free, making it possible to register fake members. The party has addressed this by responding that other parliamentary parties and several other parties also offer equally frivolous member registration via their websites. They, however, could not deny the occurrence of false accounts but hold that party administrators would clear these as soon as they are discovered.

While the established parliamentary parties employ a process in which prospective members have to sign forms prior to the membership contract, the SPP fetishizes instant data: On their website, membership statistics are updated daily, in great detail, noting things such as churn and renewal rates. Similarly, Troberg gives a US-style boosterist slant to her argumentation, with self-asserting quotes such as this one, following the 2012 raid on PRQ: "Last time I checked, we had about a thousand new members and 12,000 new likes on Facebook in a day" (Maxwell 2012). Given the critique of frivolous registrations—as well as the questionable relevance of Facebook likes—one should however ask, If the data is questionable in terms of quality, why lend it so much weight?

Many of the party's problems in terms of image and credibility could be attributed to its technocratic elements—connected not only to the male bias of the Internet/technology sector but to what I will address as a martinet, rule- and measurement-obsessed approach. The recourse to evidence-based politics is problematic in that it only recognizes those outcomes that are directly measurable, and only so in the short term. It shuns principle in favor of instrumentalism. We could compare this difference between managerialism and ideology to that between a positivist view of media effects and the theory of agenda setting. Further, advocating a complex interrelated set of regulations requires a faith in orchestrated effort, whereas managerialist politics is a politics that, in terms of regulation, is based on a faith of minimal but precise state intervention.

One example would be the case of endorsing polygamy and relationship anarchism, based on the argument that the problems affiliated to polygamous, abusive family relations could be enforced more directly by addressing the actual abuse in itself, not by sweeping legislation that outlaws also those polygamous relationships that are not abusive. The risk with this line of thinking, however, is that the more direct regulation would in fact involve a higher manual workload in terms of management.

Another example is that of drugs and alcohol. Here, a libertarian view would advocate a laissez-faire market, dealing with the more occasional cases of substance abuse separately. However, in countries such as Sweden where the legislation in these areas is both sweeping and restrictive, it has been shown that state intervention of this kind is likely to keep consumption rates down, across the spectrum, meaning that what can be experienced as a hassle for the vast majority (restricted access to alcohol) nevertheless makes a difference in the aggregated harm from alcohol:

> When the total consumption increases, the consumption of heavy consumers also increases relative to other consumers. [. . .] There are no examples of where a private system, regardless of how that system was created and is regulated, has led to lower alcohol consumption or fewer alcohol injuries compared to an earlier state retail monopoly. (Holder 2008: 16–17)

The difference could also be expressed as that of preventive (or risk-averse) policies versus policies of damage limitation. Sweeping legislation might be suboptimal, from a technocrat standpoint, but might still be the most practically efficient mode of regulation. At the same time, the regulationist model of alcohol politics in Sweden has seen an expansive array of partial liberalization, mainly as a response to the EU membership and increased ease of private import, and there does not actually seem to be much of an increase in injuries because of increased consumption, as initially expected (Svensson 2012). Regarding online pharmacies that sell synthetic drugs and avoid litigation through subtly changing the chemical composition of these drugs, there are many interesting overlaps between this phenomenon and online file sharing. Asserting formal legality through gaming the system like this could be attributed to an approach that willfully dismisses sweeping morality for a stickler perseverance.

Further, sweeping legislation has a rhetorical function: Restricted access to alcohol is an expression of a societal norm. Falkvinge's child pornography statement is a case in point. While the intent was to make for a less sweeping, more exact legislation, he failed to reflexively assess such a statement's strategic side effects, its performative aspect as a speech act.

It is precisely these areas of policy that the German Pirate Party (GPP) has championed—queer politics (lesbian, gay, bisexual, and transgender [LGBT] rights; raising the legal status of nonheterosexual relationships), drugs liberalization, increased secularization, and free infrastructure (wireless networks, public transport)—which arguably makes the party leftist-libertarian. However, the concept of post-privacy, as championed by a more select group of GPP affiliates such as Julia Schramm, makes for an altogether rather different case. Here, the mainstream Pirate Party view that personal privacy should be maximized would indeed be the more sweeping and risk-averse proposal compared to the more avowedly liberal stance of post-privacy. For a longer discussion of post-privacy, see Burkart and Andersson Schwarz (2013).

Historically, the conventional, welfare state model of sweeping, preventive regulation is deeply embedded in corporatist Swedish political discourse. However, a move toward liberal, less authoritarian leanings is now discernible among younger voters. A mere difference in attitudes toward governance is not enough to distinguish ideologies from one another; it takes more than one dimension to accurately describe voter perceptions of how the parties differ (nevertheless, rarely more than two dimensions, see Jegers & Lindgren 1992; Oscarsson 1998; Sandberg 2006; Sjöholm 2009). A move toward more anti-authoritarian, pro-liberal leanings is discernible among younger voters. The problem is that very often, these politics do not square with Swedish parliamentary politics because of the strong predisposition toward block politics; instead, the liberal leanings are expressed in one-off topics such as file sharing or are captured through engagement in NGOs or through (ecological and ethical) consumption choices.

If neoliberal policy is to be seen more as the adherence to regulation that strives to maximize market conditions (Harvey 2005; Hesmondhalgh 2008) rather than an adherence to the absence of regulation, then pirate politics marks a return to a more classical liberalism—not seeing giant financial institutions making greater returns on investments as an end in itself[3] but rather as a secondary outcome of greater latitude among individuals. At the same time, laissez-faire liberalism is agnostic to the wider markets generated, which makes it similar to neoliberalism in praising increased market exchange regardless of what is traded and why.

At the center of the PP ideas program, globally, lies IPR reform. IPR reform is based on the suggestion that civic utility would trump rights-holder benefaction and that the freer markets engendered would automatically lead to a cultural output that is more relevant to the citizens. It is a politics that is premised on a civic standpoint rather than an industrial one; however, in the current policy landscape, the civic interests in freely communicating are aligned with those of giant technology companies such as Google. It puts great emphasis on both positive externalities and the symbolic aspects of such reform. However, these arguments constantly risk turning into a simplistic insistence on the possibility of upholding the bourgeois private sphere.

It is clear that the relationship between the ex-Piratbyrån cohort and the current SPP is a strained one. Fleischer has expressed acerbic criticism of SPP on his blog. He and Eriksson are quick to point out the main distinction between Piratbyrån's approach and that of the SPP: While wanting to make a clearer distinction, so that the private realm is better protected from outside intervention, the SPP ultimately serve to reinforce the distinction between the private sphere and the public sphere, rather than continuously questioning it. Piratbyrån had little to do with having an opinion about where this border should be. It had more to do with a continuous questioning, an inquisition into the nature of copyright and the nature of digitization. Piratbyrån had less to do with the political in its reified mode (in which parliamentary seats have to be gained and populations have to be rallied for support) and more to do with the political as non-parliamentary contestation, debate, and critical reflection (often couched in the academic form).

A key event that manifests this difference would be Piratbyrån's symbolic act, in April 2007, of organizing an alternative Walpurgis celebration on a hilltop in Stockholm. Walpurgis (*Valborg* in Swedish) is an ancient, heathen ritual, characterized by the burning of bonfires, marking the arrival of spring. By burning their own book (Kaarto & Fleischer 2005), Piratbyrån symbolically asserted a non-dualistic conception of the issues pertaining to file sharing and piracy, conceptually erasing old dichotomies that they held as no longer applicable:

> legal—illegal
> private—public
> free—pay
> art—technology—life [sic] (Piratbyrån 2007)

While these dichotomies could be related to Latour's (1993) critique of modernity as an "act of purification" that originates from Kant's distinction between art and labor, the last distinction points to a more Aristotelian approach stressing art, technology, and life as interrelated.

The Walpurgis mass marks a point in time when the people loosely affiliated to Piratbyrån began realizing that the SPP had narrowed its focus—Swedish pirate politics, in its parliamentary mode, was exclusively tied to a dogged discussion on copyright and personal privacy. People such as Gerson and Fleischer have lamented that the potential breadth and depth that pertains to digital politics writ large—something that the original slogan of "welfare begins at 100 megabit" was intended to capture—was superseded by a form of pirate politics characterized by atrophy.

So, what would a digital politics that maintains both breadth and depth look like? In an article published at the apex of the file sharing debate in Sweden, I tried listing some constituents (Andersson 2009b).

First, the regulation of copyright, patent, and surveillance needs to be reformed, increasing civic representativity and accountability. In addition to the lobbying required, hacktivist-influenced politics aims at rebuilding or even constructing entirely new infrastructures that can serve as benchmarks and legitimize new behaviors.

Second, the Internet is a continuation of the brain—digital media allow for a radical undoing of traditional roles in terms of consumers, producers, and distributors. All creation relies on imitation. This begets a novel way of thinking about economic value and entrepreneurialism. Readership helps reconstitute authorship, and harnessed in the right ways, the traces left by consumption can be utilized in progressive ways. Citizen journalism as well as informal avenues for collaborative research and innovation all rely on knowledge being widely available and communicative platforms being accessible, as utilities.

Third, the value of networks cannot be measured solely in monetary terms. There are values—reputation, dissemination, appreciation, credibility, and excitement—that current capitalism does not fully account for, mainly because it lacks the tools to assess them. At the same time, the temptation to more directly be able to measure such values can also lead to information idealism and an increasingly metered society. The unforeseeable, emergent processes that result from collective aggregation mean that the ability to index and link cognitive processes is largely an experimental, precarious endeavor that carries the endemic risk that what is generated is a Pareto world characterized by extreme inequality. This can seem frightening. The legal landscape of IPR regulation can be read as being based in one mode of such suspicion toward unmanageable collectives and unexpected synergies.

It is "so 68" to highlight individuals, Palmås argued at the time (2009). Do not think "human subjects"—think "thought ecologies," think "psychogenes," think "contagions":

> Is it "post-humanist" to think in that way? Well, you can also see it as libertarian, in a Spinozan sense. Freedom is precisely the realization that the human subject is "a finite mode within the infinite modi of substance" [Spindler 2009: 24]. . . . The shift we are going through has nothing to do with "us." The only "we" that exists is that which is assembled through the thought virus. (Palmås 2009, my translation)

Much of what has been taking place is reminiscent of the unruly crowds mobilized through those grassroots processes that were intrinsic to the nascent labor movement but quickly came to be anticipated and muted by hierarchization, corporatism, and pacification.

As I have argued throughout this book, digital politics is always a politics of probabilities—a politics of risk, precariousness, and possibilities. It is a politics of exploration, of inquiring where the thresholds lie, for complex systems to be saturated above a critical level and to undergo phase transitions.

What can be read as a set of values, Eriksson (2009b) asserts, are in fact methods—a praxis, putting parameters to test (and reflexively assessing also the test itself). Digital politics hence contains a sobering agnosticism, but—much like neoliberal economic policy—this agnosticism always runs the risk of escalating into managerialism, as I have tried to exemplify.

Further, the geometric dimensionality of this politics is very different from the traditional notion, espoused by mass media and parliamentary politics, that as long as both sides be heard, the truth would emerge somewhere in the middle of this spectrum. Despite cyber attacks and scorn against the antics of old media, digital politics is less about us-versus-them and more of us-against-us (Andersson 2009b). This is meant in a literal sense: Digital agency carries a power that is often alien to itself; digital subjects have their own destiny in their own hands, which begets reflexivity. The Internet is not something that will, one fine day, be something that is held in safe hands. The Internet is something that constrains behavior yet is, at the same time, continuously performed.

5.9 SPOTIFY: IMPOSING LIMITS IN A LONG-TAIL WORLD

> Ek eventually loaded Spotify with pirated songs and sent demos to industry execs. That got them noticed. "With Spotify people don't get it until they try it," Ek says. "Then they tell their friends." (Bertoni 2012)

The intent of bringing Spotify into the narrative is that as a company—and as a technological practice—this company mirrors so much of what is found among the similar, yet less legitimate pirate sites. Spotify was founded in April 2006 by two entrepreneurs, Daniel Ek (CEO) and Martin Lorentzon (Chairman of the Board). Both had engineering backgrounds: Ek from Stockholm's KTH, Lorentzon from Gothenburg's Chalmers. Prior to founding Spotify they had been involved in the Internet start-up Trade Doubler. Ek realized that more and more people downloaded music for free via the Internet instead of buying CDs. Inspired by Napster, he began to think about a possible new solution to the problem. Spotify—the name allegedly coming from Ek mishearing one of Lorentzon's name suggestions (Bertoni 2012)—can be seen as a streaming-based music brokerage service. An important technical contribution came from Ludvig Strigeus. Already from the outset, the idea was to partner with major record companies, and after long negotiations Ek and Lorentzon succeeded, launching the service for music customers in Sweden and parts of Europe in 2008.

The content that they needed for their beta version was copied from their own and their friends' music collections (Greeley 2011). In other words, the cloud-based streaming service heralded by many people as the successor, or perhaps antidote to file-sharing, itself began as a rogue archive of non-licensed media content.

By installing the Spotify application, music can be streamed from the Spotify servers. The application can be installed on multiple devices, but users can only play music on one device at a time. The search function is essential to Spotify's operability. Additionally, users can make playlists that can be shared with other users, even administrated collectively. By connecting Spotify to your Facebook account you can show your "friends" what you are listening to and see their choices. In September 2011, Spotify partnered with Facebook, allowing users who have linked their account to Facebook to listen to songs directly in Facebook. The songs you listen to are also displayed in the Facebook news feed, a feature that has been criticized by many users for being invasive, akin to a form of mutual surveillance. Further, new customers were required to have a Facebook account, but as of August 2012 this requirement was scrapped.

Spotify is one the most typical examples of a so-called freemium business model. The service is available in three versions: a free version, financed by advertising, and two versions in which you pay a monthly fee for an ad-free application and, additionally, for mobile connectivity. Until October 7, 2008, the service was only available in a beta version for invited testers. Prior to May 2010, registration to the free service was by invite only. In May 2011 several restrictions were imposed to the free version, such as a limit on the number of times a song could be played.

Spotify, in this sense, thrives on scarcity. The initial requirement that users be invited to the service helped generate a sense of exclusivity. The subsequent restrictions on the free version, combined with the fact that only the paid version allowed mobile access, were intended to encourage users to begin paying for subscriptions. There have been third-party, unofficial software clients such as Smutefy, Blockify, and Despotify that allow users to compromise the Spotify experience—the first two muting the sound when ads appear, while the latter one working as an unofficial open-source Spotify client.

In November 2011, the Spotify Apps feature was launched, allowing for external actors to build software plugins inside the Spotify application. Launch partners included *Rolling Stone,* the *Guardian,* and Last.fm. Also the Swedish public service broadcaster SR has launched its own Spotify App. Further, after lengthy negotiations with, among others, Facebook partner and Napster founder Sean Parker, Spotify launched in North America in the summer of 2011. The first two years, the founders funded Spotify, but since then they have attracted cash from several investors in several instances. In 2012, Spotify was valued at between $3 and $4 billion.

In August 2012, the *Wall Street Journal* cited public filings, which showed that Spotify reported about $236 million of revenue (an increase of 140 percent from the $99 million it reported for 2010) but that the company also had a net loss of $56.6 million, up from $42 million in 2010 and $26 million in 2009. Another analyst has shown corresponding figures ($244 million in revenue, yearly growth of 151 percent, but with net losses of $59 million in 2011, compared to $37 million in 2010).

Spotify operates in an environment equally obsessed with data as the techno-progressivists in the SPP and the like. The difference between corporate ventures and open-source models espoused by the latter, however, is the opacity of data: Proprietary businesses such as Spotify thrive on business secrets, only making available that data which attests to their popularity. Hence, reliable user figures are hard to come by; information such as the degree of activity of its users are not disclosed. According to Grundberg (2012), the company had 32.8 million registered users by the end of 2011. Out of these, around 15 million would count as active, while 2.6 million of all Spotify users were paying users. By December 2012, total users had reached 20 million—with 5 million of them paying monthly (either $5 or $10).

In the past, up to 70 percent of Spotify's revenue has come from subscriptions. Currently, the paying customers account for 83.5 percent of the company's total revenue (Dredge 2012). Exact figures are hard to come by, but Spotify's actual revenue would be strongly correlated with its paying users. Revenues from subscriptions increased by 300 percent between 2010 and 2011, while revenues from advertising only increased by 30 percent (Jerräng 2012). Spotify revenue grew fast in 2011, but losses mounted too—Ek has attributed this to investments in local licensing rights required for every new national market entered. Here, his attitude is typical for an entrepreneur in a company's expansive phase:

> The question of when we'll show a profit actually feels irrelevant. Our focus is entirely on growth. It is priority one, two, three, four and five. . . . Our entire model is based on taking on pirate users, converting them into legal users. We don't cannibalize record industry sales but instead add money from those who previously mainly used pirate sites. (Ek, in Lundell 2012, my translation)

The notion of sectors and externalities can clearly be seen in statements such as these: Spotify is designated to harness that consumption that currently takes place in the file-sharing hinterland.

Not only was Spotify made operative only through filling its archive with pirated material. Underneath its client-server-based shell, Spotify utilizes a p2p-based form of file distribution, as the user's own connection is harnessed by the application to spread data and ease music playback for other users. Prior to its launch, its architects had tried their wings with an unmitigated file-sharing application: Before founding Spotify, Ek and chief software architect, Ludvig Strigeus, had created and managed µTorrent, one of the most popular BitTorrent clients (now owned by BitTorrent, Inc.). In early 2012, it was claimed that µTorrent had over 132 million users. As a historical phenomenon, there is a similar continuity between Spotify and µTorrent, much like the continuity between Skype and the p2p application Kazaa that Niklas Zennström launched and managed before founding Skype.

The argument that I would like to make is that, in retrospect, Spotify was perfectly designated to fill a gap that should be evident to you as a reader by now: In terms of usage and readiness to consume music via computers and other streaming devices, Sweden was a very mature market thanks to the outstanding levels of Internet penetration and usage. Especially the establishment of mobile connections was a prerequisite for Spotify to become profitable; the key incentive for users to pay for the premium version is that only this version allows you to use Spotify on mobile devices.

Further, Swedish consumers were used to file sharing. In fact, Spotify could be argued to have harnessed a behavior that already existed—making a legal version of an already established illegal behavior, especially since the actual music files that the service was making accessible by the beginning of its operation (in the beta version, before October 2008) were originally obtained through illegal file-sharing networks. Adding insult to injury, the Spotify application works by means of a p2p-based streaming protocol. At the same time, Sweden as a market for legal services offering Internet-distributed content was underdeveloped, compared to, for example, the United States or the United Kingdom (WWWF 2012).

There is a strong self-image in Sweden of having an innovative, cutting-edge music industry. Swedish national pride is often channeled through the country's institutions and innovations: Once Spotify was established, it could thus exploit the symbolic capital inherent to its position as "the future of the Swedish music industry." This is evident also in the overwhelming support that Spotify has garnered from actors such as Swedish public service radio broadcaster SR, collecting societies such as STIM and SAMI, as well as ISPs such as Telia. Constructing a financial arrangement that involved making the major record companies co-owners of the company also helped give Spotify bargaining power. Instead of demanding that the entire cost should be borne by current usage, Spotify could offer the record companies the promise of being part of future revenues from the service, thus tying it to a financial logic of speculative credit—a viable business model at the time. It should, however, be noted that 18 percent of Spotify is owned by the major record companies.

About 70 percent of Spotify's revenues reportedly go to the record companies. Just over a sixth of Spotify is owned by the four major record labels (Universal Music Group, EMI, Warner Music Group, and Sony BMG), together with Merlin (an organization representing small, independent record companies). In 208 they were offered their 18 percent share for the petty sum of €8,804.40; it is obvious that this was a negotiation piece for acquiring their licensing rights. Besides having signed contracts with IFPI, Spotify has also signed contracts with collecting societies in each country where the company operates. Spotify does not pay artists and songwriters directly. It is these rights holders—labels, publishers, and collecting societies—who distribute the money.

On average, record companies would receive just under 0.5 cents each time their song is played on Spotify; however, besides being both complex and largely secret, the figures differ from country to country and estimates vary between 0.3 and 1.1 cents. The service has therefore been severely criticized for benefiting record companies and letting artists and songwriters remain marginalized in the overall revenue calculations, negotiated at corporate level. However, Strömberg (2012) shows that the trickle-down effect regarding songwriter revenue from Spotify has increased in the Swedish market during 2011 and 2012, as a result of a combination of factors—not only a vast increase in paying listeners but also a shift in the contractual landscape.

> The contract is renewed yearly and is divided according to country. There is a basic tariff regulating the lowest remuneration that the record company gets for songs played for more than 30 seconds. In Sweden, this figure is €0.0027. But there is also a flexible tariff. It is much more complicated and is based on the total number of plays in a country, and the revenues that Spotify has accrued from this country during the preceding month. Half of the advertising revenues are to be distributed according to number of plays. The same goes for revenues from paying users, but here the share can be larger than 50 percent, based on a mathematical calculation occupying almost two pages of the contract. The conclusion is nevertheless clear: It is the revenue accrued from the flexible tariff that will be used if it becomes higher than that of the basic tariff. (Strömberg 2012: 117, my translation)

Industry insiders have confirmed to me that the major labels enjoy very good profitability from Spotify, especially in Sweden, where the service enjoys a higher ratio of paying users—and less competition from the likes of Rdio and Wimp—than in its more recent markets. It is the paying users that facilitate these higher rates of revenue, and the industry has come to love streaming services since the initial investments and financial risks are much lower than with CD manufacturing. In fact, Swedish music industry statistics indicate a trend reversal, as incomes from music streaming increased in Sweden during 2011 and 2012 to the point that industry insiders speak of a sea change, virtually all of it attributable to Spotify: In 2011, revenues from streaming surpassed those from physical copies. The amount of licensing revenues that artists and songwriters get is dependent on their licensing deal. Ten percent of the remuneration typically goes to songwriters; during 2009 the payouts resulting from this (in the Swedish market) only accrued to $80,000, but three years later the figure was twenty-four times higher (Strömberg 2012). How much each artist gets is, however, dependent on his/her particular royalty agreement.

Those record companies that are effective in negotiating fees and creating management structures that involve few intermediaries between Spotify and themselves can enjoy significantly better fares than other actors. Whereas the major labels can, more or less, directly publish songs on Spotify (many of the circumstances around these arrangements are, however, secret), smaller labels have to go through intermediaries (so-called aggregators). One example is the Swedish independent label Goldenbest Records, which enjoys a distribution agreement with Universal but does most other things themselves, thereby being able to negotiate higher royalties (Strömberg 2012). The argument could be made that Spotify consolidates major label power but at the same time empowers those small actors who have the perseverance of organizing their own recording, mastering, touring, and so on, while negotiating better-than-average licensing deals with the majors.

What the Spotify approach toward artists and songwriters suggests is thus a further entrenchment of neoliberal incentives: Artists are expected to be solitary entrepreneurs who are expected to maximize their own involvement with markets. Not only are they supposed to manage their own public relations and marketing, but also they are supposed to be good at negotiating good solutions in the B2B level, as with the example of Goldenbest Records. Middlemen are disincentivized, which can act to the benefit of artists and songwriters but makes them more closely aligned to a raw market mechanism, arguably entrenching Pareto distributions even further.

Interestingly, both TPB and Spotify have, during the last years, experimented with editorial functions, countering the Death Valley problem and attempting to aid musical discovery and serendipity. While TPB has experimented with functions such as promobay.org and temporary front page endorsements of particular artists, Spotify announced the introduction of new functions at the beginning of 2013, with the Follow and Discover browser tabs. Ek argues that this is a response to the immutability of the empty search window: the common problem in the digital media ecology of user interfaces being designated for situations when users know what they want to listen to but not for situations when one would not know what to look for (Dredge 2012). He frames it as a problem voiced by artists rather than by consumers: "Another thing we've heard a lot more recently is that artists are saying to us 'There are 20m songs now on Spotify, so how do I get heard?' We've been really thinking hard about how we solve these problems."

The relaunch of MySpace in 2013 is premised on a similar idea of artists as curators. What remains to be seen is whether this will mainly benefit those artists who are already enjoying wide popularity or whether it could in fact help also those artists further out in the long tail.

6 Critical Masses / Undercurrents and Articulations of Community

> There was madness in any direction, at any hour. If not across the Bay, then up the Golden Gate or down 101 to Los Altos or La Honda. . . . You could strike sparks anywhere. There was a fantastic universal sense that whatever we were doing was right, that we were winning. And that, I think, was the handle—that sense of inevitable victory over the forces of Old and Evil. Not in any mean or military sense; we didn't need that. Our energy would simply prevail. There was no point in fighting—on our side or theirs. We had all the momentum; we were riding the crest of a high and beautiful wave.
>
> So now, less than five years later, you can go up on a steep hill in Las Vegas and look West, and with the right kind of eyes you can almost see the high-water mark—that place where the wave finally broke and rolled back. (Thompson 1998)

The sight is intoxicating: A population of like-minded people reaches a critical mass, so that the individual subjects no longer even need to hold up a fight—the energies are already so strong that the entire situation pulls in one direction no matter what the individual actors do or say. No one is able to tell where everything will end up.

Nevertheless, writers such as Hunter S. Thompson and Joan Didion have shown that there is a dark undercurrent to such developments. The 1960s wave of utopian dreams was subjected to a backlash, as the 1970s turned into what has been described as "the Me-decade." The dewy-eyed idealism stalled. Add to that the fall of the Berlin Wall, the "death" of ideology, and the chilling effects of global capitalism, absorbing these energies. At the end of the century, it was difficult to find someone dreaming the same flower dreams as those in the 1960s counterculture. This backlash is still fresh in collective memory. The shortfalls and illusions inherent to idealism were, arguably, more apparent in 1999 than in 1968, begetting reflexivity and, partly, cynicism. Most people are rather aware of the mistakes of previous generations, which makes political organization all the more complicated. It is not as easy to gather citizens under a unifying banner, as these citizens would be pickier regarding the unifying theme. The pragmatism of sacrificing some of your minor disagreements in the service of a greater cause seems to have been replaced by a pragmatism of picking and mixing only those issues that are seen as being of most value to oneself. At the same time, some truths are still held as self-evident—most notably, the idea of safeguarding totalities to maintain personal privacy and freedom—but as so many of these truths hinge on the continued maximization of individualism, they easily fall prey to the pragmatism and egoism.

Making matters even more complicated, the very awareness of the situation being characterized by these new modes of pragmatism makes for further self-caution; tendencies toward cynicism are always present, and people know this. As I pointed out earlier, this knowledge can be formulated as heeding the us-against-us inherent to digital politics—we could call it a politics of interiority—rather than the less reflexive us-versus-them—a politics of exteriority. The activist is, in this sense, her own worst enemy.

The entire Pirate Bay controversy shows how communications protocols lie at the heart of contemporary technopolitics. In fact, the first pages of the district court verdict (April 2009) consisted of a long discussion about the BitTorrent protocol, the perhaps most slippery agent of all agents involved in this court case: What is this? What is its nature? Where does the criminal intent lie? Who performs the criminal act? Whose fault is it? At the same time, file sharers who I have myself interviewed—alongside those voices that have found expression through various accounts in online forums—hold that file sharing is as natural an element online as trees would be in the forest. They too embrace the mainstream technologist view: The principle that the entire Internet is in fact based on file sharing. What becomes apparent, when noting the overt conflict at hand, is that the users and administrators of file-sharing technology see as natural that which other actors see as an aberration. Different actors want the Internet to be different things, and because of this, conflicts are enacted that result in people being put in prison. Ontology—the description of its nature, or essence, of technological reality—is in itself political.

To say that the Internet is essentially based on p2p from the outset is to highlight one of the network's central organizational principles. Arguing, instead, that the network should be organized according to a principle in which, for example, anonymity should not be made possible is to highlight a different organizing principle.

Any such act—where the network is said to be this or that, where the network's essence or nature is highlighted—seeks to highlight an organizing principle over another. This is what is meant by the term *ontopolitics*, introduced by sociologists of science and technology such as Stengers (1997) and Mol (1999). Hopefully, this book will show that the Internet cannot actually be reduced to just one of these diagrammatic structures. It is its complex layer-by-layer design that makes networks variable and fickle. What hackers often do, for example, is break up a layer, changing its functionality, or accessing its underlying, more elementary layers. Conversely, programmers create applications that add new layers of functionality on top of the underlying TCP/IP structure. All file-sharing applications work in this way, arguably utilizing the underlying, physical server-client structure as well as the TCP/IP suite in technically more efficient and productive ways, allowing for decentralized, swarmlike functionality between users.

In this sense, the Internet is truly stupid—at least in three respects. Firstly, it is a stupid, mute and blind network of networks that merely channels data. Secondly, we have the "stupid" file sharers who relentlessly keep sharing material in an unregulated fashion, although the record industry is said to be bleeding. Third, we could provocatively note the relative stupidity, bordering on autism, which characterizes the true geek—in other words, how some of those who built the Internet infrastructure constructed it mainly because it was possible and for good fun, however, not perhaps devoting much further thought, intention, or prediction of the impact of this construction.

Taking this dogged stupidity into consideration, it is perhaps easier to understand the paternalistic impulse to govern the Internet: Not only is the emancipated user, in this sense, a simple-minded creature—technology makes the user endowed with considerable power as well. We will return to the topic of user empowerment in the next chapter.

6.1 LEECHING AND SEEDING: INFRASTRUCTURES PRESCRIBE BEHAVIORS

Peer-to-peer-based file sharing can be thought of as a mass utility resulting from the harnessing of individual opportunism. The number of participants in the BitTorrent network is literally countless—never possible to overview in its entirety. It is the dark matter of the global media ecology.

Having noted that individual opportunism drives the sharing, one must also keep in mind the deferral of responsibility the infrastructure allows. File-sharer argumentation is always relational to an entity bigger than the individual, preexisting before he or she joins the network. File sharing depends on infrastructures that are conditional—or prescriptive—to the actual usage.

My respondents seemed to shun from openly expressing this idea. This was partly surprising but might indicate the extent to which p2p-based file sharing has become a widely embraced technology in Sweden, ubiquitous to the point of being normative and thus made partly invisible.

The respondents' reluctance to describe the phenomenon as normative can also be attributed to methodology: More complex, or controversial, modes of reasoning tend to only appear after an escalation of the interview process. In a self-reflexive elaboration of desires, motivations, and actions, many such processes might remain unarticulated, unintentional, or simply not visible to the individual. My respondents did, however, note a form of normativity that they mainly associated with human collectives—more explicitly, the communities that establish the rules for engagement. For me, such normativity is simultaneously embedded in the infrastructure, but this seemed less obvious to the respondents.

The term *prescription* comes from science and technology studies—more specifically, actor-network theory. It refers to the process by which technologies prescribe certain behaviors back to humans. In contrast, *delegation* is the term for humans assigning tasks to nonhuman objects. Slack and Wise (2002) note that technology usually prescribes behaviors back to all who encounter them, not just those who initially delegate the task. "In this way," Slack and Wise maintain, "technologies are moral. They impose 'correct' behavior and foster 'good' habits. . . . In addition, the technology may be discriminatory" (p. 494). The file-sharing network becomes a preexisting collective, an institutionalized mass entity that users are destined to always relate to, either by hacking it (opening the black box; Winner 1977) or by accepting its designated standards and procedures.

Lanier (2006; 2010) has argued that in some aspects, digital networks are in fact the opposite of malleable. Despite their genealogy within countercultural and activist circles, p2p networks (in their ossified form) exert a technocratic influence of their own, although not necessarily malevolently. The tacit knowledge that millions of other individuals are using the networks—constituting a people's movement—adds further weight to this implicit normativity of sharing. One of the tropes used by the SPP at the time was to frame file sharing as a common activity, indeed as common as broadband itself. This, to me, was a central constituent of the entire debate on this topic.

Similar to the notion of false consciousness, much of this prescription can be accused to only exist in the mind of the researcher. Perhaps it is haughty to assert that the researcher would be equipped to see things differently, more clearly. Hence, I would like to insert a word of caution. This equipment is the sociological knowledge contained in theory; merely a tool for discovering particular aspects or dimensions of social reality.

In what follows, I will propose a rather complex, sophisticated argument based on such knowledge; it is not the ultimate story of file sharing in Sweden—merely a brief intervention, an attempt to understand differently.

6.2 DONORS AND HOARDERS

Similar to blood donation, online file sharing is a decidedly stranger-to-stranger mode of exchange that requires large-scale infrastructure and considerable institutionalization, realized by a complex arrangement of institutional actors who come to act as anonymizing proxies (in the case of file sharing, hardware-software assemblages; in the case of blood donation, mutually cooperating medical clinics). Further, the exchange is made possible thanks to its participants' beliefs in the efficacy of the overall system; this dedication to operability seems to be a more likely explanation than altruism.

Moreover, p2p networks can be leeched—tapped for content—much as blood banks can. Compared to blood, however, tapping of cultural products would in most cases rely less on (physical) need than on (psychological) desire. Tellingly, the conventional broadcast model presupposes a similar arrangement in which the audience perceives a glut of public goods (non-rival, non-excludable) as being available "on tap" (Andersson 2012a).

Regarding the organizational distinction between those facilitating the sharing and those performing it, contemporary file sharing is highly complex and dependent on the particular protocol or network in question. Even as the act of accessing a file from a torrent swarm is akin to tapping into a glut, the default setting of BitTorrent also makes each user a co-uploader while downloading. Hence, a leecher is a temporary seeder as well, at least during the window of time that the user is plugged into the network.

Peer-to-peer-based file sharing is similar to blood donation in yet another way: Both thrive on simultaneity. Both require that the content is actively held in circulation—kept fresh. To meet demand, such simultaneity would, in turn, beget a constant increase in material resources (bandwidth, storage space); see Steiner (2003: 148).

As the latter half of this book turns to the sociality and identity implicit to being a file sharer, it is interesting to observe that leechers are quite often criticized by file-sharing activists. They are seen as free riders, either unserious newbies, or worse, parasites. While the scorn directed toward these can be attributed to a morality of duty (returning favors, paying dues, etc.), the strong reliance on different kinds of technological determinism that I have explored would suggest that what is more acute is the affirmation of systemic efficacy. If everyone would leech, the continued operability of the system would be jeopardized. What is perhaps more interesting than the scorn put on leechers, however, is the dismissal of what my respondents referred to as a data hoarder mentality.

The ratio systems that used to be a common feature in early instantiations of digital sharing (e.g., BBSs, DC hubs, FTP sites) and still are (on exclusive, private torrent sites), helps establish a data hoarder disposition that some of my respondents saw as outmoded. Moreover, they saw this hoarding as less morally justifiable than their own, more spontaneous and, therefore, allegedly less calculating behavior. Probably, this distancing could also be attributed to the invocation to a scene of semiprofessional, dedicated uploaders; an image that has been common in the mass media debates. As some respondents differentiated between pirate copying (for monetary gain) and private copying (without such gain), they associated data hoarding with the former of these categories, because it introduces a calculating, monetary logic into the file exchange. This could also be compared to Slater's (2002) observations of how degrees of formal order and different forms of valorization are imposed, so as to sustain some kind of normative framework. Scarcity is somehow invented to maintain a moral order. Ratio systems would in effect prescribe certain behaviors, assigning certain functional roles to the user. This attests to the theory of infrastructures being prescriptive. If we return to the analogy of blood donation, it similarly configures morality—and, by extension, the actual quality of the goods circulated—via its institutional setup, most notably in those countries where monetary reimbursement is deliberately deemphasized to constitute only a minor motivation for the donors (Titmuss 1971).

Distancing oneself from the alleged behavior of more heavily invested file sharers can also be read as a typical example of Othering—letting negative characteristics of a phenomenon become attributed to people other than oneself.

6.3 A POLITICS OF PROBABILITY

We will see that very few users are in fact active in the administration and regeneration of networks and hubs. Still, most users nevertheless act as partial or occasional reproducers or media activists in the sense that their participation acts as a small splinter that adds to uphold the network in question. We are now reaching the Gordian knot of tangled agency as explored by the likes of Latour (2005), Hernes (2008), and Galloway and Thacker (2007). If there is one thing to be learned from TPB, it is how it illustrates distributed agency. When acquiring a movie via BitTorrent, the default setup of the system automatically makes each downloader simultaneously upload while downloading, and moreover, the system turns this act into yet another addition to the statistics that attest to the popularity and, in effect, gravitas of TPB as an actor in the media ecology.

This adherence to the sticky, slimy mass agency of the networks could be argued to be hidden mainly from view from the user; it might even be largely subconscious. Still, users are not entirely without intentionality: Their participation is an expression of their desire toward the content, and to be a user is to desire the actual exchange—and hence, access—to be sustained.

The infrastructural setup of BitTorrent makes these processes mundane. With the uploading function integrated into the act of downloading, an act that would otherwise be associated with activism—seeding—is hidden, almost as an afterthought. It is nevertheless a very important afterthought, as the superabundance of content circulating would arguably be reduced were it not for this function.

The critical mass generated is not invisible—it can be seen—but, as a totality the exchange is forever non-overseeable. As there is no macroview of the phenomenon, the actual hive of exchange can never be directly visualized, only second-guessed. The ongoing file sharing is only apprehended by means of a rather myopic, close-up view (Latour 2005: 181) that assesses the macro only by way of inference, or reflexive guesswork. Digital politics are always subject to assessment and estimation, hence the endless recursion to probabilities on both sides of the copyfight.

Further, the mass itself lacks faciality. Bauwens (2002) quotes Michael Hardt (2002):

> The traditional parties and centralized organizations have spokespeople who represent them and conduct their battles, but no one speaks for a network. How do you argue with a network? (Bauwens 2002)

As a network would contain movements that are too disparate, seemingly too contradictory to form a unified opposition in the traditional sense, Hardt argues that the force of networks is instead exerted as a form of undertow. Of course, it could be argued that this undertow makes itself visible through those material artifacts that carry its discursive messengers (user forums, FAQs, how to documents) or that enable the actual exchange (servers, cables, personal computers, software code). The distributed agency of the peers is reinforced in the physical exchanges and, hence, actually perpetuates the material networks at hand. Simply put, without peers, without content, no network.

This distributed agency leaves traces, in sheer aggregated numbers of data up- and downloaded, in the occasional logging of IP addresses and in the indexical inscriptions of its discursive artifacts. This traceability in turn compromises the "quasi-invisibility" that de Certeau associates with traditional consumption, as everyday consumption and hand-to-hand dissemination are normally thought to be acted out in clandestine, individually scattered, largely unrecognized ways (de Certeau 1984: 31; Buchanan 2000: 93). With file sharing, what we are seeing is an aggregation of these earlier fragmented acts on a near-industrial, hyperefficient scale. Singular acts that may individually seem banal are accumulated, and the alternative tinkering, the establishment of expedient shortcuts (and the do-it-yourself ethos that they comprise) slowly become societal norms. Simultaneously, the material networks and discursive artifacts generated become indicative of the sheer scale of the exchange.

Cooper (2001: 17, 34) draws on Simmel (1971) in acknowledging that mass—as an aggregate of either human agents or cultural objects—usually appears to be quite transient. In terms of relating to vast, electronically mediated masses, the individual is forced to resort to probabilities rather than certainties. Likewise, the technical configuration of BitTorrent never guarantees sustained availability of the circulated products. Users tap in and out of networks very rapidly, making user presence highly transitory. Users searching for particular content on a file-sharing network have to rely on the probability of finding it. Police officers searching for signs of delinquent behavior have to make estimates and "shots in the dark." Heavy users, bordering on the criminal, must similarly assess the risk of getting caught.

The copyfight debate ultimately resorts to these probabilities time and again. The entertainment industry argues that file sharing hurts sales, but full causation can never be positively proven because this argument relies on a probability calculation. The debates on possible legalization of or crackdowns on file sharing rely on similar estimates. The file sharers I interviewed also made similar approximations, estimating the possible risks, damages, or benefits affected by file sharing. The risks are minimal, VT (m21) maintained, stressing personal knowledge and skill as factors that reduce the likelihood of getting caught.

6.4 FILE SHARING AS A PART OF THE ENTERTAINMENT ECONOMY

The collectivist claims of the cyberliberties activists—"sharing is caring" and the like—frame the activity in a way that makes it seem radically different from the earlier accumulation and exchange of cultural products. It is framed as a boon to a more communal, collective, and nonprofit form of consumption. However, much of what characterizes BitTorrent distribution suggests otherwise.

Sure, one could argue that the ripped .avi and .iso files that carry the digitized mainstream movies that circulate via BitTorrent in effect constitute artifacts of their own, ontologically different from a purchased DVD or even a downloaded legal file (which most often comes with digital rights management (DRM) that makes it expire at a certain time). An Internet user can actually live her entire life as a cultural consumer without ever opening a legally produced DVD sleeve. In this sense, her experience of film as a cultural artifact would be an affair largely autonomous from the expectations of the mainstream corporate establishment. At the same time, the pirated titles tend to be the same titles as those in commercial circulation.

However, from what is indicated by my empirical data, purist consumption habits of this kind would constitute a rather extreme behavior, given that virtually all file sharers interviewed in my own study noted the permeability between pirate and legitimate consumption. Almost all of them did occasionally purchase DVDs. Some of them specifically noted the practicality of illegal files for giving a preview of whether a movie was actually worth a purchase.

The fact that p2p makes massive data exchange possible without a monetary valuation of the content exchanged does not, however, remove it from the economic realm. File sharing is still an economic activity, having economic repercussions and generating externalities, and it still requires outposts of institutionalization and safeguarding. Despite being labeled anticommercial, it still helps spread the mainstream products that the corporate establishment want us to consume.

> Was not Marx's very quarrel with the utopian socialists based on the insight that the problem of domination in capitalist relations cannot be solved at the level of distribution, no matter how egalitarian such distribution might be? (Brown 1995: 14)

File sharing, as a means of cultural exchange, can therefore never be equated simply with resistance—because it thrives on the same capitalist system of cultural exchange that it forms part of. As most of the data circulated is industry generated rather than user generated, the sharing can be read as a tacit satisfaction with the existing output of these cultural industries. The controversy does not so much apply to what content is circulated, as to *how* it is circulated. This goes beyond a mere question of access; it has to do with what engagements and interactions with cultural content are at all possible. Whereas TPB highlights such controversies, IPR industry representatives such as Antipiratbyrån and IFPI have repeatedly strived to depoliticize it, framing it as a simple police case. In contrast, the SPP has tried to push the issue in the other direction, pitching themselves as a kind of citizens' movement of the information society, framing file sharing as an essentially voluntary phenomenon with little or no profit motive.

Still, to depict p2p-based file sharing in such a blue-eyed way is equally misleading. File sharing has economic repercussions, and the operation of hubs, indexes, and websites that facilitate the sharing can be made economically profitable. However, it is equally important to note that the Swedish court rulings found that TPB had in fact not been a profitable operation (Fleischer 2009a; Andersson & Snickars 2010); the earnings generated from advertisements (equivalent to $150,000) only covered the expenses that were required to run the site, and barely so. As a contrasting case, the entrepreneur Kim Dotcom, running the New Zealand-based Megaupload service that was raided in 2012, made it part of his persona to brag about how profitable it was to run a file-sharing hub.

Both Megaupload and TPB illustrate how agency always spills over: that it is hard to maintain a pure identity in a phenomenon that is as complex as file sharing. As Palmås (2010; 2011) notes, when running a torrent index one is simultaneously an activist and an entrepreneur. The file-sharing structures tend to be uniquely interactive and collaborative, in many ways akin to the Web 2.0 paradigm in that they emphasize openness, participation, and reliance on free, user-generated content. They have the potential to serve as facilitators for anyone to become an occasional activist. On p2p networks everyone has an opportunity—though not an obligation—to be a contributor as well as a recipient.

Any act of consumption that currently makes use of these infrastructures is often deemed by the entertainment industry and its allied lawmakers to be transgressive, or activist-like, by virtue of the perceived sheer illegality of the phenomenon. Using a file-sharing hub is, in this view, to be contaminated by it.

In this sense, the phenomenon becomes politicized less by the file sharers' own intent and more by the potentialities inherent in the technology in its current legal and economical context and the ways these potentialities are strategically employed by the people administering the actual infrastructures, such as the administrators behind TPB.

6.5 THE ALEXANDRIAN AND THE BABYLONIAN

A familiar problem for librarians and archivists is that archival endeavors require active labor—especially so in an era of digital storage, where data has to be migrated constantly. The fickle, non-guaranteed presence of nodes on p2p networks, constantly jetting in and out, on and off (as nodes on file-sharing networks come and go), and the illegality of the entire operation mean that the content is never guaranteed to stay in one place. One could think of *Alexandrian* versus *Babylonian* ways of storing data: The first term would allude to the classic library ideal—centralized, hierarchical, overseeable storage. The latter term alludes not only to more scattershot, unreliable, fickle, decentralized, nebulous archiving but also to the less highbrow forms of content often catered for by these means of storage: pornography, novelty pop tunes and C movies, schlocky and lightweight products that users might never have paid money for—yet download anyway, out of curiosity and novelty.

These two idealized modes of circulation can of course also be compared to Raymond's (1999) concept of "the cathedral and the bazaar"; decentralization here being what prompts a disorderly but highly resilient archive, hard to survey or oversee, akin to what Ernst (2008) has called the *an-archive*. A telling example would be the way historical manuscripts survived the occupation of Timbuktu during 2012–2013, during an Islamist insurrection throughout northern Mali, as these manuscripts were held in domestic residences, scattered across the city.

Reynolds (2011: 59) describes YouTube as perhaps the most telling emblem of a similarly disorderly media ecology. It allows for a rapidly ramped-up convenience of access but is at the same time largely dependent on the output of the mainstream corporate entertainment industry, as a lot of the material on YouTube is simply rebroadcasted audiovisual entertainment and news clips. It is a disorganized, messy public reservoir, offering a stupefying range of content—from ultra-obscure live footage to the most widespread viral "funny clips"—however, with "crummy image and sound quality" and plenty of repetition and "damaged copies," Reynolds notes, drawing on Hilderbrand (2009). This helps induce a kind of Google-addled, associative "drift," reminiscent of Carr (2010), where "artifacts from different eras are jumbled promiscuously and linked by a latticework of criss-crossing associations" (Reynolds 2011: 62).

But elsewhere on the Web, also the Alexandrian finds an outlet, as "all kinds of official organizations and amateur associations are assembling well-managed cultural databases whose contents are available to the general public" (ibid.). Reynolds mentions institutions such as the British Library, the National Film Board of Canada, organizations such as UbuWeb, and specialist blogs. I would add as my examples two metadata databases native to the Web and built in a Wiki-like way: the Internet Movie Database (launched in 1990) and Discogs (launched in 2000). These are user-driven, collectively managed information databases currently rivaling any established public or proprietary database, yet they do not contain any audiovisual content (except occasional snippets of video or sound to preview artifacts). They are highly reliable resources with a low degree of deformation or misinformation.

Also those underlying protocols that are seen to allow for relative disorder in some parts of the Web are found to engender highly sophisticated, immensely organized archives, outperforming those of established, richly funded national archives. The cineaste community explored in my 2012 study is one of the more talked-about torrent trackers in terms of archival stringency and depth. This order can only be imposed through the strict content policy on the site, involving detailed restrictions on what content is allowed and curatorial selections of works highlighted almost every month, from Luis Buñuel to Iranian cinema, from 1950s science fiction to Hammer films and avant-garde jazz, from Krzysztof Kieslowski to Marguerite Duras.

BitTorrent is a protocol that is designated to engender relatively orderly networks. Pouwelse (2004) has accounted for how moderators collaborate in BitTorrent communities to weed out incorrect or polluted content. This makes torrent links relatively labor intensive but much more accurate in terms of content quality and easy to use for its vast group of end users. With BitTorrent, polluted content is much less of a problem than compared to, for example, FastTrack, the network that was made infamous in 2002 by the spyware- and adware-riddled software clients such as Kazaa and Morpheus.

Similarly, Soulseek, which used to have a rather significant user community with over a million registered user names and 100,000 users logged on during peak hours, was even at that point mainly geared toward alternative, non-RIAA-affiliated material, thus remaining largely scot-free in the eyes of legal authorities (Mennecke 2003). With its simple user interface and few formal filters for quality or genre, Soulseek is analogous to the original mp3 exchange hubs of the early century: The requirement for metadata or comprehensiveness is low; the degree of missing, incomplete, badly rendered or polluted files, hence, varies greatly. However, with the dedication to actually make files available often comes a dedication to maintain a good integrity of this kind, which means that from time to time, precarious yet impressively comprehensive collections are made available.

6.6 FEW ACTUALLY CONTRIBUTE

While the popularity of file sharing serves as an indication of a general acceptance of so-called piracy, the active, sustained uploading of material is what is more controversial in that it is what upholds the durability and quality of the networks as pools of content. Yet, many investigations of the nature of participatory online networks show that relatively few users contribute with new, unique content and that many more download material without actually contributing to any considerable extent. Oram (2000) quotes a study that found out that only 2 percent of Gnutella users actually contributed content. Similarly, on Usenet News the ratio of posters to total readers was only about 7 percent. "Perhaps the gift economy is a little less public-spirited than its promoters suppose? A lot more receiving/taking than giving is evident," May (2002: 102) claims, referring to a survey quoted in the *Economist* (2000). According to this survey, the amount of users who offered no files to download for other users (i.e., who only received and did not contribute content) was a lavish 70 percent of the group of about 31,000 people who connected to the Gnutella file-sharing system during the twenty-four-hour survey period. In another study, those who shared their CD collections did not contribute evenly. A mere 20 percent provided 98 percent of the material. Indeed the most generous 1 percent served up about 40 percent of it (Adar & Huberman 2000). Approximately 26 percent of Gnutella users shared no data; these users were clearly participating to download data and not to share (Saroiu et al. 2002). Another study found that less than 10 percent of the IP numbers on a particular network filled about 99 percent of all p2p bandwidth (Sen & Wang 2004).

With BitTorrent, every minute the user stays online after the download is completed is significant, because the entire file then acts as a seed, being available to other users. Pouwelse (2004) has shown that only 17 percent of users remained online longer than one hour after they finished downloading. After ten hours this number had gone down to 3 percent, and after one hundred hours it was a mere 0.34 percent. The Research Bay survey (Andersson Schwarz & Larsson 2013) also shows that the group of users who labeled themselves uploaders constituted a small minority of around 5.3 percent.

Another example of how long-tail distributions mean vastly different interpretations of what constitutes sensible cultural distribution can be found in the Pirate Bay trial in which Sunde's defense attorney Peter Althin asked him about the amount of copyrighted material administered by TPB. Sunde told the court that he had carried out a survey of a random 1,000 torrents from the tracker and that 80 percent of these titles were not copyrighted. However, had the prosecutors then asked whether these titles were as popular as the remaining 20 percent, the answer would most likely have been no. The 80 percent of obscure, non-copyrighted material at the tail of the Pareto distribution says very little about the extreme circulation of those titles that spike at the popular end of the diagram. I have repeatedly analyzed TPB's own charts, listing the one hundred most popular titles, and those charts tell a radically different story: Virtually all of these titles are copyrighted works being circulated without the consent of the rights holders. This is concurrent with findings enumerated by Levine (2011: 55).

Liebowitz et al. (2003) have similarly shown that Kazaa traffic was highly concentrated around a small minority of large, popular items. The user behavior they noticed was very pronounced: As few as 2,500 files (a mere 0.8 percent of all detected files) accounted for as much as 80 percent of the traffic. Thus, also the traffic inside the actual file-sharing systems can be found to follow a power-law distribution (Ripeanu et al. 2002).

> While the figures for downloading music are almost certainly understated, the low levels of "creative" behaviour are more surprising and do little support to the notion that the Internet is an intrinsically more sympathetic environment for mediated activity. Blogging and online discussions are undertaken vigorously but, thus far, only by a minority of enthusiasts rather than the general online population. The figures demonstrate that the Internet is more commonly used as a tool of individual research and connection rather than as a site of mass-mediated production and interaction. (Freedman 2006: 285)

Jenkins (2007) refers to a study (Lenhardt & Madden 2005) that might initially suggest the opposite interpretation: It claims that 57 percent of US teens who use the Internet could in fact be considered media creators. However, their definition of a *creator* is very broad. It is taken to mean someone who has "created a blog or webpage, posted original artwork, photography, stories or videos online or remixed online content into their own new creations." This begs the question of how long-lasting, accessible, and politically relevant the content produced is. Enzensberger's (2003) is a classic rebuttal of the idealism of activist media uses:

> For the prospect that in future, with the aid of the media, anyone can become a producer, would remain apolitical and limited were this productive effort to find an outlet in individual tinkering. Work on the media is possible for an individual only insofar as it remains socially and therefore aesthetically irrelevant. The collection of transparencies from the last holiday trip provides a model of this. (2003: 266)

Without determined collective organization, "the individual, so long as he remains isolated, can become with their help at best an amateur but not a producer" (ibid.). To mobilize the inherent productive powers in the new, granular, dispersed media in any effective way, these powers need to be systematized, or at least aggregated. This does not of course remove the possibility of local, tactical, limited political movements taking place, but as such, these would remain comparatively limited, if not even unnecessarily exclusive, he argues. To truly make a difference, the aggregation has to be purposeful, and its local instantiations have to have potential beyond the trivial; they have to be part of a body that is overseeable, accessible, and visible to the public eye. As Shirky (2008) has pointed out, most user-generated content is not actually intended for mass consumption: It is merely personal communication in a public forum. Ironically, this insight has itself become something that file-sharing proponents have picked up on, when sharing is primarily framed as an exchange among private individuals, taking place in the private realm. Defining file sharing exclusively in such a way is, however, problematic.

As the Google PageRank algorithm has made apparent, different Web pages have vastly different popular impact. Certainly, the Internet is often said to be premised on a nonhierarchical information exchange in which everyone enters on equal terms. Yet, someone is always "more equal" than the rest, to paraphrase the common aphorism. Open infrastructures quickly become susceptible to corruption, hostile takeovers, or strong-arm actors who can bypass the background noise, the low-level chatter of masses occupying themselves with ceaseless mutual exchange. Isolated amateur production lends itself to be politically neutralized because of this very isolated, amateur character. Hardin's (1968) lament on "the tragedy of the commons" has been an influential way to conceptualize this. In the contemporary debate on pirate politics, this stance has, however, been questioned and even directly opposed:

> Every commons, Hardin argued, would sooner or later be destroyed because all participants essentially acted as rational, utilitarian profit maximizers and the self-interest was higher then concern for the common resource. Research by the political scientist Elinor Ostrom (1990) however showed that Hardin's findings were only true under specific conditions and that other conditions existed where collective commons management was indeed possible. (Medosch, 2008: 83)

I will not expand on this debate at any further length here, but suffice to say that the optimistic presupposition that the endless space online would disprove Hardin's thesis is itself disproved by the fact that the attention span of human beings is limited and can be saturated. There is asymmetry of importance in a cognitive sense too, as we (largely subconsciously) acknowledge how differing regions of the surrounding mental ecology is assessed and encircled according to different criteria.

6.7 ONLINE SOCIALITY AND GESELLSCHAFT

In this book, we are seeing how file sharing prompts us to revisit a generation of early modern thinkers who were largely each others' contemporaries: Gabriel Tarde (1843–1904) and Vilfredo Pareto (1848–1923), but also

Ferdinand Tönnies (1855–1936). Here I will try to connect some concepts of the latter with more contemporary developments within social theory.

Tönnies distinguished between *Gemeinschaft* and *Gesellschaft* as sociological categories (they can be translated, subtler connotations aside, as "community" and "society"). Individuals in *Gemeinschaft* are unified by common practices and affinities. They are subject to mutual responsibilities and duties toward the community that they are embedded within (Tönnies 2001: 22). The most typical expression of *Gemeinschaft* would be the bourgeois family. In contrast, *Gesellschaft* refers to associations that lack shared customs and mutual bonds. *Gesellschaft* rarely or never takes precedence over personal self-interest.

Taking the individual as the central unit of network society is a contested matter—Castells (2000) sees the actual network as the central unit, whereas Van Dijk (2006) puts more emphasis on molar formations such as individuals, groups, or organizations as central units of network society. As has been pointed out by Castells (2001: 1), there is no return to an era before the network society—the network is in this sense the message (Lovink 2003: 45). Lehmann et al. (2007) point to the ontological premises underlying this, resulting in the recognition of a number of totalities: Everything consists of complex networks, interlocking into one another (Kampmann Walther 2007); the Internet consists of numerous such complex networks, and these are all embedded in a wider network, namely the "general economy" (Jenks 2003: 107), which thrives not only on constructive processes but on Schumpeterian creative destruction, and Bataillean excess and wastefulness alike.

Wittel (2001) has seized on Castells' macrosocial ontology to identify a "network sociality": Here, the logic of information exchange engenders a type of sociality that is markedly different from that of *Gemeinschaft*. Instead, social encounters become discretionary, intense but often brief. Traditional units such as the family become increasingly fragmented and challenged by competing forms of social organization, running parallel with the tendencies toward a more thoroughgoing individualization (as observed earlier, see Section 5.1). Castells (2004: 196) confirms similar tendencies.

First of all, network sociality is biased toward short-lived, strong relationships; the "strength of weak ties" (Granovetter 1973). Further, it encourages the merging of work and play. Both of these tendencies—the promiscuous but strategically detached nature of socializing and the increasingly informal nature of labor—are enabled and mediated by digital technology. Wellman's (2002) concept of "networked individualism" is parallel to Wittel's in that it seizes on how the Internet has made individual communication less place bound and more network bound; people are presumed to interact with one another based more on interest and affect and less on demographic or geographic factors. As I have argued, if file-sharer sociality depends primarily on factors such as knowledgeability, access, and familiarity, the fact that it is demographically dominated by young people and males is relegated to only be a secondary upshot of these more primary factors.

As Christensen and Jansson (2012: 220) point out, much has happened during the decade since Wittel and Castells formulated their theses. Instead of a general shift toward sociality in "open systems" (Wittel 2001: 64), interpersonal relationships are increasingly channeled through SNSs that are at the same time globally expansive and allowing for "refined regimes of closure, and the making of (deterritorialized) enclaves" (Christensen & Jansson 2012: 221). Exclusion and closure works in new ways: Not only is online networking taking place in much more variegated ways—with different degrees of technological sophistication regarding the degree of how social ontology is tuned—but also networks are bounded by what Bourdieu (1984) observed as social fields in which the need for status, influence, and respectability "necessitates various forms of symbolic boundary maintenance and distinction" (Christensen & Jansson 2012: 220).

One effect of groupings based on shared interests would be that they give the participants the opportunity to, in a comparatively safe environment, experiment with their online personas and develop "thick descriptions" (Geertz 1993) about their own norms and ideals. As this would allow for a reflexive approach, it is potentially transformative. Nevertheless, that online sociality would be increasingly characterized by information rather than narratives is directly contradicted by the rise of SNSs such as Facebook and their ongoing refashioning of the self; platforms that encourage narrativity of a markedly different kind from that of the solitary author and the secluded literary text, in that they make for ongoing, unbounded narratives seemingly without beginning or end, and therefore are disorienting. Sontag (2007: 224–225) criticizes both television and the Internet for this narrative drift.

Further, Christensen and Jansson argue, social control in the traditional sense of *Gemeinschaft* is still overlaid on top of the heterogeneous online infrastructures. If "broadcasting cultivates a form of *reasonable* subjectivity, characterized by a willingness to listen and openness to other viewpoints that is essential to the maintenance of a shared public life" (Barnett 2004: 65, in Christensen & Jansson 2012: 235, their emphasis), "new online social media cultivate an exclusivist subjectivity marked by desire to control the inflow and outflow of public utterance, engendering a paradoxically traditional *and* novel sense of *Gemeinschaft*" (p. 235). Personal privacy emerges as a tactical asset, akin to symbolic capital, in (semi)public life, modulated for complicity in surveillant practice. This could be compared to the opportunist uses of the system in Section 5.2.

Of course, this form of disposition would vary greatly between different types of social fields—and, as Christensen and Jansson note (ibid.), reflexivity as such is not always the desired logic of practice. In my own study, I have come to compare the social structures engendered by file sharing primarily to *Gesellschaft*, and only secondarily to *Gemeinschaft*: Notwithstanding the prevalence of online communities, a vast amount of file sharing takes place without users having to subscribe to, or even make contact with, communities or individuals in the online realm. The high-tech gift economies of the Internet appear primarily to accommodate the overall efficacy of networks, rather than being used for close-knit, communal purposes (Barbrook 2005).

The turn to post-social theory (Knorr-Cetina 2001) is an interesting aspect of Wittel's (2001: 64–65) analysis that can be seized on here. The notion of post-sociality is not to claim the decline of the social, but rather a shifting of social activities away from humans and toward objects. In Latour's philosophy, this shift is rooted in modernity, which he and Knorr-Cetina associate with "the collapse of community and the onset of individualization" (Knorr-Cetina 2001: 521); the lifeworld is more and more characterized by interactions with technological hybrids, something that crashes the myth of a social realm separable from the nonhuman realm.

Leyshon (2003) characterized early p2p services such as Audiogalaxy and Gnutella as "inverse" gift economies, since the objects shared through these were "not actively 'given' by one actor to another" (p. 554). These high-tech gift economies should be seen as institutional arrangements that enable actors with needs or desires to "take" from those with resources, albeit at no cost to the latter, because of the nature of digital reproduction (ibid.) Of course, as these networks are all intermeshed with other online and off-line networks—hacker spaces and the like—it can be argued that apparently weak social ties are interspersed with friendship networks, both online and off-line, consisting of strong ties. For instance, when Twitter acquaintances share links to copyrighted files, this is not really a case of stranger-to-stranger exchange but a mode of exchange more reminiscent of early p2p networks such as Napster and chat applications such as IRC.

Certain elements of online file sharing suggest an amplification of *Gesellschaft*-like properties, while the tendency to rhetorically invoke the trope of community somewhat underplays the institutionalized, semi-anonymous, and depersonalize characteristics that can also be found in more close-knit, secretive communities. It thrives on the pooling of resources between millions of strangers, principally through weak ties (Currah 2007: 474). This partially contradicts the tendency to see it as gift economy (Cooper & Harrison 2001; Giesler 2006; Skågeby 2010; Zerva 2008; Bauwens 2012) in the vein of the tight-knit communities that were described by Mauss (2002).

Especially BitTorrent and cyberlockers can be seen as mass-scale phenomena, at least in countries such as Sweden where the usage is common. In these modes, vernacular sharing has many similarities with the corporate cloud metaphor, not least since both legal and illegal instantiations of such clouds involve a conditionality in terms of their visibility: There is always a back end to the services, hidden to ordinary users. There is also something of a set horizon that is always dependent on the user's standpoint. We are seeing how these phenomena mirror each other, and both effectuate economies of naked competition—tendencies that are so strong that they have to be ameliorated through the implementation of editorial functions that guide users and curate content.

6.8 "CHARISMATIC AUTHORITY" AND THE HONORABLE MANAGEMENT OF CULTURE

All is not *Gesellschaft*. Like Lindgren's (2009) informants, several of my own respondents expressed great concern for collectivism and shared a utopian notion of sharing as an actual positive force in society. Whether this was lip service or the expression of a genuine investment in community was hard to tell, however.

As we have seen, many smaller, dedicated communities of sharing still exist, alongside the more mass-oriented cyberlockers such as Rapidshare, Mediafire, and the recently subdued Megaupload. Those respondents in my 2012 study who were found in connection with a private torrent tracker did of course express a clearer dedication to community. However, many of these new communities tend to be of an ad hoc kind and are often based around links that, after all, lead back to these more anonymized mass repositories.

Strategic sovereigns are nominated (Andersson 2009a) through a process akin to something arising out of a substrate—an articulation that can be named and recognized, indicating that a larger movement is going on (Melucci 1989). Through "homesteading" (Raymond 1999) actors come to inhabit and "claim their own territory" in the otherwise nebulous topology of computer networks. A website is a spatial site located on a server somewhere on the planet, liable to the jurisdiction of whatever country it is hosted in, but it is simultaneously a textual entity, experienced as a despatialized entity—more akin to invocation than to traversal of physical space (Chesher 1997)—independent from geographical location, and capable of representing gigabytes of arbitrary data. The establishment of a successful Internet site is thus a double endeavor: It is both a spatial location and a semiotic move.

We will see that also in those supposedly depersonalized hubs that are found in the file-sharing world, a form of honor is found, connected to the act of hosting an archive or service. In providing platforms for sharing and for voicing dissent toward the established entertainment industry, the increasing autonomy gained by actors such as TPB, private torrent sites, Soulseek, Zeropaid, and TorrentFreak is more akin to the concept of positive liberty than to negative liberty.

Regardless of whether we are talking about open torrent indexes such as TPB and EZTV, literary archives such as Aaaaarg, Library.nu, and Avaxhome, or private hubs serving specialist interests, the freedom to upload copyrighted content that is hosted on and/or orchestrated by a dedicated service is an act that is not devoid of responsibility. With this freedom comes an obligation, I would argue, to act in an honorable way regarding the access to the content. This is, however, dependent on what the intended audience deems as honorable. This notion of virtue can be applied both to the individual users and to the site administrators; the responsibility of the latter of course is more extensive than the former.

In a forthcoming article (Andersson Schwarz 2013a) I draw on Benkler and Nissenbaum (2006) and O'Neil (2011) in developing a theory around site administrators, noting how their prioritizing of technical efficacy is similarly a form of appeasement of users. There are many parallels to the author principle outlined by Derrida (1995): the paternal and patriarchal principle of being the upholder of an archive, the upholder of institution, domiciliation, and filiation.

This reification of the author function is apparent also in alternative, allegedly more civic licensing schemes such as Creative Commons (CC), particularly through the emphasis on attribution. CC allows users to share and remix works, as long as they make sure to quote the original author.

Further, it is instructional to consider the honor/virtue that is bestowed also to those ordinary users who upload: the pride of seeders. The Indian respondent in my 2012 study argued that seeding was noble:

> I really admire the uploaders who take the effort to upload serious arthouse films. . . . File sharing is noble down to the core. I mean, think of it a person sharing a file he may have brought it for a high price is giving away that material for free to others irrespective of who the end user may be [sic]. That is as noble as any cause can be. It's like the patent system. If you didn't patent it then any XYZ can use it without paying any money. There is nothing nobler than this. (EC, m23, India, 2012)

When I replied that the user nevertheless spreads the author's work without permission, he began by stating that the depiction of it as "stealing" was false, as every author would see his/her work being enjoyed, then he pointed out that politicians and industrialists were corrupt. This, to me, is a clear example of taking only a specific viewpoint—that of the domestic/consumer view.

Another user was a bit more ambivalent:

> I think most of them are probably a bit like me, they are aging white males with a useless hobby but with education, and they dedicate their digital life to the love of cinema, which is a foolish thing to do, and as such definitely honoursome. . . . In the case of communities like [NN], [gratitude] shows by being active on the forums and seeding (seeding, seeding, seeding . . .). (UE, m40, Netherlands, 2012)

At the same time

> Since sharing (in the sense of seeding in a good ratio) is such an easy thing to do, you cannot say that users who are good seeders are motivated by the noble goal of Mutual Sharing. They may just as well be motivated by the vain goal of "getting lots of scene points." (ibid.)

We need to recall that intra-forum appreciation is compromised by the fact that users are normally only known to one another by their pseudonymous avatars. Regarding manifesting pride externally, in one's daily life, this would entail not only a pride of particular behaviors, but also of being part of a movement as well. T-shirts attesting "proud pirates" are highly indicative of this and tie back to the romantic, revolutionary air of such outsider aesthetics, manifesting support and influence toward those tragic, sacrificing actors who put their lives on the line building infrastructures. With legal ventures such as Spotify, such heraldic potency would arguably not be found in these in the same way; if a person wears a Spotify logo it is more likely to do with either the status of being an early adopter or—for a Swede—an assertion of nationalistic pride.

In the late nineteenth century appropriation of honorability, as outlined by Ruskin (1997), it is synonymous with sacrifice. The honorable actor is the fighter/warrior/martyr "whose mission is to die" (p. 175). It is important to differentiate between dissimilar types of hubs and services; the pirate literature site Aaaaarg.org has, for example, been lauded for being neutral, nimble, and discreet, whereas Megaupload was brash and overtly commercial in its interface design. The architect behind the former, Sean Dockray, keeps a low profile but has been praised for having the kudos to run Aaaaarg in the face of adversity. Similarly, TPB, when Sunde was still its spokesperson, enjoyed similar appraise among activists and pirate affiliates while simultaneously insisting that TPB, as a service, should be seen as a mute utility, impartial to what is exchanged on it.

Sunde keeps insisting on TPB's role as mere conduit, a neutral space or place where people in general (the hazy, never fully overseeable collectives) are able to share stuff; in February 2013, when the Swedish antipiracy organizations threatened the SPP with legal action, because of the SPP's hosting of TPB, he invoked this neutrality. Whether TPB, despite its name, allows for significant other uses than illicit sharing of copyrighted material is, however, as we have seen, a matter of interpretation.

On the other hand, there are many secretive, private BitTorrent hubs, such as the one in my 2012 study, whose administrators remain anonymous, and we have file-sharing networks such as Soulseek that have managed to exist under the radar for more than a decade, where the administrators are much more secretive but have briefly appeared, under their own names, in online forums (nevertheless keeping an extremely low profile).

It is therefore telling that Spotify's Daniel Ek also manages to fall in line with this type of user-centric appeasement. Playing the card of technological smartness benefits the image of Spotify as an outsider when compared to the established entertainment companies but equally an ally to those in favor of a more efficient management of domestic technologies and increased customer utility. Coming from a small, peripheral country adds to the underdog appeal of such an actor. The engineering heritage also benefits Spotify in this respect; there is a humility that those actors can afford who prove themselves by the silent running, the quiet efficacy of their product.

At the time of writing—after the guilty verdict of aiding copyright crimes on a vast scale—the founders of TPB have seen their lives ruined, or at least gravely circumscribed. In that sense, they fit the bill for being tragic actors—fighters whose mission is to die. Per Sundin, CEO of Universal Music Sweden, is quoted as having stated, off the record, in the summer of 2011 that TPB had acted as a catalyst for systematic change:

> Without The Pirate Bay, the industry would not have changed so much as it did. Without The Pirate Bay, Spotify would never have seen the light of day. (Sundin, in Svanell 2013)

This quote echoes Schumpeter's concept of creative destruction: how capitalist economic development arises out of the destruction or reconfiguration of some prior economic order, or prior forms of wealth. Tellingly, it is possible to trace an unconcerned, agnostic approach to this destructive dialectic among both entrepreneurs on the neoliberal end of the political scale, as well as among the activists steeped in more socialist ideal. Quite much of what will lead me to argue that there are shared managerialist and technocratic elements between both groups comes from my detection of a certain wanton attitude to conservation of infrastructural architectures and habitual settings. There is a strong progressivism of delivery platforms (for lack of a better word) on both sides of the copyfight rift. Ironically, both groups could at the same time be said to espouse a nostalgic approach to the actual content shared; Reynolds (2011) makes the case that we are living through "retromania," as the back catalog of popular culture only keeps growing, making it harder and harder to create something entirely new. Moreover, the latter group—leftist, often academic proponents of promiscuous copying—tends to have, as I have said earlier, an archivist approach to culture: Much of Fleischer's and Edin's critiques of Spotify focus on its actually very limited archival breadth. In the hyperbolic affirmation that Spotify enjoys in Sweden, it is often overlooked that it is merely a subsystem (a clearly delimited one, we might add) embedded in larger, much more open and intermingled systems of circulation.

Tellingly, it is this invocation to potentially even deeper archives and even better metadata that forms the charge in advocating an uprooting of older infrastructures in favor of faster, more comprehensive, more decentralized ones: "Hopefully, the efforts of The Pirate Bay will inspire those who will make The Pirate Bay totally irrelevant" (Fleischer, in Reddit 2013a).

7 Technologies of the Self / Subjectivities Engendered by Mass-scale File Sharing

With great power there must also come—great responsibility! (Spider-Man, 1962)[1]

Although several of my respondents were contributors to file-sharing communities, few of them professed explicit political inclinations. Still, virtually all of the people I interviewed—both in 2006 and 2012—took a wary, if not distanced, stance toward established media corporations. The general consensus was that the entertainment industry makes too much profit and prices of CDs and DVDs are too high. In some cases respondents coupled this critique with the particular argument that Sweden is generally overpriced and that it is often cheaper to import goods from foreign-based online retailers.

File sharing can be seen as a potent example of user power, not only in terms of the manifestly (co)productive forces of activism and seeding but also in terms of more conventional consumer power: File sharing empowers audiences in terms of making consumption choices (voting with your feet), in terms of the freedom to designate your own delivery platform (freedom to tinker), and in terms of supporting those infrastructures that you appreciate (this latter aspect, however, being circumscribed by the restricted abilities to donate money to actors such as TPB).

Lindgren (2009) argues that the file sharers see their activities as mundane, convenient, self-evident, and—at first thought—not particularly political. I agree with this, but I would not primarily attribute this to the distancing effect of computer use that Lindgren observes, but rather to different forms of visibility and habit. Overt politicization appears to be something that only a minority is engaged in. But when this minority is part of managing the actual platforms and orchestrating the sharing, as with TPB and Piratbyrån, they can engage also the less politically inclined users to fall in and out of roles that perform a political function, for example, voting online in favor of issues framed by the cyberliberties activists.

What is central in this chapter is that the tendencies outlined herein all relate back to those totalities and structures outlined in the preceding chapters. As we have seen, file sharing as an ongoing, never fully overseeable superabundance is perhaps overly abstract to invoke, in terms of lending it political weight. In contrast, a people's movement or folk sport is to formulate it as a valid collective, to give it a more rhetorically powerful, organized form.

This discursive invocation appears to be charged with attempts to objectify it, to bequeath it with validity, by way of referring to other factors: not only the ontological stability and the normativity offered by the evident popularity and ubiquity of the infrastructures. By invoking the history and perceived nature of the Internet, a generality is offered that lends weight and provides stable and coherent coordinates for the justification, "subject to general assessment" (Boltanski & Thévenot 2006: 12). But the prescriptive material framework alone does not fully justify the sharing. More universalizing regimes of justification were invoked, such as the idea of progressive adoption of the functionally most optimal technologies and the primacy of individual latitude over authoritarian order. My respondents primarily justified their sharing by holding that it would have, on the whole, a positive impact on society, and some even doubted that file sharing would have any detrimental impact on society at all, as the link between falling sales of audio CDs and file sharing is hard to establish. Some seemed to think that the impact of file sharing was only negative for certain industries. This echoes the findings by Hinduja (2003) among users of unlicensed, illegally copied software, who denied that fiscal harm was exacted on manufacturers because of their illicit copying of software.

I criticize the technocratic impulse implicit to the cyberlibertarian ethos. This is not so much a Heideggerian critique (a lament of the *Gestell* of technocracy) but rather, it should be read as a critique of the managerialist approach to politics that sees everything as utilities and demands everything to be metered: seeing the price of everything and the value of nothing.

7.1 FIRST AND FOREMOST A QUESTION OF TECHNICAL ABILITY

One of the things noted, already in my fieldwork in 2006, was that active file sharers seem to share a propensity for exploration—not exclusive to youth or gender but rather to personal inclination. Despite a language of sharing, various Internet-activist commentators, as well as my own interviewees, have tended to use decidedly individualist explanation models, emphasizing individual ability above any particular other demographic factor. This ability is facilitated by high levels of computer literacy and access to broadband. In addition, what is required is a strong personal inclination to govern one's own media consumption, to discover new media texts, and to explore new technologies—in short, to manage a media consumption that is personally experienced as autonomous.

Individual specialization involves a plethora of categories; some of them miniscule, perhaps even banal (especially in a chronological sense, as subjects might often only adhere to them at very short intervals); others more long-lasting, even comprising entire life projects. Some are more fundamental to one's personal identity than others. Thus, my own heuristic is to avoid the assumption that certain categories would define identity in an a priori way. A person may be a computer user, a sci-fi fan, a girlfriend, a tourist, a car driver, a parent, a file sharer or pirate—the list can be virtually endless—but it would be methodologically unsound to decide in advance which category would have more bearing than others in determining this person's identity in relation to certain contexts. We all jump in and out of such roles continually. This is central to the concept of "actants," found in Greimas (1966), later taken up by Latour (1993). An actant is a structural role or, rather, a functional operator that various actors—human and nonhuman—can embody. Any such actor relies on a range of associations to other human and nonhuman actors to function. This insight is central also to Searle's social ontology, described in Section 1.1.

The various subjective valuations people make of such constitutive roles can be accessed by way of empirical analysis. Lindgren's study (2009) is similar to mine, and he reaches the conclusion that in the file-sharing world, moral issues tend to be given ad hoc solutions, as no prior benchmark exists for many of the new behaviors enabled online. However, to assess this is not necessarily only done by means of ethnography. The example of file sharing shows the importance of the material, infrastructural settings, and external contexts, such as the ways the topic is discursively framed in society.

File sharing entails several roles or functional positions. One can simultaneously be, for example, a seeder, a leecher, a data hoarder, a deviant, a commoner, an IP number, a numeric entry in a website's statistics, an unwitting redistributor, or a highly intentional evangelist. How such roles are subjectively conceptualized depends on the mode of reasoning; this mode of reasoning, in turn, depends on the subjective position of the person advocating or justifying certain uses. A record company lawyer would make different conclusions than a working-class teenager. Many respondents emphasized privacy and efficacy as each user's individual responsibility. Often, they attributed the problem to individual users making the decision to use or abuse the system, where it was "up to oneself" to decide whether to "keep up" with these new technologies or remain "left behind."

The barriers of access involved (in terms of skills as well as material setup) and the primacy of directed, purposeful action (actively pulling the content desired, rather than making do with what is pushed toward you) resonates strongly with the ways one's individual self is increasingly managed as a reflexive project (Rose 1999; Bauman, in Beck & Beck-Gernsheim 2002). Here, older, more rigid, pre-given categories such as class, profession, or gender are thought of as becoming less determining for what identities individuals form. Dean (1994: 193) speaks of "a culture of the self and self-improvement," whereas Rose (1999) elaborates how the "entrepreneurial self" in fact partly grew out of a corporatist, humanist Scandinavian rationale in which work was increasingly seen as an essential component of self-fulfillment, prompting people to scrutinize their own lifeworld and to aim to maximize both pleasure and efficiency, treating all areas of life as projects to be managed.

File sharing, and similar knowledge-demanding activities on the Internet that aim to open up the black box of technology (Winner 1977), could be said to share with the hacker discourse on free and open-source software (FOSS) a "*transposable* model for new legal possibilities composed of an aggregate of practices, licenses, social relationships, artifacts, and moral economies" (Coleman 2004: 509, italics by author). Thus, these practices and economies enter "a wider public debate on the limits of intellectual property primarily through visible cultural praxis" (ibid.). As laws and norms become ossified in code (Lessig 1999; Galloway 2004), when the black box is opened, "what is purported to be a 'singular' field of intellectual property law" (Coleman 2004: 509) is opened up into multiple possible areas of renegotiation, each demanding new modes of justification.

7.2 SHARING AS "MUTUAL EXPLOITATION"

A lot of file-sharer discourse relies on confirming the scale and pervasiveness of what is already happening on the Internet. Perhaps this is why the technological determinism card is so often attached to the proponents of unmitigated file sharing: The teleological, ontological argument that the Internet has certain properties that have always been there and that are now harnessed in previously unanticipated ways makes these technological progressivists a likely target for accusations of a blindly technocratic approach to culture. This reference to carrier neutrality was also one of the arguments that Sunde used when being criticized for allowing links to gruesome footage to remain indexed by TPB (Andersson 2009a).

File sharers mainly assess the situation as citizens and cultural consumers. From this point of view, the individual is always relative to totalities bigger than the self. From a policy viewpoint, however, it is senseless to talk about totalities, as such argumentation will only digress into ever wider circles. As we have seen, the justification for different social phenomena has to be specified through particular registers, concerns, or ideologies (Boltanski & Thévenot 2006).

The general devotion shared by file sharers—regardless how inclined one would be toward activism—appears to be toward the functioning of the overall technical system. File sharers seem to value technical feasibility and operability more than what is shared on the network, or who speaks for the network. In a 2004 study (Svensson & Bannister 2004), it emerged that the file sharers were more outraged by issues of network integrity (i.e., spamming and viruses) than by the unregulated dispersal of music, video, and software. Regarding pornography, the answers were mixed, but regarding child pornography the antipathy was as strong as that for computer viruses. As Linde and Lindgren (2007: 122) have observed, the overall concern appears to be for how technology can improve the world—a user interest that Piratbyrån creatively tried to harness into a more politicized stance. This is similar to the US context, outlined by Burkart:

> What cyberlibertarians share . . . is a psychological, social, and, especially, political orientation to the Internet: as an aspect of their lifeworld, it is basic to their sense of personal identity, culture, and society. . . . They share a commitment to preserving aspects of the Internet that they see as critical to the autonomous development of people and communities, free of unwanted intrusion and legal interference by the state, and free of state-sanctioned economic monopolies. (Burkart 2010: 82)

Both Lindgren (2009) and Burkart (2013) compare the politicization of file sharing with the environmental movement, as everyday behavior is harnessed for ends that can benefit both the ecology at large (as file sharing would benefit open access, wider range of content, greater functionality, and allowance for tinkering and hacking) and that can serve to benefit the political weight of the movement as well, as the incidence of such behaviors would attest to popular relevance. Quite a few of my respondents in the 2006 study noted that what is good for overall network efficacy and accessibility is ultimately good for each node involved. Hence, they tended to value uploading more than downloading, as contribution to the common pool is the very activity that makes this pool at all possible.

Despite stressing individual competence and efficacy, the respondents' discourse tended to locate moral responsibility primarily in the collective rather than the individual—that is, in the network architecture or infrastructural institutions that this collective helps constitute and is itself constituted by. This was especially so for those forms of responsibility pertaining to those side effects of file sharing that were seen as (potentially) negative. The individual choices were not seen as unwitting or innocent—indeed, individual, self-determined, and highly pragmatic choice was seen to be equally paramount—but the moral justification for these choices was shifted from the individual to the collective. The respondents seemed to struggle to see any real negative effects of file sharing, and when the prospect of such potentially negative effects was raised, it was seen as never entirely the individual's fault but rather attributable to the aggregated, hazy collective.

LS (f25) maintained that in terms of her own usage of DC++, the concept of sharing was indeed "rather secondary":

> I would call it a [collective] mutual exploitation. . . . It might be that "taking" is active, whereas "giving" [sharing] is a passive act. . . . The giving [sharing] is for me a necessary evil in order to get something out of it, egoistically, basically. . . . It would have been more controversial

> if it was a social revolt against the market and the powers that be, but I think that it the reason it appears as such a revolt is an unconscious effect of it being so easily accessible. To challenge the market in order to lower prices might have been an initial idea, but not a deliberate act for many users.

Besides showing how the sharing is embedded within wider capitalism, here the act of sharing (or "mutually exploiting") appears to be externalized as part of the rules of participation, embodied in the material infrastructure (the requirement to maintain a good ratio) and coupled with social netiquette (the common courtesy of this particular network).

There was strong awareness of this individual gratification, and many everyday file sharers reveal typical traits of leeching. This is also mirrored in the slogan "sharing is caring," which can be read as a normative statement urging online participants to share their newly acquired content and to not merely leech. Arguably, the slogan's popularity indicates a need for such a plea. It acts as a reminder: Making the downloaded file available for a while longer is to care for the community. Another parallel can be made to blood donation: Such a reminder is akin to reminding blood donors that what they do is morally commendable.

For a researcher, it is vital to see that the expedient character of p2p infrastructure potentially lends itself to meaningful outcomes (truly open, accessible, decentralized, user-generated archives as a reachable utopia) as well as obvious abuses—such as the prevalence of deliberately corrupt and morally questionable files, pirate copying for monetary gain, and purposely abusive leeching practices. To be sure, not all such outcomes would be deliberate, or even the result of one human actor alone. Many of these systematic problems arise out of complex aggregates—emergent phenomena beyond one person's intent.

The infrastructure addresses such problems through adjustments to the protocols that facilitate the exchange (Galloway 2004). Interestingly, norms and rules can be read as applying a protocol logic also to those parts of the complex aggregate that allow for human action and intent. If ratio systems are rather hard, nonnegotiable rules, imperatives such as sharing is caring act to establish norms—but these are, by their very nature, more negotiable and open to interpretation.

7.3 END USERS: EASE, PSEUDONYMITY, AND ABSENCE OF SACRIFICE

The distinction between seeding and leeching is nowadays, as we have seen, rather hard to make. The online economy is a meshwork of interconnected public and private resources, many of which can be accessed at little expense to participants. One thing I noted in my fieldwork was how often the sharing was justified by invoking this ease. If managing a hub is, as we saw, characterized by sacrifice, the act of accessing data is typified by absence of sacrifice. This strays from Mauss's (2002) definition of gifts, as these essentially require sacrifice on behalf of the giver.

Further, online sharing was also justified by declaring it a central part of the human right to take part in culture (Ross 1998; Shaver & Sganga 2009). Yar (2008) and Patry (2009) have noted how the copyfight dichotomization catalyzes arguments around alleged rights. Basing one's arguments on rights risks polarizing the debate and appeals to different kinds of fundamentalism. "There should be no guaranteed right to live on one's hobby (culture)," SZ (m31) maintained—an example of seemingly unambiguous opposition to both the Lockean myth of property as a natural right and the romantic myth of an individual, sole author (Yar 2008)—yet, contrastingly, "it is everyone's right to be able to participate and take part of all culture" (SZ, m31).

However, when deconstructing these kinds of arguments, we see that they might as well be performative speech acts, serving to position the person who utters them against an allegedly corrupt creative industry. This was noted in the Research Bay survey in which the assertion that there are too many middlemen was stronger among the more devoted uploaders than those users who held that they "only download." Similarly, when pressing further, or framing the question in a different way, respondents tended to agree that struggling artists and musicians who have ambitions should have the means to at least be able to carry out their projects.

This framing of the conflict might be typical of Sweden, perhaps stemming from an underlying civic disappointment with an extensive public sector that is seen to benefit large numbers of unemployed people—alongside (smaller numbers of) state-subsidized artists, actors, and musicians. Arts funding throughout welfare-oriented countries such as the United Kingdom, France, Germany, and Sweden tends to be criticized for systematic favoritism in selection of beneficiaries. Nevertheless, some respondents made subtler amendments to this rights argument. LB (f42) pointed to how moral concerns sometimes arise in the online file-sharing communities:

> If you hang out in a file-sharing community, pretty often the discussion "Should this be downloaded or not?" occurs. It can be due to slightly different reasons—for example, if it's a charity CD with famous artists. . . . A different reason can be if you think that a film, song or whatever is of Good Quality [sic], and therefore should be invested in.

Different affinities and valuations (the ability to preview material plays a role here) play a part in constituting this sense of rightness and morality. PN (m15) problematized the civic "right to take part in culture" argument, asserting that culture has never been totally free and that many musicians in fact rely on reimbursement. VG (m22) noted the corporate, constructed nature of these perceived rights: "The music-, computer-, film- and entertainment industries create needs which capital can't satisfy!" LB (f42) noted that this perception of consumer rights partially results from a strong discourse of creativity and opportunism that I associate with post-Fordist capitalism:

> The same creativity that production companies have been able to thrive on, that has been sold with massive PR campaigns, and reached a position in our lives as something we *must* have, but have been driven to pay dearly for. Paradoxically, we now see ourselves as having a god-given right to film, music etc. Very much so—I think—because it's exactly that attitude that the big companies have sold to us throughout the years. Does that mean you *have* to get it for free? No. But do you get to have the right to become filthy rich from your song because of that? I don't think so.

Now that music and film are appreciated as natural elements of everyday culture, a habit of expecting to be able to access these staples for free appears to have taken hold: an expectation, among file sharers, of a constant flow of new cultural material, fresh blood for the leeches.

The argument found among ordinary citizens, ordinary cultural consumers, is standpoint dependent in that it does not place any a priori urgency on a particular sector; instead the care for the cultural sectors takes place in a secondhand way. It is in the consumers' interest that the material on offer is of good quality—and if a sector is manifestly harmed, that would affect the output. Yet there is no guarantee that the file sharers would make amends to practice new ways of reimbursing artists and creators, as the creation of new films and new music is, after all, not as vital to the sustenance of society as is the production of food and shelter, or labor markets. I did not perceive any real sense of urgency in these everyday file-sharers' views on the music, gaming, and movie industries.

As we have seen, file sharing attests to a radicalization of a wider trend toward promiscuity of choice; it thrives on the ability to virtually anonymously, and with very little sacrifice, try out different products and services. A certain degree of liberal promiscuity is encouraged in consumer society, but as soon as it becomes radicalized—to the point of freely disposing of artifacts, and adopting alternative circulatory infrastructures—it becomes controversial.

The Internet has always been characterized by a high degree of semi-anonymity, or pseudonymity. Not only does its vastness, granularity, and semi-obscurity make for a "disappearance in the crowd" and a statistically insignificant risk of getting caught, but also it has—until the recent emergence of walled gardens—allowed for a rather arbitrary nature of usernames and avatars, as the IP number is the only entry that can implicate users. And IP addresses can be masked. At least among those file sharers who are more dedicated than the average Internet user, a common tactic has been to resort to dedicated services for anonymity; VPNs, proxies, seed boxes.

Karaganis et al. (2012) show that 70 percent of US 18- to 29-year-olds claim to have acquired pirated music or video files, and a comparable number of respondents (69 percent) think that Internet activities "should not be monitored." Around 20 percent of respondents aged 18 to 65 deliberately encrypt their Internet traffic, while only around 4 percent use IP-masking tools such as TOR. It is also not surprising that exclusive, closed communities such as the private tracker that I examined require high degrees of security and anonymity; users of such networks are even vetted to gain membership. This determination and privacy praxis was manifest also in the Research Bay data: Of the respondents who answered the survey question on anonymous practices (N = 67,473), 17.8 percent acknowledged to have used VPNs or similar services for hiding their IP-addresses. Another 51.4 percent did not use anonymization services but showed an interest in using one. A correlation between frequent uploading and anonymization was found. Within the minority of users who upload files nearly every day, 30.9 percent used an anonymization service, while only 14 percent of those who said they never upload files at all did so.

The study also found that paid versions of VPNs or similar services are more common in northern Europe compared to the rest of Europe. A smaller group of "core uploaders" use anonymity services to a greater extent than the average file sharer. Online anonymity in the file-sharing community can be seen as an active countermeasure against legal action that is perceived as illegitimate, and there seems to be a widespread willingness among file sharers to be more anonymous (Larsson et al. 2012b: 273). There is a notable paradox here: It is relatively cumbersome, not easy, to anonymize one's surfing—but once having done so, ease and convenience is restored, even amplified.

In a recent Swedish historiography of privacy, Fleischer (2012b) connects the erosion of the private sphere with the post-2007 emergence of cloud services. He connects this to a development in which popular faith has shifted from financial institutions ridden by debt and commodities markets entering a state of crisis to the possibility of massive future revenues from behavioral data, unsurpassed in its sophistication and comprehensiveness. One of the other linchpins of the Swedish debates on file sharing and digitization, Palmås (2011b), has called this mode of surveillance a "panspectric" one: It differs from "the panoptic sort" (Gandy 1993) in that it does not hinge on compiling (primarily visual) data about certain selected bodies, but rather, it compiles information about all subjects at the same time, within more registers than the visual, using computers to select the segments of data relevant to its surveillance tasks (DeLanda 1991: 206).

In some ways, resorting to this dialectic of cloud services is a re-enactment of the already familiar dialectic of the "immaterial economy" (Robins & Webster 1999). Fleischer points out that these data centers, although appearing as neutral intermediaries—allowing for radically increased convenience—also allow for panspectric surveillance on a previously unmatched scale and, moreover, are obliged to disclose sensitive information to government agencies. For this to pass, popular attitudes toward privacy would have to be changed: In January 2010, Facebook CEO Mark Zuckerberg declared that privacy should no longer be regarded a "social norm."

Fleischer contrasts this historical development with the Swedish debate on state surveillance that reached a critical point with the so-called FRA law, enacted on September 25, 2008, when the four government parties agreed to abide by the decision to forcibly connect all the country's telephone and Internet operators to a governmental eavesdropping authority with access to all communication across national borders (Fleischer 2012b: 113). Both Piratbyrån and the SPP were, for once, united in their rallying against this development. Sadly, he argues, the outrage over state surveillance seemed to trickle out over the subsequent years. Debates on privacy have come to appear more like an arms race between commercial and governmental actors in which civic actors are left dejected on the wayside, resorting to arguing about which one would be the greatest evil.

In survey work, Bjereld and Oscarsson (2009) examined public attitudes toward the FRA program. The law was much more well-known among educated and politically interested people than among people with low education and low political interest, and also Internet use was decisive. Attitudes also followed the traditional political rift between opposition and government. The researchers did not see the resistance to the FRA law and the urge to legalize file sharing as the embryo of a new social movement, but they hold that both of these issues can be seen as an expression of new political dividing lines that partially correlate with age, Internet use, and left-right ideology.

In a survey two years later, a majority of Swedes expressed awareness of online privacy risks (Jansson 2010: 263). These respondents were tested for three types of privacy: electronic transactions, governmental surveillance, and social media. A correlation emerged between high usage of social media and a reduced perception of risk with regards to it (p. 273). Familiarity with electronic transactions also revealed a similar correlation. Respondents interested in technology were considerably less concerned about privacy risks within social media and electronic transactions than those who were not interested in technology. However, technology-savvy users were more skeptical of government supervision. This skepticism can be explained partly by gender differences, but perhaps also by correlations between interests in technology and pragmatism on the one hand, and between commitments to culture/politics and personal privacy as a perceived priority on the other.

Here, a historical explanation to the success of Spotify and panspectric SNSs such as Facebook can be found. In addition to the originally rather weak awareness and antipathy toward government surveillance in Sweden (its citizens having had little direct experience of this, compared to, e.g., the German population), even less awareness and antipathy can be said to exist toward the much newer phenomenon of corporate surveillance.

7.4 AN OSCILLATION BETWEEN AUTONOMY AND SOLIDARITY

Among the file sharers that I interviewed there was a strong emphasis on personal autonomy, the freedom to tinker, the taking charge of one's own consumption habits, and the retaining of one's own privacy. This ethos, I would argue, has been central to Western culture and popular attitudes since the emergence of a postwar subject who embraces hedonic, post-materialist values such as self-fulfillment and individualism; as we have seen, this ethos enjoys a particularly wide currency in Sweden.

The Internet allows for the enactment of these values, but ironically it does so in an expedient, highly functional, and, in many ways, cybernetic way—reminiscent of the cold war origins of computing and digital networking. Information, as a concept, allows linear machine logic to mask the uniquely human ability to maintain circular and contradictory logic (Gleick 2011; see also McCulloch 1988).

At the same time, the cybernetic premise that was embedded in the Internet infrastructure from the outset is equally a product of hippy values, furthering a self-reliant, frontier mentality—in many ways, an unmistakably US ideal of self-governance: I want to take advantage of the information that I want; no one should be allowed to stop me. I want to be able to link together the information that I want; no one will herd me in any direction. I want my privacy; no one should be able to monitor me. Burkart (2010) succinctly points to the conflicted nature of this ethos:

> It is caught between political anarchism and communitarianism. It is also caught between anti-systemic and anti-capitalist tendencies on the one hand, and merely anti-establishmentarian and reformist approaches on the other hand. Commitments oscillate between autonomy and solidarity as foundational norms. (Burkart 2010: 82)

This can be illustrated by Raymond's argument (2000) that hacker culture is implicitly libertarian but channels this anti-establishmentarian impulse through "radical sharing" and "worldwide cooperation" (ibid.), to maximize operational efficiency.

7.5 AN OSCILLATION BETWEEN DIFFERENT FORMS OF TECHNOCRACY

File sharing constitutes a constant engagement with technocracy; the risk of, time and again, falling into the *Gesellschaft*-like managerialism of culture versus the possibility to, paradoxically it might seem, use technology against such tendencies, while at the same time consolidating other aspects of digital life. File sharing thus becomes tied to the management of the self.

Bakardjieva (2009) has acknowledged how everyday life is politicized by means of what she terms "subactivism":

> [A] kind of politics that unfolds at the level of subjective experience and is submerged in the flow of everyday life. It is constituted by small-scale, often individual, decisions and actions that have either a political or ethical frame of reference (or both) and are difficult to capture using the traditional tools with which political participation is measured. (Bakardjieva 2009: 92)

An even more useful concept might, however, be Feenberg's (1999: 108) notion of a "technical micropolitics." Burkart (2010) outlines the ways in which consumers, when being addressed as clients to content-delivery services, are apprised to the difference between this markedly technical, managerial mediation of their (previously largely tacit) private consumption: "a relatively new kind of role for consumers in privatized media markets" (p. 73). This, again, prompts individual reflexivity, as "the changes are hard for people to get used to, particularly when the new terms governing their interactions with corporations are based on unilateralist contracts created by the service provider" (ibid.). Burkart exemplifies this unilateralism by noting the assertion included in the Apple iTunes store end-user agreement, which gives Apple the right to change the terms of use for downloaded music files without notice.

A technologically mediated role, relationally defined as a client, is asserted through the terms of use, not only through legal discourse but also primarily through the code that governs use in less ambiguous ways. In a country such as Sweden, this clientelization becomes doubly coded, through the nature of being a small country at the periphery of the center. No wonder that the response to this is to look for other, similarly prescriptive logics found in the technological infrastructures. Accordingly, the Kopimi movement asserts a technical primacy to their (albeit woolly) politics: "According to Kopimi all truths can be summarized in one sentence: 'The Internet is right.'" (Piratbyrån 2009: 5).

Through technical micropolitics, individuals driven by civic enlightenment become lay activists through individual, nonmandatory engagement. This argument is very similar to Bakardjieva's notion of subactivism but could be said to put even less emphasis on a dedicated activist identity or predisposition among these individuals. According to this view, micropolitics only come into place in those instances where conflict is at hand:

> Who are the actors involved in this new type of politics? Not citizens as such, but individuals who are directly affected by a particular technical decision. (Feenberg 1999: 120)

The temporary assignment that ordinary Internet users are put into when engaging with unregulated copying of copyrighted content—to be a file sharer—could be interpreted as the outcome of such effects. When noting what enables these temporary roles, Feenberg's account mirrors Oram's historiography of file sharing (2001), as he too notes that a peculiar kind of emancipation that has been central to the development and extension of today's Internet, increasingly "adding human communication functions to systems that were originally destined to handle data" (p. 121, 126). Entirely black-boxed technical systems can be changed, given enough civic intervention and accumulation of micropolitical acts.

Because of the accumulated, totalizing functioning of systems and networks, their renewed agency can, however, become dominant in its own way. Given enough people illicitly copying for their own use, this quickly becomes the norm in itself.

One of the beauties of such a conception of political intervention is that it does not presuppose any form of predetermined hegemony or false consciousness, which would imply that the strategic, ruling entity is a fixed one, to which the tactics would merely be forced to react. On the contrary, hegemony is instead seen as the upshot of whichever side finds itself in the dominant position. Similarly, hegemonic forces can arise on a macro scale from aggregated local interactions without hegemonic intent. The strategic endeavor here is to orchestrate or harness these forces, something that TPB has continued to do throughout the last decade, making it an emblem of file sharing.

The key insight from my analysis of Spotify, and its endemic Facebook integration, is that we are seeing an increase in references to it, a veritable spotification of the mind, a spotification of the technological imagination. In this sense, Spotify—as an alleged remedy to crises of untrammeled digitization in the cultural economy—has had a contagious quality: It has engendered the proclamation of things such as "a Spotify for books," "a Spotify for movies," "a Spotify for games," and "a Spotify for photography." Spotify becomes part of an alluring grand narrative of Internet-enabled "solutionism" (Morozov 2013) and—from a Swedish perspective—becomes part and parcel of a technocracy with good intentions. Just as citizens now do all their dealings with banks, insurance companies national and private, real estate brokers, money transactions, and secondhand markets through semi-autonomous, privately owned cybernetic systems, their cultural lifeworld becomes increasingly arranged within a similarly cybernetic regime. One is left out from invitations to events such as parties and social gatherings—in fact, even getting to know about them is often restricted without having a Facebook account—and hyperlinks no longer represent links to social objects that could be publicly shared, instead the link requires a Facebook or Spotify log-in.

When this is all hailed as convenient, what is hidden are all the problematic aspects of such privately owned, surveillant infrastructures; the fact that they can act as bottlenecks for access and allow prying government authorities to monitor citizens; the fact that they do not act as public spaces, effectively restricting the right to assembly; the fact that the archival breadth offered on these platforms is severely restricted; and so on. As we have seen, the Swedish approach to privacy and modernization involves a high degree of defeatism toward these developments. Efficacy and convenience—combined with the self-assured pride of "a small country doing well" thanks to brands that are seen as highly successful and progressive—are seen to, all too often, trump such civic concerns.

In this sense, resorting to file sharing can ironically be seen as a retrograde maneuver, in that it is akin to going back to what was once the norm, before Spotify. Noting the technical premises for these modes of usage, it is to return to a somewhat barer form of internetworking, but not necessarily more technocratic—in fact, arguably less so given the more closed, more determining mode of operation of these newer cybernetic systems.

7.6 REGULATION OF THE INDIVIDUAL IN CONTROL SOCIETIES

As Burkart (2010) has shown, online life is caught also in an oscillation between self-regulation and regulation from above. Commercial, sequestered portals such as iTunes and Facebook would supplant everyday fan behavior (e.g., music sharing) with a form of voluntary self-surveillance, in which community members knowingly adhere to standards and cultivate their obedience to personally gain from it. Like the self-regulation in p2p environments, this self-surveillance is voluntary. Yet, different infrastructures allow for altogether different scopes for action, and the infrastructures for p2p-based file sharing clearly allows for a wider range of such normalized uses and behaviors than commercial, proprietary infrastructures. File sharing allows for great latitude when it comes to the end user, however, requiring both knowledge and directed action on the side of the user, and an overarching ubiquity and standardization in terms of infrastructure.

The embrace of these freer, albeit largely unmitigated habits hinges on a recognition that there is a need—or even perhaps inevitability—for voluntary self-regulation as the primary mode of regulation in the context of digital media. This inevitability could either be attributed to what many of my interviewees referred to, the "unstoppable" nature of file sharing, or it could be attributed to the inherent individual freedom of citizens and consumers to engage with the technologies and media at their disposal. As routinely pointed out by cyberliberties activists, effective and complete curbing of file sharing would entail an effective and complete curbing of private communication over the Internet.

Interestingly, however, the former of these two arguments is only valid when approaching file sharing on a general, aggregated level and not in the local instantiations—as these are often, as has been shown in a number of contexts (Morozov 2011; Hindman 2008), subject to regulation and censorship. Sure, this censorship is never entirely comprehensive, always subject to leaks or re-routing, but in a Gaussian view of society, they are effective enough so that significant majorities are left out.

The file-sharer argumentation, as we have seen, is, however, not prone to Gaussian modes of reasoning. Rather, it focuses on interpretations of demographic distributions in which even the slightest lapse in completeness allows for leaks that engender new, popular appropriations. I have called this dilemma the Pandora problem (Chapter 2). Arguably, this aspect of the file-sharing debate makes for a revealing benchmark of what actually constitutes "risk society" (Beck 1992) or "control society" (Deleuze 1992), relying on universal modulation, computer-based surveillance, individuals twinned to their data selves, distributed self-adaptation, perpetual training, a capitalism of higher-order production and circulation, the ethos of the corporation seeping into every pore of social order. "Even art has left the spaces of enclosure in order to enter into the open circuits of the bank" (1992: 6).

Here, freedom seems manifest, but freedom is compromised by the latent tendency for agency to flow over, to engender new externalities. The need to regulate this overflow is sometimes expressed in totalizing rule either of the old, disciplinarian kind or of the new, modular, surveillant kind. However, as a result of the latent totalitarianism in such modes of control, democratic societies see to it that regulation is instead enacted as voluntary self-regulation (however induced through incentives, or all-out appeals). The extent to which regulation takes this latter form can be argued to be a measure of its degree of democracy. However, this turn to voluntary discretion can also be seen to rest on a central political difference: Either the argument centers on the need, implementation, and management of efficient markets (the libertarian anti-copyright argument), or it hones in on the promise of new forms of solidarity (much as Piratbyrån's emphasis on shared experiences and ecological concerns for the digital realm).

7.7 DIGITIZATION PLACING COMMUNICATION WITHIN A TECHNOCRATIC LOGIC

According to Beck (1992; 1994), contemporary societies are increasingly being affected by prescriptive, totalizing structures that have global reach. Often these decisive structures are products of phenomena that are emergent in their own right, and have no single point of causal agency, transgressing political disputes such as the copyfight dichotomy, as these prescriptive structures emerge quite independently of the effects and sometimes conflicting opinions held by the actors involved. As we have seen, the principles of material accumulation and maximization of both personal gratification and of functional efficacy are, for example, shared by both sides of this alleged dichotomy—and so is the shared appreciation of new infrastructures, increased functionality: more speed, less friction.

Many of these formations take on a strongly universalizing, globalized character. This often acts as a normative, prescriptive force for society at large, in that its effects appear unavoidable and ubiquitous. There is a peculiar standardization that goes hand in hand with individualization. Many of the defining structures of our era appear to have this emergent, aggregated, ubiquitous, and prescriptive character at their roots: transnational communication and global media, the global financial economy, the global environment, and so on. Similarly, the Internet can be understood as a heterogeneous, global network of networks, which is based on unrestricted file sharing—yet hugely standardizing in that it begets the common use of certain protocols and techniques.

As the overall exchange is governed by technical protocol and machine-readable code, some particularities inherent to digital communication come into play, for better or for worse: The nature of data as machine-readable traces bound to a physical carrier (Hayles 1999) makes it possible to trace circuits of civic communication in entirely new ways. This is what allows file sharing to be potentially monitored and ultimately policed—although the sheer superabundance of the phenomena makes any totalizing attempt at this a practical impossibility. This is also something that the file sharers themselves seem highly aware of, prompting a perhaps cynical attitude toward both state and corporate surveillance.

Secondly, code facilitates new uses, but similarly, these uses are premised on a system that translates old media into forms governed by an informational logic—a logic that is operative and efficacious, and thus, in a sense, technocratic. When cultural products are encodeable as information, and thereby malleable, expedient, and duplicable, it becomes easy to see them more as raw data than as precious artifacts.

Lanier (2011; 2013) has proposed a way to recapture civic agency and middle-class clout, based on Nelson's prototypical *Xanadu* hypertext system "where people buy and sell each other information, and can live off of what they do with their hearts and minds as the machines get good enough to do what they would have done with their hands" (Lanier 2011).

What he proposes is a micropayments system, quite like Flattr, but way more far-reaching and all-encompassing, where each "bit" of information or data generated by individuals would bear the memory, or inscription, of who the originator of this piece of data was, enabling the system to remunerate this originator for each reuse, or reiteration of said piece of information. Giving credit where credit is due, so to speak, recognizing the original incipient ad infinitum. Despite the laudable intent of people such as Lanier and Nelson, such a proposal also sounds a lot like the kind of informational idealism that is so typical of Silicon Valley, recently criticized by Morozov (2013) as a form of Internet-centrism: Given that we construct a good enough information system, problems will be solved, obstacles overcome, and conflicts ameliorated.

There are several risks inherent to a universal micropayment system such as this. First of all, if it is inconclusive, it would end up only benefiting those who are most influential anyway; much in the vein that the Google PageRank algorithm or the distribution of Wikipedia contributions already work. There will always be small groups of people who contribute more, and whose created objects will be downloaded more often. However, if the proposed system is universal enough—so that otherwise unrecognized labor will be recognized too (much like Lanier has noted: flower arranging, dating, drink mixing, etc.)—the system will eventually encompass enough human activities to remunerate all but the most idle.

But there would still be a problem of delineation: The system will always have an inside and an outside, and the risk is that this will create vast political and economic rifts. Who is to say what should count? Is hoovering more valuable than drink mixing? Who is to decide? Who coordinates it? What interests would these coordinators have? Is there not a risk for corruption or bias at the heart of this coordination? Ultimately, it would have to be a "perfect" system, including an almost incomprehensible range of human actions imaginable and not yet imaginable.

Further, it is my conviction that data is inherently qualitative, arising in interaction with human agency—to think otherwise would be to adopt Shannon and Weaver's fallacy of reifying information as a quantitative essence (Gleick 2011). This results in yet one more problem: How to unambiguously define the cognitive contributions that the system is thought to address by making them trackable and putting a value on them. One could draw this epistemological problem even farther: How do you delineate a unit of fact?

In short, information idealism is to confuse culture with a system. The exponents of such idealism can be said to adhere to a managerialist mindset toward knowledge and culture—something that unites Internet-centrists (Morozov 2013) regardless of stripe. In management, you need certainty—verifiable data—a condition shared by both "black hat" hackers and "white hat" entrepreneurs.

I would hypothetically propose that very much of the emphasis on the role of IPR in contemporary culture can be attributed to this martinet approach. As the user has to internalize the system to subvert it, there is a problem in that also those who act to reform or outmode copyright in fact serve to reify it. Creative Commons (CC) operates through the belief that licensing systems actually shape culture. To advocate CC, or a similar alternative license, is to put a strong belief that such licenses actually have an effect. With the case of CC, because it actually builds on the currently existing copyright regime to begin with, the hypothesis that it would in fact act to reinforce the affirmation of the role of licensing would be particularly strong.

In this perspective, schemes such as Unlicense or Kopimi are liberating because they serve to negate a license mindset by operating on the basis of no license. They emphasize non-metered, informal modes of appropriation and attribution. In many ways, such total disregard of licensing can be interpreted as being based in trust rather than distrust in the public appropriation of the work.

Authors putting their works under Kopimi do not hold that if it were not for an explicitly stated license, other people or institutions would abuse their work. Instead, their approach is based in the (perhaps more hazy) realization that some of the reappropriation of your work will attribute you as an author, some of the reappropriation will not. In a way, disregard of explicit licensing means an increased reliance on a Gaussian distribution of probability, in terms of how one's work will be appropriated.

7.8 THE MOLAR AND THE MOLECULAR: HUME AND SOCIAL DEMOCRACY

Social democracy is, thanks to its grassroots origins, to be thought of as distinct from authoritarianism or more precisely, vanguardism. Nevertheless, it contains authoritarian elements and tendencies. These tendencies can be seen especially in social democracy's historical mode of defending the national interest (as in the case of Swedish self-interest regarding the power blocs of the Cold War) and in the workers' movement strategy of maintaining "a popular front strategy of inclusion made in the language of the old vanguardist rhetoric of exclusion" (Wark 1997b). This can also be seen in the movements for public education and health that Berggren and Trägårdh (2006) write about.

Wark (1997b) has argued for a rejection of the dichotomy of vanguardism versus social democracy (a dichotomy that he blames on the philosophical heritage of Hegelian dualism). He holds that this rejection can be achieved by rephrasing the connection between the Deleuzian concepts of the molecular and the molar, emphasizing that it would be a mistake to think of these concepts as polar opposites. Rather, one needs to see how the molecular flows through the molar, and also constitutes it. The dichotomy of either-or tends to blind us to the possibility of an and-also, he explains, as if it was all a question of either social democracy or vanguardism, of either molar coherence or molecular atomism.

Deleuze and Guattari (1983) interpret politics as a process of flux that always has an unpredictable outcome. They criticize the notion of capitalism as a repressive machine and suggest that it could be opposed from within by redirecting the creativity and multiplicity of its immanent flows. Political mobilization is generally seen as a ground-up process, from the molecular toward the molar—with the ultimate molar structure of the infrastructure as the most global systemic element, encompassing the entire system in question or, indeed, even complex assemblages of systems. Wark notes that Deleuze's first book (1991) was on Hume, leading Wark to argue that the war-against-all libertarianism of the Californian ideology actually owes more to Hobbes than to Hume and thus tries to envisage a more benevolent political ecosystem:

> Rather than think of the state as a limit to the free action of individuals, why not think of it as a productive rephrasing of those powers and desires in ways that produce a collective good? . . . Rather than think of abstract human individuals as existing in as pure atoms, why not think instead of the actual clumps and packs in which people actually live their lives? These, Hume notes, are not characterized by the war of all against all that is thought to prevail in a pure state of individualism. Rather, we find that within any self-organizing human group, the group is bound together by feelings of what Hume calls sympathy. The role of an institution is not to limit the competition of individuals, but to extend the sympathy one might feel for an immediate group to a more abstract social collectivity. (Wark 1997b)

However, an obvious critique is appropriate here: If the state is not to be seen as the repressive leviathan of the Hobbesian legacy, but rather as a benevolent entity, Wark's political ideal is only focusing on one of the two ways in which this entity takes on a benevolent character. What Wark emphasizes is a typical Anglo-American appreciation of the state as a heterogeneous conglomerate of interests—an empirical experiment in plurality.

But as the Swedish example shows, the state (as a molar entity of a globalizing or totalizing kind) can also be seen as the facilitator of molecular freedom, in systemic terms. The overarching molar structure delimits a range of action, within which molecular agents are granted various energies and possibilities for redirecting the immanent flows of the system as a whole.

While the act of political mobilization, in its conscious and intended form, is a ground-up movement, from the molecular to the molar, the prescriptive agencies allowing or disallowing for this action all stem from the configuration of the system as a whole. Hume's understanding of the state, Wark maintains, is one in which the state is seen as a "productive rephrasing" of the multifarious powers and desires of individuals "in ways that produce a collective good" (1997b), rather than one of the state as a limit to free action. This is concurrent with the Swedish concept of liberty.

Further, all conscious political mobilization creates visible entities that become possible targets for critique and counterattacks. As we have seen, although it is a common trope to think of p2p as based on typically networked, nonhierarchical formations, the political wing of unauthorized file sharing tends to generate molar formations. Wark points out that such formations tend to generate entitlements and spokespersons:

> Institutions create entitlements. Entitlements to space, to time, to language, to appearances. Entitlements to a future, to the present, to various pasts. There are all kinds of entitlements. When they come into

> conflict, there is often no way of adjudicating between them. . . . Among the many entitlements that require constant renegotiation involve those of speaking. Who can say what, when and in what manner? Who owns the past? Or the future? Or at least, who is entitled to speak of it? (Wark 1997a)

To speak for the network or for the institution is an act that generates an entitlement. The deterritorializing tendencies of p2p networking are seen here to be contrasted by reterritorializing, molar tendencies of political mobilization. The question is to what extent this mobilization is conscious or non-intended. The formation of strategic structures such as TPB is the intentional work of a few activists, but only made possible through the harnessing of a wide range of actors and agencies, both human and nonhuman.

Scandinavian-style, benevolent corporatism (where the state would effectively sanction large portions of unrestricted file sharing) could be argued to constitute a rather conventional social-democrat position on these matters. Compared to the position that advocates retribution against civil file sharers, and acts for the protection of specific trade interests (i.e., more delimited molar structures, particular to trade associations and the conglomerates of transnational firms on behalf of which these associations act) this social-democrat position acts to safeguard the global (or national) molar structure of the public interest, the aggregated welfare of civic actors. However, I would argue, a central problem for rallying support around these concerns would be the shifting political emphasis from Gaussian interpretations of society toward the power-law ideology and cultural managerialism implicit to the network society: Propositions for broadband levies or cultural flat rates suggest that all citizens should collectively contribute, across the board. This flies in the face of those managerialists who hold that intervention should be as minimal and precise as possible. Why should the majority pay for that which only a minority is involved in? As I have argued, this is a source of atrophy not only for the idea of a shared commons, but potentially for politics as a whole.

However, there are other reasons for technologists to adopt this welfarist view, since it can be said to be concordant also with the technological argument of the inevitability of unrestricted file exchange. As cyberliberties activists lay claims to safeguarding the global structure of a healthy (carrier-neutral, scalable, flexible, open) Internet-as-utility, they do so by arguing that high degrees of molecular freedom must be retained on the level of the individual machine or user. As this book has shown, this notion of a molecular, granular freedom is a direct function of the universalizing protocol logic: Molecular agency is premised on its system-wide integration.

This managerialist view on culture crops up in Spotify's micropayment scheme, in Lanier's (2013) proposition of a form of granular repayment system, as well as in Sunde's Flattr venture. The idea of a highly granular micropayment system is directly comparable to Hayek's idea of catallaxy and, as we have seen, the utopian promise expressed by early digital pioneers such as Nelson. In this context, Sunde is highly interesting in that he combines the disruptive, prankster-like streak of cyberliberties activism with a utopian belief similar to that of Lanier's and a self-professed socialist dedication (this is what really sets him apart from his US counterparts). It is somewhat telling that Sunde, in 2013, connected the care for the individual citizen-producer (those alleged 99.9 percent who, in Sundes view, are *not* living off their creative labor) with the social-democrat idea of an overarching, government-based welfare system (cultural flat rate):

> I think that Flattr is somewhere along where I would have done it. But then again, most of the people actually creating things have almost nothing of their actual income from the copyright of the works. 99.9% make their living on working in grocery stores, gas stations, office work or whatever. Rather put a system in place where culture is supported by the government, which it is partially today. (Sunde, in Reddit 2013b)

This recourse to extreme granularity and its odd reliance on totalities was seen also in my respondents' argumentation, both in the sometimes sardonic individualism of plugging into the infosphere and making as good use of it as one would be able to—"Some make use of today's technology, others don't understand it" (PG, m24)—and in their remarks that the punitive means of policing would surpass the actual crime, a conditional, totalizing phenomenon requiring equally totalizing solutions to fully quench it: "Since file sharing is so extremely decentralized, it is a bit like shooting a mosquito swarm with a bazooka" (ES, m17).

By contrast, the industrialist (or unionist) position of the copyright lobby would claim to be safeguarding the much more local, molar structures of various trade associations or business interests. While the molecular-totalitarian position adheres to a normative ontology of the Internet that accentuates the inevitability of unrestricted file exchange, this molar-unionist position can be said to argue for a normative ontology of the Internet in which exchange is regulated, safe, and sanctioned by institutionalized, accountable providers. Both of these positions give rise to discourses that are internally cohesive and sensible, at least when assessed by their own standards. When reciprocally compared, however, they become incommensurable—hence the seemingly endless lack of consensus.

Further, while the argument is that copyright in its current form fails to serve the 99.9 percent who are not financial stalwarts harvesting interest on proven blockbusters, the recent critique of digital labor goes to show that a new form of rentier capitalism has emerged that harvests the profits that come from owning and controlling also the delivery platforms. This is a harder problem to address than dismissing the workings of copyright simply by distributing content in alternative ways; it is harder to rally populations toward a dismissal of these platforms, as citizens have become largely dependent on them.

8 Conclusion / Cultural Consumption and Piracy

File sharing, as outlined in this book, could be devised as a race between vernacular, bottom-up attempts at recapturing utility out of developments within entertainment technology. In this sense, hacks or exploits are always one step behind the industrial innovation that precedes them: For blu-ray hacks to come about, there first has to be an infrastructure for blu-rays. For applications such as Mp3get or aggregation sites such as mp3juices.com to come about, there first has to be an infrastructure for mp3-based music. In this sense, infrastructure precedes civic appropriation. File sharing could thus be considered a cunning, truly tactical reappropriation, in the way de Certeau (1984) conceptualizes this condition.

He argues for everyday consumption to be labeled as tactical, because it involves poaching (a form of making do with whatever is at hand) and is largely decentralized, provisional, and ultimately quasi-invisible. I would argue, however, that this notion is being increasingly turned on its head by the solidifying effects of digital networking: The generative forces inherent to consumption are here being materialized in new, previously unexpected ways. The acquisition and exchange that makes consumption possible is visualized in numeric charts, listing the popularity and thus accessibility of each film, album, or computer game. The exchange is routinely monitored both by market analysts (BigChampagne, TrendMaze, and Outbrain) and by legal enforcers (IFPI and RIAA). It is an exchange that is traceable—if not on the individual level then most certainly on the aggregate level. The concept that Hayek (1978) described as catallaxy or what I call *information idealism* turns on this traceability as well: By enumerating previously quasi-invisible, dispersed, granular acts of consumption and by inferring estimates and causal relationships, structural considerations can be made.

This has value for the proponents of unmitigated sharing, in that they can point to the ongoing exchange as a valid, substantial sphere of consumption that, in some way, has to be accounted for—for example, when assessing popularity of certain acts or popular attitudes and sentiments. Also activism and mobilization rely on such inferred data; only when an agency that would otherwise remain dispersed is accounted for can it be argued to be a latent or explicit consumer uproar or a latent or explicit people's movement.

But it also has value for those who hold that this sharing should not remain unmitigated: Regulators act to trace consumption to assess grounds for redistribution through collecting societies or broadband levies. Likewise, litigators and agents act to police end users and file-sharing facilitators. Such policing can take place either through active investigators such as Antipiratbyrån or by forcing ISPs to monitor traffic, policing file sharing by proxy.

Regarding the openness industry—infrastructural Internet actors such as Google, Oracle, and Amazon, hardware manufacturers such as Apple and Samsung, and telecommunications companies such as Verizon and Telia Sonera, who all benefit from a continuation of unmitigated civic sharing—it somewhat falls into a middle position, between these two ends of the spectrum. They want to be able to trace the ongoing consumption patterns to serve the output of advertising networks so their ads correspond to intended target groups in the most efficient ways.

A range of continuities have been observed, between unregulated, illegal modes of circulation and consumption and those modes of consumption that—from the viewpoint of user experience—might appear very similar (as was shown in the intermezzo). From the viewpoint of infrastructure, however, these legal services harness p2p functionality but do so in considerably different ways than their forerunners. The aggregated agency constituted by file sharing can, in countries such as Sweden, be argued to be so efficient, durable, and widespread that it can be argued to constitute a new, secular, vernacular norm. What was originally an intervention is repeated and attains permanence.

Strategy, in de Certeau's (1984) account, is characterized by a double sovereignty. It need not be interpreted only as a literal command of a place or space, but as a mode of agency that also commands the rhetorical, discursive upper hand—actual hegemonic power to dictate what counts as truth and validity in any discursive argument. At the same time, there is a vernacular bias to the technologies of file sharing; they only gain collective weight in the form as referents in the ongoing argument, yet very rarely file sharers come together and perform their sharing, in person, face to face, or in public. The illegal aspect of the phenomenon has this effect. It is officially frowned upon, and it is rarely something one flaunts publicly. Yet it takes place, in the privacy of one's domestic sphere.

File sharing is therefore caught in the hinterland between official, public life and unofficial, private life. Because its services and infrastructures (hubs, applications, sites, and indexes) can rarely be fully assimilated into the formal, legal economy, it remains part of a shadow economy where adoption is highly reliant on hearsay and rumors and efficient usage requires tacit knowledge, learned, community- or subculture-specific codes and expectations. Unmitigated file sharing—as it stands today, being outlawed and hence never endorsed by governments and subsequent educational institutions—assumes technical and cultural skills that are not taught by any official institutions. Hence, I would argue, it can never—at least not in its present form—be a fully democratic technology. Here we see one of the first paradoxes of vernacular file sharing: It is not for everyone, yet the minority making use of it is so large and considerable that it becomes a valid media form in its own right—even normative among certain demographic groups.

Further, it is my belief that this vernacular bias of domestic technologies is deeply problematic, in that despite mobile privatization, "bringing the world to one's home"—as Williams (1974) argued that television would do—the world is always and forever bound to be mediated through this domestic nexus. The particular vantage point is always framed by one's own interests. In this sense, the problems of misrepresentation that are endemic to news coverage—ignoring conflicts far removed from viewers, while over-affirming conflicts that lie closer to home—is not only attributable to the shortsighted editorial policies of professional media producers but also can be traced back to the situated interests of the audience. Despite best intentions by programmers and editors, audiences will often veer toward the smallest common denominators and quick gratification.

Similar problems riddle the phenomenon of economic imagination. The copyfight makes it excruciatingly apparent that participants in the debate refuse to see two steps ahead and admit the actual complexity of the economic world. This could be for strategic reasons as well—vested interests that force people to cling on to programmatic viewpoints. The work of Grassmuck (2010), Liebowitz (2011), and others shows us that even the academic society struggles with the complex abstract models of causality that are required. It is therefore little surprise that the enemies of unmitigated file sharing tend not to see the positive network effects or externalities or that consumer expenses are funneled elsewhere, toward other sectors or types of goods, when less money is spent on audio CDs. The proponents of unmitigated file sharing, on the other hand, often struggle to see the problems with free culture removing incentives for precisely those actors who do not act within corporate structures driven by requirements to generate returns on investment. How can those actors—independent, struggling artists—be expected to invest time and effort into creating new, innovative culture with any degree of ambition, when digitization appears to help make sector after sector more precarious than before?

Tan (2010) has characterized TPB as an enabler of countervailing power of a virtual, globalizing kind. My conclusion is that while counteracting scarcity and opening up for sampling new cultural repertoires, file sharing nevertheless adds to the current tendency of world markets taking on long-tail characteristics.

In a forthcoming article (Andersson Schwarz et al., 2013), different ways of imagining piracy will be outlined. It is important to see how piracy is simultaneously a countercultural position, a material intervention, an exploit of flows, an intervention into the property regime, and a challenger to bourgeois privacy. Many of the Piratbyrån-affiliated thinkers have tended to embrace explanatory models of affect and flow and ontologies that are open-ended. In Serres' (2007) exploration of parasitical relations, these tendencies combine. In French, the word *parasite* refers to three things: a biological parasite, a social parasite (a guest who gives praise and flatters for food), and static (interfering signal). The parasite, as a relational configuration, thus reveals power balances; it prompts the question of who is the host and who is the client. It also questions social unity; it prompts us to see how truly open-ended structures become untenable to the observer. As cognitive beings, we are always reluctant to imagine a herd of cats, a swarm, a flock, a shoal, relationships-of-exteriority (i.e., the open, emergent model of the ecosystem; DeLanda 2006). We invent words that transform the untenable, irresolvable openness into closed-off, delimited concepts, translating the untenably molecular and hazy (the undertow, the gas, the mosquito swarm) into molar form (Wolfe 2007: xii).

It questions inclusion, as the subject of knowledge must take the Other of knowledge seriously; as the observational problem in cybernetics (e.g., Luhmann, Bateson) highlights, "noise" is always already part of the signal, and "noise" begets new systems (Wolfe 2007: xiii). For Serres, human relations form "a parasitic chain," endless exploitative relationships that become reliant on one another (p. xv). Tellingly, both capitalism and piracy thrive on exploitation; it can even be argued that it is inherent to their structure to exploit. Piracy—especially in its third-world incarnations—can thus be seen as a violent, dark twin of neoliberalism that "exploits back" (Philip 2005), engendering new counter-economies (Medosch 2008). Cicero is sometimes said to have described pirates as "the enemy of all" (Heller-Roazen 2009). The notion has been with us since antiquity, but Serres twists it even further; in his ontology, the act of interfering with alleged piracy forces also the enforcer to become an interloper. In this sense, there is no way to fight a pirate without becoming one. One might ask, Who reacts to whom? Who is the parasite, the leech, the vampire—when also multinational corporations are seen to base their profit-making operations on a mode of rentier capitalism? Who drives development in this cyclical dialectic of piracy and counter-piracy? International law develops as a response to free trade and piracy; at the same time, actual maritime piracy accelerates thanks to international communications such as airlines, shipping, trade routes, and the Internet. Piracy has always been interrelated with speed and mobility. Moreover, the pirate is constructed as a transitional entity, a step toward new social realities. Pirates expose the overall, structural change that happens around them. Because people are dissatisfied with the conditions, the pirates can exploit this discontent—pirates are, in this view, only exponents, indicators of wider change. By being pests, minor groups can become major actors in public contestations. They prick the fallacies and inconsistencies of existing structures and, by doing so, leverage influence.

A radical form of innovation is thus enabled, but can it retain its power, once assimilated? Can it remain as radical, once harnessed or funneled into a legal, corporate structure? TPB exemplifies this confusion. It was populist and radical at the same time; a treasured identity, brimming over with symbolic capital while—arguably—itself pauperized in terms of monetary capital. During the trial, it was often noted that the site itself constituted a semi-commercial entity. The court verdict suggested that it was not to be seen as a company, but nevertheless as a commercial entity, operating "on a commercial scale." They had a cash flow, but no profits were proven. "Commercial scale" marks a shift in the legal terminology: It is intentionally more vague than "commercial purpose." In a Latourian perspective, TPB is a hybrid that disrupts established structures while revealing the arbitrary nature of the ontological dichotomies that modernity is premised upon. Likewise, it calls into action dialectics of privacy, as it both interlopes the established split between private and public (intervening, challenging, and rejecting it) and catalyzes it (affirming it, and shedding light on it).

Kopimi was deliberately thought to evoke other connotations than merely those of maximizing access to data—it is designated to interrogate the ontology of digital life, while also exploring the capacities for community building. The cloud would, in this sense, be understood as a counterrevolution to file sharing: In the Swedish mainstream discourse of popular mass media, Spotify was heralded as a replacement to file sharing—but to the likes of Fleischer, commercial services such as Spotify are anathema to it, as they merely give you access as a consumer, not as a member of a community.

It is therefore ironic that Spotify has recently announced that they are adding precisely those functions that would make it more constitutive of a community. Similarly, Facebook acts as a commercial appropriation of the community building that was once at the heart of online life. The example of private torrent trackers that I have turned to in this book shows that similarly editorial, community-building functions are constantly added also to the BitTorrent functionality. The difference is one of origin and intentionality: The torrent indexes and sites are built by fans for fans and can be argued to hinge on a different kind of secrecy than that of the commercial stalwarts (still, also the trackers are problematic in many ways, as they, for example, engender altogether new technocratic logics). Facebook, on the other hand, makes for a totalizing platform where the back-end functionality is kept secret and impossible to interfere with, while the private trackers act as granular enclaves, trying to remain altogether secret by hiding under the radar—but with more internal openness and mutability, once allowed inside.

8.1 AGAINST CYBERNETIC TOTALISM

Several debates are suffused under the file-sharing heading. It has become clear to me that many actors speak different languages, come from different standpoints, and consequentially, highlight different modes of justification. We could differentiate between the macro, the micro, and the meso. In fact, many of the debates prompted by ex-Piratbyrån members and by everyday file sharers relate to totalities: the alleged impossibility of imposing regulation as a result of the totalizing aspects of digitization. But that is a different form of reasoning than that found among industry representatives. In these latter, more sectorial modes of justification, a meso-level perspective is adopted, and the concerns are for particular industries, unions, or sectors. Regarding the micro level, this seems interconnected with the macro level in that the close-range observations of file sharers themselves tend to be bolstered with justifications that invoke the macro issues.

This mode of argumentation thus tends to hinge on a more dour, fastidious mode of reasoning, in some ways more pernickety toward what cannot or should not be done. I connect this with a more academic approach toward innovation: interpreting innovation in an absolutist way. Contrastingly, within industrial modes of reasoning innovation is often used to simply connote newer, more efficient ways of doing things. The former stance can be exemplified by Žižek's (1991: 102–104) dismissal of advertising and its conservative "pathological narcissism" while the latter can be exemplified by Florida's (2002) enumeration of "creativity" as a measurable quantity. Hence, debates on the impact of file sharing on CD sales are in many ways distinct from debates on the more philosophical implications of digitization as a totalizing practice. Still, they relate to each other, as the former can be seen as a case study testifying to some elements of the latter.

The micro is related to the macro in yet another way: They both accentuate a systemic interrelation between the very granular (the local) and the very total (the global), a property that lies at the heart of power-law dynamics. Both regulated and unregulated file sharing are concurrent with an apparent, technocrat belief in catallaxy, and that supply can match demand in more granular ways if applying inductive, algorithmic approaches—a line of thinking that stipulates that the world is broken and should be mended with more, and better data. This chimes with many of my observations of file sharers: First, the belief that leaving cultural content free on the Web will somehow favor a natural selection, where the best works will be adopted by audiences in an emergent way, and second, the belief that audience interest and output offered can be matched by means of algorithmic induction from data.

Both of these problems have historically been remedied thanks to the two main functions that record labels have: marketing and A&R. But these have been appropriated by way of a mode of audience interpretation and prediction that is mainly based on a meso-level approach, almost always requiring Gaussian probability equations.

Being a researcher-in-residence at an advertising agency has taught me that planning, in the creative industries, is more of a hermeneutic than a cybernetic science. Trying to predict audience whims and tastes is less an induction and more a daring proposal based on tacit knowledge and an impressionistic analysis of the world. Simply put, a gut feeling. Historically, this has been at the heart of advertising and the cultural industries; they rely on the mutability of *semiosis*, the fact that social reality cannot be modeled by mathematical reasoning alone, especially not in advance (Jessop 2004). Of course, this often leads to suboptimal conclusions, artifacts of the many traps of commonsensical reasoning (e.g., detecting causal relations where there are none, overestimating bias; Watts 2011). Still, if we adopt a Gaussian mode of estimating also this fallibility, the aptness of decisions tends to pan out as a bell curve over time: some decisions being really bad, most of them average, and some really good.

Of course, the music industry is a sitting duck among technologists and proponents of file sharing. It is often noted—among my respondents, in survey work, and on online message boards—that the industry is crooked, that its selection and output is biased, and that cronyism and vertical integration ("Payola") is rife. I would not dispute the many historical anecdotes that attest to this, but if catallaxy is a form of belief in aggregated positive effects of markets, so is the belief that market logic—in a Gaussian mode of reasoning—also tends to favor a somewhat functional matching of supply and demand, in slightly different ways than those currently in vogue. The functions of A&R and marketing can not be reduced to mechanical induction alone, and there is a case to be made for dedicated human interventions into the flatness of inductive data.

Nevertheless, the Spotify example shows us that there is a lot to be learned also from the data-driven, scale-free model as well: Industry insiders attest to the more long-term approach to planning involved in this mode of management, as the window of marketing is extended over time. If, in the record sales model, artists were required to be successful within two weeks upon release, now the window is elongated up toward thirty-six months. Spotify lends itself to a long-tail model where shelf space becomes irrelevant, thus benefiting back catalogs (Strömberg 2012). Regrettably, what is represented on Spotify is still, however, only a small, delimited selection of the virtually endless long tail out there on the Internet.

Further, the emphasis has shifted toward touring and licensing, also prompting a more long-term, granular approach to management. The digital ecosystem as a whole seems to engender much more eclectic approaches to licensing; A&R takes place in an environment suffused with SNSs such as Twitter, Instagram, and Facebook, alongside streaming services such as YouTube and Soundcloud, that act as showcase platforms. The function of mixing and mastering has also become more decentralized; an increasingly common arrangement is that artist license their finished, mastered work on a per-song basis, as we saw in Section 5.9.

During the last decade, it has been clear that reluctance toward signing new acts increased significantly; in the Nordic market, the dramatic drop in CD sales among younger consumers meant that artist acquisition extended primarily to acts that would appeal to older age groups. The currently optimistic state of the Swedish music industry—post-Spotify—means that major labels express a more willing attitude toward signing new acts and, markedly, also acts appealing to younger audiences.

8.2 THE PARADOXES OF FILE SHARING

Still, unregulated file sharing remains extremely popular. Approximately 1.3 million Swedes file-share illegally, and the figures show few signs of decreasing. In 2011, the drop in illegal music file sharing was not even 1 percent. At the same time, 2.5 million Swedes consume music through streaming: 36 percent of the population (aged 15–74). Of this group, 40 percent paid for streaming (Widlund 2012).

What is more, the Swedish music industry's overall growth, including both domestic markets and exports, was 4 percent between 2010 and 2011, which was higher than Sweden's overall economic growth. Most of this was attributable to growth in revenues from concerts and touring (7 percent growth in 2011), whereas total revenues from recorded music and from licensing actually decreased by 1 percent during the same year (Portnoff & Nielsén 2012: 23).

The situation seems to be genuinely contradictory. As a way of crystallizing some insights from my overall study, one can seize on the many paradoxes that file sharing and digitization seem to entail. I will briefly list some of them here, beginning with two paradoxes that, according to Mansell (2012), are common to the contemporary Internet era.

The paradox of information scarcity. Information is initially costly to produce, therefore intellectual property rights are required as temporary monopolies that are thought to ensure protected innovation, diversity, and growth. At the same time, information is virtually costless to reproduce and the optimal incentives for innovation, diversity, and growth occur when it is freely distributed.

The paradox of complexity. "The architecture of the Internet on one level in the system may suggest heterarchy, but this does not eliminate hierarchical relationships among other components of the communication system" (Mansell 2012: 182). The Internet makes possible both exogenous and endogenous systems. Further, on some levels it engenders radically expansive scopes for agency, whereas on another level, it engenders binaries and a limitation of agency. File sharing does not only allow for the former features; it also engenders binaries and limitations of agency, such as the fact that any artwork, as soon as it is digitized, becomes subject to illicit copying.

The paradox of superabundance. Digitization makes cultural artifacts more accessible, consumption more convenient, and the cognitive reference library much wider, thereby increasing the value of culture. But it equally makes artifacts less scarce and more ephemeral, thus decreasing their value. When asked about this, one respondent answered:

> Yes, more fleeting. What has been lost: Materiality, concentration, true love for culture (mostly). What has been gained: Speed, Access, Universality. So there are good and bad things about it. I think more about the bad things though, as i feel people who keep praising the internet for all the freedom and information it gives us are rather naive and often stupid. (CI, m30, Germany, 2012)

The paradox of digital affordances and allowances. Just as the existence of different file formats apprises us to the malleability of data, or as the different ways of organizing data apprises us to network structures, people involved in file sharing tend to be highly aware of what can and cannot be done, given the material preconditions of digital networking. However, this knowledge is not in any way objective; it is discursively charged with norms, beliefs, and tactical speech acts. Focusing on the absolutes ("copies will always be leaked") and potentials ("Orwellian surveillance will ensue") risks an ignorance of pragmatist actualities; partial regulations are, after all, more efficient than no regulations at all (at least in a Gaussian ontology).

The paradox of free flow (Section 2.2). Those who defend the currently unregulated circulation online do so with an eye to the future (techno-utopianism) but could equally be said to hark back to a past state of limited copyright legislation and pre-industrial ways of producing culture.

The paradox of reappropriation. File sharing might appear a radical disavowal of entertainment industry circulation, but at the same time enacts a reappropriation of its products.

The paradox of hosting (Section 5.6). The illicit hubs in the file-sharing universe rely on encryption, secrecy, and closure. They thus resemble the legitimate hubs of neoliberal capitalism, prompting the question whether they in fact are hubs of the same economy, only of a rogue, non-sanctioned kind.

The paradox of centrifugal communication. TPB champions piracy as a mode of copying that leads to distributed, decentralized networks of communication. A successful copy subverts the legitimacy of its original and thereby subverts positions of authority. Still, the popularity of TPB as a monolithical actor at the center contradicts this (McKelvey 2012). The more efficiently this function is enacted, the hub itself increases in importance: the value of molecular data striving toward zero, the value of the orchestrator or platform striving toward infinity (Shapiro & Varian 1999).

The paradox of industrial alignments. We have seen that the claims of pirates to defend consumers against certain corporations at the same time makes the same pirates (unwitting?) bedfellows with other global corporations, such as those within the openness industry. There is a disingenuous side to cyberlibertarians who exclusively rally against the invasive surveillant practices of the entertainment industry while turning a blind eye to, for example, Google's surveillant practices.

The paradox of cultural stewardship. The same pirates claim a concern for culture but at the same time allow for an atrophy of the cultural exception, no longer seeing culture as special in terms of its conditions of production.

> How can the Socialists, who are in favor of regulation for everything—for finance, for the workforce—want to totally deregulate culture? (Olivennes, in Levine 2011: 202)

Among my respondents I found a doggedly relativist, almost nihilistic approach to cultural labor—regarding both the work embedded within cultural artifacts and the conditions for cultural work:

> Work? Which work? You play guitar on the podium, I enjoy, I pay. The concert gets recorded, some chinese workers get exploited to produce CDs and what more, I hope they get paid for their work. My internet provider maintains a network that allows me to download and share the recording, I hope the guys who do the maintenance work get paid for their work. (UE, m40, Netherlands, 2012)

The paradox of state individualism. Swedish pirates claim a concern for the general population, yet at the same time embrace a radical individualism:

> If I want it, I take it, 'cause I can. It might be [im]moral to some people but I think it's up to me to decide. (Sunde, in Levine 2011: 202–203)

This odd volatility between abstract collectivism and individual atomism is easier to understand after having observed the totalitarian dimensions in the Swedish social contract (Section 5.2).

The paradox of regulatory evasion. The TPB representatives claim a civic interest while supporting exploitative capitalist structures and evidently striving to avoid paying taxes. Levine (2011: 205) is one of the few authors who has accounted for this underreported aspect of TPB's administrators. In this book, I have also pointed to the lamentable, demeaning nature of the site's advertising and much of the content circulated through it. Further, if file sharing is said to benefit the rights holders whose work is shared (e.g., by sparking further interest in consumption, or by outsourcing costly A&R and marketing operations through forcing upcoming authors to market themselves), it should follow that the major multinational entertainment corporations would be its main beneficiaries.

Notes

NOTE TO CHAPTER 1

1. E.g., the 1970 Fair Credit Reporting Act; the 1986 Electronic Communications Privacy Act; the 1988 Video Privacy Protection Act; the 1992 Cable Television Consumer Protection and Competition Act; the 1998 Children's Online Privacy Protection Act; and the 2000 Safe Harbor amendments.

NOTES TO CHAPTER 2

1. Rigamonti (2006) shows that common law countries (e.g., United States, United Kingdom, Australia, Ireland, and New Zealand) have partially introduced the civil-law concept of moral rights into their legislation, albeit as a set of rules rather than as a founding concept.
2. Bauwens has borrowed this phrase from evolutionary psychologist John Stewart.
3. The idealism implicit in much of this praise of p2p is observable in Röttgers's (2003) formulation "p2p: Power to the people" and the P2Pnet.net slogan, "person-to-person, people-to-people, peer-to-peer, 'puter-to-'puter."
4. The authors observe a first generation of directives directly affecting copyright: Computer Programs Directive (91/250/EEC), Rental and Lending Directive (92/100/EEC), Satellite and Cable Directive (93/83/EEC), Copyright Duration Directive (93/98/EEC), Database Directive (96/9/EC), and Resale Rights Directive (2001/84/EC); and a second generation, more thoroughgoing and horizontally interlinked: Information Society Directive (2001/29/EC) and Enforcement Directive (2004/48/EC).
5. Signifying a totality too large to be entirely rationalized (Bataille 1991); cf. also Braudel's (1982) notion of "material life."
6. Computer/Internet industry PACs contributed with almost $7 million, telecom services and equipment PACs with $2.4 million, telephone utilities PACs with $6.3 million (OpenSecrets.org 2013).

NOTES TO CHAPTER 3

1. All references in this style (initials, gender and age, year of interview) indicate references to respondents.
2. Another cinephile tracker / community that I have chosen to leave anonymous.

3. Part of the fieldwork for my masters dissertation.
4. Out of thirty-two users approached, sixteen actually responded. Out of these sixteen, eight people went through the entire interview process.

NOTE TO CHAPTER 4

1. For a current list of such proxies, see http://about.piratereverse.info/proxy/list.html or http://mirrorbay.net.

NOTES TO CHAPTER 5

1. Including Magnus Eriksson, Rasmus Fleischer, Sara Sajjad, Marcus Kaarto, Palle Torsson, Ibrahim Botani, Daniela Alba, Martin Fredriksson, Ayman Taki, Tobias Andersson, Mikael Altemark, Marcin de Kaminski, Julien Nebbout, Kristoffer Smedlund, and Fredrik Edin.
2. The 301 does not involve formal sanctions, as the United States gave up unilateral sanctions under 301 during the Uruguay round. However, the leaked cables indicate that diplomatic pressures would nevertheless be enacted.
3. Neoliberal economic policy, in the Friedmanesque legacy, appears to me as putting the interests of capital first and civic exchanges second. The devotion to low inflation—at the expense of unemployment rates—serves the interests of capital and is at the same time thought to have trickle-down effects benefiting the wider economy: a bonafide externality if there ever was one.

NOTE TO CHAPTER 7

1. The quote has earlier historical roots. It can be traced back to Voltaire. The sentiment is also found in the Bible (Luke 12:48).

References

Abbate, J. (1999) Inventing the Internet. Cambridge, MA: MIT Press.
Abramson, P. (2011) "Critiques and Counter-Critiques of the Postmaterialism Thesis: Thirty-four Years of Debate." Paper prepared for the Global Cultural Changes Conferences, Leuphana University, Lüneburg, Germany. March 11.
Adar, E. & Huberman, B. (2000) "Free Riding on Gnutella." Technical report, Xerox PARC, August. Also in First Monday, 5(10).
Alexander, J.C. (ed.) (1990) Durkheimian Sociology. Cambridge: Cambridge University Press.
Andersen, B. & Frenz, M. (2007) "The Impact of Music Downloads and P2P File-Sharing on the Purchase of Music: A Study for Industry Canada." Industry Canada, Intellectual Property Policy. October 12.
Anderson, B. (1991) Imagined Communities: Reflections on the Origin and Spread of Nationalism. Revised ed. London & New York, NY: Verso.
Anderson, C. (2006) The Long Tail: Why the Future of Business is Selling Less of More. New York: Hyperion.
Anderson, C. (2009) Free: The Future of a Radical Price. New York: Hyperion.
Anderson, N. (2008) " 'Can I Resell My MP3s?': The Post-Sale Life of Digital Goods." Ars Technica, Dec 18. http://arstechnica.com/tech-policy/2008/12/post-sale-life/
Andersson, J. (2009a) "For the Good of the Net: The Pirate Bay as a Strategic Sovereign." Culture Machine, vol. 10, Pirate Philosophy issue, 64–108.
Andersson, J. (2009b) "Sätt stopp för vi-mot-dom-tänket på nätet." Newsmill, April 27. http://www.newsmill.se/artikel/2009/04/27/satt-stopp-vi-mot-dom-tanket-pa-natet
Andersson, J. (2009c) "Jonas Gardell är rädd för den otyglade demokratin." Newsmill, May 18. http://www.newsmill.se/artikel/2009/05/18/jonas-gardell-r-r-dd-f-r-den-otyglade-demokratin
Andersson, J. (2010) "Peer-to-Peer-Based File-Sharing Beyond the Dichotomy of 'Downloading is Theft' vs. 'Information Wants To Be Free': How Swedish File-sharers Motivate their Action." PhD thesis. Goldsmiths, University of London.
Andersson, J. (2012a) "The Quiet Agglomeration of Data: How Piracy is Made Mundane." International Journal of Communication, 6: 585–605.
Andersson, J. (2012b) "Learning from the File-Sharers: Civic Modes of Justification Versus Industrial Ones." Arts Marketing: An International Journal, 2(2): 104–117.
Andersson, J. & Snickars, P. (eds.) (2010) Efter The Pirate Bay. Stockholm: Mediehistoriskt arkiv.
Andersson Schwarz, J. (2013a, forthcoming) "Honourability and the Pirate Ethic." In: T. Baumgärtel (ed.) The Pirate Book: Global Piracy and Other Inadmissible Approaches Towards Intellectual Property Rights. Amsterdam: Amsterdam University Press.
Andersson Schwarz, J. (2013b, forthcoming) "Catering for Whom? The Problematic Ethos of Audiovisual Distribution Online." In: V. Crisp & G. Menotti (eds.)

Besides the Screen: The Distribution, Exhibition and Consumption of Moving Images. London: Open Book Press.
Andersson Schwarz, J. & Larsson S. (2013, forthcoming) "On the Justifications of Piracy: Differences in Conceptualization and Argumentation between Active Uploaders and Other File-sharers." In: J. Arvanitakis & M. Fredriksson (eds.) Piracy: Leakages from Modernity. Los Angeles, CA: Litwin Books.
Andersson Schwarz, J., Schillings, S. & Fleischer, R. (2013, forthcoming) "Pirate Imaginaries: Different Ways Of Conceptualizing Piracy." Popular Communication: The International Journal of Media and Culture.
Andriani, P. & McKelvey, B. (2011) "Managing in a Pareto World Calls for New Thinking." Management, 14(2): 89–118.
Ang, I. (1991) Desperately Seeking the Audience. London: Routledge.
Ang, I. (1996) Living Room Wars: Rethinking Media Audiences for a Postmodern World. London: Routledge.
Antoni, R. (2007) "Morgondagens publik: Attityder och vanor kring film och bio på 2000-talet." In: S. Holmberg & L. Weibull (eds.) Det nya Sverige, 367–378. Gothenburg: SOM-institutet / Göteborg University.
Arvidsson, A. & Peitersen, N. (2013; in press) The Ethical Economy: Rebuilding Value After the Crisis. New York: Columbia University Press.
Atton, C. (2004) An Alternative Internet. Edinburgh: Edinburgh University Press.
Bakardjieva, M. (2009) "Subactivism: Lifeworld and Politics in the Age of the Internet." Information Society, 25(2): 91–104.
Barabasi, A.L. (2002) Linked: The New Science of Networks. Cambridge, MA: Perseus.
Barbrook, R. (2005) "The Hi-tech Gift Economy." First Monday, 3(12). (Orig. 1998.) http://firstmonday.org/ojs/index.php/fm/article/view/1517/1432
Barbrook, R. (2007) Imaginary Futures: From Thinking Machine to the Global Village. London: Pluto Press.
Bard, A. & Söderqvist, J. (2009) Kroppsmaskinerna: Manual till den moderna människan. Stocksund: Hydra.
Barlow, J. P. (1996) "A Declaration of the Independence of Cyberspace." Davos, Switzerland, February 8. http://w2.eff.org/Censorship/Internet_censorship_bills/barlow_0296.declaration
Barnett, C. (2004) "Neither Poison or Cure: Space Scale and Public Life in Media Theory." In: N. Couldry & A. McCarthy (eds.), 58–74. Mediaspace: Place, Scale and Culture in a Media Age.
Barry, A. (2001) Political Machines: Governing a Technological Society. London: Athlone.
Barry, A. & Slater, D. (eds.) (2005) The Technological Economy. London & New York: Routledge.
Barry, A. & Thrift, N. (2007) "Gabriel Tarde: Imitation, Invention and Economy." Economy & Society, 36(4): 509–525.
Bataille, G. (1991) The Accursed Share: An Essay on General Economy, Vol. 1: Consumption. New York: Zone.
Bauwens, M. (2002) "Peer to Peer: From Technology to Politics to a New Civilisation?" http://www.itu.int/osg/spu/wsis-themes/contributions/others/pEERNewP2P.doc
Bauwens, M. (2012) "Gift Economy." P2Pfoundation wiki. http://p2pfoundation.net/Gift_Economy
Bayaan, I. (2004) "Technology and the Music Industry: Effects on Profits, Variety and Welfare. Emory University." Working paper. March.
Baym, N. & Burnett, R. (2009) "Amateur Experts: International Fan Labour in Swedish Independent Music." International Journal of Cultural Studies, 12(5): 433–449.
Beck, U. (1992; trans. M. Ritter) Risk Society: Towards a New Modernity. London, Thousand Oaks, CA, & New Delhi: Sage.

Beck, U. (ed.) (1994) Reflexive Modernization: Politics, Tradition and Aesthetics in the Modern Social Order. Cambridge: Polity Press.
Beck, U. & Beck-Gernsheim, E. (2002) Individualization: Institutionalized Individualism and its Social and Political Consequences. London, Thousand Oaks, CA, & New Delhi: Sage.
Bell, D. (1962) The End of Ideology: On the Exhaustion of Political Ideas in the Fifties. Revised ed. New York & London: The Free Press.
Bell, D. (1976) The Coming of Post-Industrial Society: A Venture in Social Forecasting. New York: Basic Books.
Benkler, Y. (2006) The Wealth of Networks: How Social Production Transforms Markets and Freedom. New Haven, CT, & London: Yale University Press.
Benkler, Y. & Nissenbaum, H. (2006) "Commons-based Peer Production and Virtue." Journal of Political Philosophy, 14(4): 394–419.
Bennett, C. (2008) The Privacy Advocates: Resisting the Spread of Surveillance. Cambridge, MA: MIT Press.
Bennett, W.L. (2003) "New Media Power: The Internet and Global Activism." In: N. Couldry & J. Curran (eds.) Contesting Media Power, 17–37. London: Rowman and Littlefield.
Berggren, H. & Trägårdh, L. (2006) Är svensken människa? Gemenskap och oberoende i det moderna Sverige. Stockholm: Norstedts.
Bertoni, S. (2012) "Spotify's Daniel Ek: The Most Important Man in Music." Forbes Magazine, January 16. Web edition.
Bjereld, U. & Oscarsson, H. (2009) "Folket och FRA." In: S. Holmberg & L. Weibull (eds.) Svensk höst: Trettiofyra kapitel om politik, medier och samhälle. SOM-rapport, 46: 293–298. Göteborg: SOM-institutet.
Blackburn, D. (2004) "Online Piracy and Recorded Music Sales." Department of Economics, Harvard University, Draft. December.
Blomqvist, U., Eriksson, L-E., Findahl, O., Selg, H. & Wallis, R. (2005) "MusicLessons: Deliverable 5: Trends in Downloading and Filesharing of Music." Research paper, KTH. November 30.
Bode, K. (2009) "113,000 Have Signed Up For Pirate Bay VPN." DSLReports.com, April 9. http://www.dslreports.com/shownews/113000-Have-Signed-Up-For-Pirate-Bay-VPN-101820
Boldrin, M. & Levine, D.K. (2013) "The Case Against Patents." Journal of Economic Perspectives, 27(1): 3–22.
Boltanski, L. & Chiapello, È. (2007) The New Spirit of Capitalism. London: Verso.
Boltanski, L. & Thévenot, L. (2006; trans. C. Porter) On Justification: Economies of Worth. Princeton, NJ, & Oxford: Princeton University Press.
Bolter, J.D. & Grusin, R. (1999) Remediation: Understanding New Media. Cambridge, MA, & London: MIT Press.
Boon, M. (2010) In Praise of Copying. Cambridge, MA, & London: Harvard University Press.
Bourdieu, P. (1984; trans. R. Nice) Distinction: A Social Critique of the Judgment of Taste. Cambridge, MA: Harvard University Press.
Braudel, F. (1982) Civilization and Capitalism, 15th–18th Century. Vol 2. New York: Harper and Row.
Braun, D. & Giraud, O. (2001) "Models of Citizenship and Social Democratic Policies." Paper prepared for the 29th Joint Sessions of Workshops, Grenoble. April 6–11.
Brennan, T. (2006) Wars of Position: The Cultural Politics of Left and Right. New York: Columbia University Press
Brown, W. (1995) States of Injury: Power and Freedom in Late Modernity. Princeton, NJ: Princeton University Press.

Brown, W. (2003) "Neoliberalism and the End of Liberal Democracy." Theory & Event, 7(1): 1–43.
Bruns, A. (2008) Blogs, Wikipedia, Second Life, and Beyond: From Production to Produsage. New York: Peter Lang.
Buchanan, I. (2000) Michel de Certeau: Cultural Theorist. London, Thousand Oaks, New Delhi: Sage.
Burchell, G. (1993) "Liberal Government and Techniques of the Self." Economy and Society, 22(3): 267–282.
Burkart, P. (2010) Music and Cyberliberties. Middletown, CT: Wesleyan University Press.
Burkart, P. (2013) Pirate Politics. Cambridge, MA: MIT Press.
Burkart, P. & Andersson Schwarz, J. (2013, forthcoming) "Post-privacy and ideology: a question of doxa and praxis." In: A. Jansson & M. Christiansen (eds.) Media, Surveillance and Identity: A Social Perspective. New York, NY: Peter Lang.
Burkart, P. & McCourt, T. (2006) Digital Music Wars: Ownership and Control of the Celestial Jukebox. Lanham, MA: Rowman & Littlefield.
von Busch, O. & Palmås, K. (2006) Abstract Hacktivism: The Making of a Hacker Culture. London: Openmute.
Callon, M. (1998) "Introduction: The Embeddedness of Economic Markets in Economics." In: M. Callon (ed.) The Laws of the Markets, 1–57. Oxford: Blackwell.
Cammaerts, B. & Meng, B. (2011) "Creative Destruction and Copyright Protection: Regulatory Responses to File-sharing." In: Z. Sujon & D. Tambini (eds.) LSE Media Policy Brief 1, March. London: London School of Economics.
Cardiff, D. & Scannell, P. (1987) "Broadcasting and National Unity." In: J. Curran, A. Smith & P. Wingate (eds.) Impacts and Influences: Essays on Media Power, 157–173. London: Methuen.
Carpentier, N. (2011) "New Configurations of the Audience? The Challenges of User-Generated Content for Audience Theory and Media Participation." In: V. Nightingale (ed.) The Handbook of Media Audiences, 190–212. Malden, MA, & Oxford: Blackwell.
Carr, N. (2010) The Shallows: What the Internet Is Doing to Our Brains. New York: W.W. Norton & Company.
Castells, M. (2000) The Rise of the Network Society, Second Ed. Cambridge, MA, & Oxford: Blackwell. (First ed. 1996.)
Castells, M. (2001) The Internet Galaxy. Oxford: Oxford University Press.
Castells, M. (2004) The Power of Identity, Second Ed. Cambridge, MA, & Oxford: Blackwell. (First ed. 1997.)
Cenite, M., Wang, M.W., Peiwen, C. & Chan, G.S. (2009) "More than Just Free Content: Motivations of Peer-to-Peer File Sharers." Journal of Communication Inquiry, 33(3): 206–221.
de Certeau, M. (1984; trans. S. Rendall) The Practice of Everyday Life. Berkeley, CA, Los Angeles, CA, & London: University of California Press.
Chaudhry, P.E., Chaudhry, S.S., Stumpf, S.A. & Sudler, H. (2011) "Piracy in Cyberspace: Consumer Complicity, Pirates and Enterprise Enforcement." Enterprise Information Systems, 5(2): 255–271.
Chen, Y., Shang, R. & Lin, A. (2008) "The Intention to Download Music Files in a P2P Environment: Consumption Value, Fashion, and Ethical Decision Perspectives." Electronic Commerce Research and Applications, 7(4): 411–422.
Chesher, C. (1997) "The Ontology of Digital Domains." In: D. Holmes (ed.) Virtual Politics: Identity and Community in Cyberspace, 79–92. London, Thousand Oaks, & New Delhi: Sage.
Christensen, M. (2008) "Contentious Terrain in EU Information Society Policies: Media Pluralism and Freedom of Expression." Mediekultur: Journal Of Media And Communication Research, 24(45): 80–92.

Christensen, M. & Jansson, A. (2012) "Fields, Territories and Bridges: Networked Communities and Mediated Surveillance in Transnational Social Space." In: C. Fuchs, K. Boersma, A. Albrechtslund & M. Sandoval. (eds.) The Internet & Surveillance, 220–238. London: Routledge.

Cisco (2010) "Cisco Visual Networking Index: Forecast and Methodology, 2009–2014." White paper. May 30. http://www.cisco.com/en/US/solutions/collateral/ns341/ns525/ns537/ns705/ns827/white_paper_c11–481360_ns827_Networking_Solutions_White_Paper.html

Coleman, G. (2004) "The Political Agnosticism of Free and Open Source Software and the Inadvertent Politics of Contrast." Anthropological Quarterly, 77(3): 507–519.

Coleman, G. (2012) Coding Freedom: The Ethics and Aesthetics of Hacking. Princeton, NJ, & Woodstock: Princeton University Press.

Condry, I. (2004) "Cultures of Music Piracy: An Ethnographic Comparison of the U.S. and Japan." International Journal of Cultural Studies, 7(3): 343–363.

Cooper, J. & Harrison, D.M. (2001) "The Social Organization of Audio Piracy on the Internet." Media, Culture & Society, 23(1): 71–89.

Cooper, R. (2001) "Interpreting Mass: Collection/Dispersion." In: N. Lee & R. Munro (eds.) The Consumption of Mass: A Sociological Review Monograph, 16–43. Oxford, UK, & Malden, MA: Blackwell.

Crawford, S. (2013) "Captive Audience: The Telecom Industry and Monopoly in the New Gilded Age." New Haven, CT, & London: Yale University Press.

Curien, N. & Moreau, F. (2005) "The Music Industry in the Digital Era: Towards New Business Frontiers?" Laboratoire d'Econométrie, Conservatoire National des Arts et Métiers, Paris. February 9.

Currah, A. (2007) "Managing Creativity: The Tensions between Commodities and Gifts in a Digital Networked Environment." Economy and Society, 36(3): 467–494.

Daly, S. (2007) "Pirates of the Multiplex." Vanity Fair, March 2007. http://www.vanityfair.com/ontheweb/features/2007/03/piratebay200703

David, M. (2010) Peer to Peer and the Music Industry. London & Thousand Oaks, CA: Sage.

Dawkins, R. (1976) The Selfish Gene. Oxford: Oxford University Press.

Dean, J. (2009) Democracy and Other Neoliberal Fantasies: Communicative Capitalism and Left Politics. Durham: Duke University Press.

Dean, M. (1994) Critical and Effective Histories: Foucault's Methods and Historical Sociology. New York & London: Routledge.

DeBeer, J.F. & Clemmer, C.D. (2009) "Global Trends in Online Copyright Enforcement: A Non-neutral Role for Network Intermediaries?" Jurimetrics, 49: 393–396.

DeLanda, M. (1991) War in the Age of Intelligent Machines. New York: Zone.

DeLanda, M. (1996) "Markets and Anti-markets in the World Economy." In: S. Aronowitz, B. Martinsons & M. Menser. Technoscience and Cyberculture, 181–194. New York, NY and London: Routledge.

DeLanda, M. (2006) A New Philosophy of Society: Assemblage Theory and Social Complexity. London & New York: Continuum.

Deleuze, G. (1991; trans. C.V. Boundas) Empiricism and Subjectivity: An Essay on Hume's Theory of Human Nature. New York: Columbia University Press. (Orig. 1953.)

Deleuze, G. (1992) "Postscript on the Societies of Control." October, 59 (Winter): 3–7.

Deleuze, G. & Guattari, F. (1983; trans. J. Johnston) On the Line. New York: Semiotext(e).

Denning, D.E. (1990) "Concerning Hackers Who Break into Computer Systems." Proceedings of the 13th National Computer Security Conference. Washington, DC: Georgetown, 653–664. October.

Deptford.TV (eds.) (2006) Deptford.TV Diaries. London: Openmute.
Deptford.TV (eds.) (2008) Deptford.TV Diaries II: Pirate Strategies. London: Openmute.
Derrida, J. (1995) "Archive Fever: A Freudian Impression." Diacritics, 25(2): 9–63.
Deuze, M. (2012) Media Life. Cambridge: Polity Press.
Donders, K. & Moe, H. (eds.) (2011) Exporting the Public Value Test. Göteborg: Nordicom.
Dougherty, H. (2010) "Facebook Reaches Top Ranking in US." Experian Hitwise report. March 15. http://weblogs.hitwise.com/heather-dougherty/2010/03/facebook_reaches_top_ranking_i.html/
Dredge, S. (2012) "Spotify's Daniel Ek: 'We Want Artists to be able to Afford to Create the Music They Want to Create.'" The Guardian, December 6. http://www.guardian.co.uk/technology/2012/dec/06/spotify-daniel-ek-interview
Ebadi, S. & Johansson, M. (2009) "Music File Sharing: Genius Technology or Copyright Infringement?" MA dissertation, Jönköping International Business School, Jönköping University. January.
ECA (2010) "USTR issues Special 301 Report on Global IP Enforcement." Game Politics blog, Entertainment Consumers Association, May 3. http://www.gamepolitics.com/2010/05/03/ustr-issues-special-301-report-global-ip-enforcement
Economist (2000) "Free Music, Free Ride?." Editorial, August 24. http://economist.com/displaystory.cfm?story_id=342345
Enzensberger, H-M. (2003) "Constituents of a Theory of the Media." In: N. Wardrip-Fruin & N. Montfort (eds.) The New Media Reader, 259–276. Cambridge, MA, & London: MIT Press. (Orig. in New Left Review, 1970.)
Eriksson, M. (2007) "Talangfunktionen." Blay blog, November 22. http://old.blay.se/2007/11/22/talangfunktionen/
Eriksson, M. (2009a) "Om teknikdeterminism." Blay blog, February 7. http://old.blay.se/2009/02/07/om-teknikdeterminism/
Eriksson, M. (2009b) "Fwd: Jonas Andersson om nätpolitik." Blay blog, April 27. http://old.blay.se/2009/04/27/fwd-jonas-andersson-om-natpolitik/
Eriksson, M. (2010) "Accelerationism III: Eskalationism, pirateri och den absoluta horisonten för mänskligheten." Blay blog, September 17. http://old.blay.se/2010/09/17/accelerationism-iii-eskalationism-pirateri-och-den-absoluta-horisonten-for-manskligheten/
Ernst, T. (2009) 6 miljoner sätt att skjuta en älg på: En berättelse om musikindustrins uppgång och eventuella fall. Göteborg: Reverb.
Ernst, W. (2008; trans. T. Andersson) Sorlet från arkiven: Ordning ur oordning. Göteborg: Glänta. (Orig. 2002.)
Etzioni, A. (1968) The Active Society: A Theory of Societal and Political Processes. New York: Free Press.
European Commission (2009) Communication on the Application of State Aid Rules to Public Service Broadcasting. 2009/C 257/01. October 27.
Falkvinge, R. (2011) "Cable Reveals Extent of Lapdoggery from Swedish Govt on Copyright Monopoly." Blog post, September 5. http://falkvinge.net/2011/09/05/cable-reveals-extent-of-lapdoggery-from-swedish-govt-on-copyright-monopoly/
Feenberg, A. (1999) Questioning Technology. London: Routledge.
Findahl, O. (2006) "Thieves or Customers? File-sharing in the Digital World." In: P. Cunningham & M. Cunningham (eds.) Exploiting the Knowledge Economy: Issues, Applications, Case Studies, 1833–1840. Amsterdam: IOS Press.
Findahl, O. (2009) Unga svenskar och Internet 2009. Stockholm: .SE (Stiftelsen för Internetinfrastruktur).
Findahl, O. (2012) Svenskarna och Internet. Stockholm: .SE (Stiftelsen för Internetinfrastruktur).

Findahl, O. & Selg, H. (2005) "The Downloaders: Who They Are and What They Are Doing?" eChallenges Conference Paper / MusicLessons. October.
Fiske, J. (1989) Understanding Popular Culture. London: Unwin Hyman.
Fleischer, R. (2004) " 'Content Flatrate' and the Social Democracy of the Digital Commons." Nettime mailing list, July 13. http://www.nettime.org/Lists-Archives/nettime-l-0407/msg00020.html
Fleischer, R. (2006) "Att avveckla upphovsrätten: ståndpunkt eller riktning?" Copyriot blog, February 5. http://copyriot.blogspot.se/2006/02/att-avveckla-upphovsrtten-stndpunkt.html
Fleischer, R. (2008a) "Re 'Paid in Full.' " In: Deptford.TV (eds.) Deptford.TV Diaries II: Pirate Strategies, 98–100. London: Openmute.
Fleischer, R. (2008b) Autumn Talk, Part 4: The Method of Kopimi. Copyriot blog, October 30. http://copyriot.se/2008/10/30/autumn-talk-part-4-the-method-of-kopimi/
Fleischer, R. (2009a) "Tingsrätten avfärdade åklagarens påståenden om miljonvinster." Copyriot blog, April 18. http://copyriot.se/2009/04/18/tingsratten-avfardade-aklagarens-pastaenden-om-miljonvinster/
Fleischer, R. (2009b) Det postdigitala manifestet. Stockholm: Ink.
Fleischer, R. (2010a) "Pirate Politics: From Accelerationism to Escalationism?" Copyriot blog, January 13. http://copyriot.se/2010/01/13/pirate-politics-from-accelerationism-to-escalationism/
Fleischer, R. (2010b) "Endast det redan kända laddas ner—eller?" Copyriot blog, November 28. http://copyriot.se/2010/11/28/endast-det-redan-kanda-laddas-ner-%E2%80%93-eller/
Fleischer, R. (2010c) "Femton gastar på död mans kista: Om framtidens nätpolitik." In: J. Andersson & P. Snickars (eds.) Efter The Pirate Bay, 259–280. Stockholm: Mediehistoriskt arkiv.
Fleischer, R. (2012a) Musikens politiska ekonomi. Stockholm: Ink.
Fleischer, R. (2012b) "Molniga tider: Om integritetsdebattens förlamande dialektik." In: J. Dalunde (ed.) Integritet i en digital värld: Sju texter om individ och internet, 109–124. Stockholm: Fores/Ivrig.
Fleischer, R. (2013) "Medhjälp till medhjälp till medhjälp till . . . Internet blir rättsobjekt när Piratpartiet dras till domstol." Copyriot blog, February 19. http://copyriot.se/2013/02/19/medhjalp-till-medhjalp-till-medhjalp-till-internet-blir-rattsobjekt-nar-piratpartiet-dras-till-domstol/
Florida, R. (2002) The Rise of the Creative Class. New York: Basic Books.
Franklin, M. (2009) "Who's Who in the 'Internet Governance Wars': Hail the Phantom Menace?" International Studies Review, 11(1): 221–226.
Freedman, D. (2003) "Managing Pirate Culture: Corporate Responses to Peer-to-Peer Networking." International Journal on Media Management, 5(3): 173–179.
Freedman, D. (2006) " 'Old' Media Resilience in the 'New Media' Revolution." In: J. Curran & D. Morley (eds.) Media and Cultural Theory, 275–290. London & New York: Routledge.
Fria Tidningen (2006) "Journalistförbundet tar upp beslagtagna servrar med Bodström." July 1. http://www.fria.nu/artikel/7425
FTC (2012) "Protecting Consumer Privacy in an Era of Rapid Change: Recommendations for Businesses and Policymakers." Federal Trade Commission report. March 26.
Fuller, M. (2005) Media Ecologies: Materialist Energies in Art and Technoculture. Cambridge, MA, & London: MIT Press.
Galloway, A. (2004) Protocol: How Control Exists after Decentralization. London & Cambridge, MA: MIT Press.
Galloway, A. & Thacker, E. (2007) The Exploit: A Theory of Networks. Minneapolis, MN: University of Minnesota Press.

Gandy, Jr., O.H. (1993) The Panoptic Sort: A Political Economy of Personal Information. New York: Westview Press.
García-Álvarez, E., López-Sintas, J. & Zerva, K. (2009) "A Contextual Theory of Accessing Music: Consumer Behavior and Ethical Arguments." Consumption, Markets & Culture, 12(3): 243–264.
Gayer, A. & Shy, O. (2006) "Publishers, Artists, and Copyright Enforcement." Information Economics and Policy, 18: 374–384.
Geertz, C. (1993) The Interpretation of Cultures. London: Fontana Press. (Orig. 1973.)
Geiger, C. (2009) "Copyright's Fundamental Rights Dimension at EU Level." In: E. Derclaye (ed.) Research Handbook on the Future of EU Copyright, 27–48. Northampton, MA: Edward Elgar.
Ghersetti, M. (2009) "Ladda ner, streama, fildela." In: S. Holmberg & L. Weibull (eds.) Svensk höst: Trettiofyra kapitel om politik, medier och samhälle, 391–398. SOM-rapport 46, SOM-institutet, Göteborg University.
Giarin, A., Nuccio, M. & Montagnani, M.L. (2012) "Digital Music: An Empirical Analysis for an Evolution of Legal Consumption To Contrast Piracy." Quaderni ASK: Università Commerciale Luigi Bocconi.
Gibson, O. (2005) "Online File Sharers 'Buy More Music.'" The Guardian, July 27.
Gibson, O. (2008) "File Sharing 'May Be Good', Says EMI Executive." The Guardian, April 3.
Giddens, A. (1998) The Third Way. Cambridge: Polity Press.
Giese, M. (2004) "Community Property: Digital Music and the Economic Modalities of Transmission and Ritual Modes of Communication." Journal of Communication Inquiry, 28(4): 342–362.
Giesler, M. (2006) "Consumer Gift Systems." Journal of Consumer Research, 33: 283–290.
Giesler, M. & Pohlmann, M. (2003) "The Anthropology of File Sharing: Consuming Napster as a Gift." In: P.A. Keller & D.W. Rook (eds.) Advances in Consumer Research, vol. 30, 273–279. Provo, UT: Association for Consumer Research.
Gleick, M. (2011) The Information: A History, a Theory, a Flood. New York: Pantheon Books.
Goldberg, D. & Larsson, L. (2013) "Här är fjolårets alla piratdomar." IDG.se., January 24. http://www.idg.se/2.1085/1.488144/har-ar-fjolarets-alla-piratdomar
Goldstein, P. (1994) Copyright's Highway: From Gutenberg to the Celestial Jukebox. New York: Hill & Wang.
Granovetter, M.S. (1973) "The Strength of Weak Ties." American Journal of Sociology, 78(6): 1360–1380.
Grassmuck, V. (2010) "Academic Studies on the Effect of File-sharing on the Recorded Music Industry: A Literature Review." Projeto de Pesquisa de Grupo de Pesquisa em Política Pública para o Acesso à Informação Escola de Artes, Ciências e Humanidades. São Paulo: Universidade de São Paulo. May 14.
Greeley, B. (2011) "Daniel Ek's Spotify: Music's Last Best Hope." Bloomberg Businessweek, July 13.
Greimas, A.J. (1966) Sémantique structurale. Paris: Presse universitaires de France.
Grosse Ruse-Khan, H. (2009) "Time for a Paradigm Shift? Exploring Maximum Standards in International Intellectual Property Protection." Trade, Law and Development, 1 (1): 56–102.
Grundberg, S. (2012) "Spotify to Launch in Canada." Wall Street Journal, August 22.
Gustafsson, A. (2008) "Tidigare dömda fildelare." Computer Sweden, May 5. http://www.idg.se/2.1085/1.159681
Gustafsson, S. (2009) "Fildelningen går under jorden." TT/Dagens Nyheter, June 20. http://www.dn.se/kultur-noje/nyheter/fildelningen-gar-under-jorden

Gustavsson, M. (2012) "Anakata kan aldrig bli mer än en antihjälte." Expressen, October 7. http://www.expressen.se/kultur/anakata-kan-aldrig-bli-mer-an-en-antihjalte/
Habermas, J. (1987; trans. T. McCarthy) Lifeworld and System: A Critique of Functionalist Reason. Boston, MA: Beacon Press.
Hadley-Kamptz, I. (2011) Frihet & fruktan: tankar om liberalism. Stockholm: Natur & Kultur.
Hafez, K. (2007; trans. A. Skinner) The Myth of Media Globalization. Cambridge & Malden, MA: Polity Press.
Halbert, D. (1997) "Discourses of Danger and the Computer Hacker." Information Society, 13: 361–374.
Hall, S. (1980) "Encoding/Decoding." In: Centre for Contemporary Cultural Studies (ed.) Culture, Media, Language: Working Papers in Cultural Studies, 1972–79, 128–138. London: Hutchinson.
Hardin, G. (1968) "The Tragedy of the Commons." Science, 162 (3859): 1243–1248.
Harding, S. (2004) "Rethinking Standpoint Epistemology: What is 'Strong Objectivity?'" In: S. Harding (ed.) The Feminist Standpoint Theory Reader: Intellectual and Political Controversies, 127–140. London & New York: Routledge. (Orig. 1993.)
Hardt, M. (2002) "Porto Alegre: Today's Bandung?" New Left Review, 14: 112–118.
Hardt, M. & Negri, A. (2004) Multitude: War and Democracy in the Age of Empire. New York: Penguin.
Hart, K. (2004) "From Bell Curve to Power Law: Distributional Models between National and World Society." Social Analysis, 48(3): 220–224.
Hart, K. (2010) "Models of Statistical Distribution: A Window on Social History." Anthropological Theory, 10: 67–74.
Harvey, D. (2005) The New Imperialism. Oxford: Oxford University Press.
Hayek, F.A. (1978) Law, Legislation, and Liberty, Vol. 2: The Mirage of Social Justice. Chicago: University of Chicago Press.
Hayles, N.K. (1999) How We Became Posthuman: Virtual Bodies in Cybernetics, Literature and Informatics. Chicago, IL: University of Chicago Press.
Heller-Roazen, D. (2009) The Enemy of All: Piracy and the Law of Nations. New York: Zone.
Hellweg, E. (2004) "Digital Movie Forecast: BitTorrential Downpour." Technology Review.com, October 19. http://www.technologyreview.com/computing/13824/.
Hernes, T. (2008) Understanding Organization as Process: Theory for a Tangled World. London & New York: Routledge.
Hesmondhalgh, D. (2007) The Cultural Industries, 2nd ed. London, UK, Los Angeles, CA, & New Delhi, India: Sage.
Hesmondhalgh, D. (2008) "Neoliberalism, Imperialism and the Media." In: D. Hesmondhalgh & J. Toynbee (eds.) The Media and Social Theory, 95–111. London & New York: Routledge.
Hilderbrand, L. (2009) Inherent Vice: Bootleg Histories of Videotape and Copyright. Durham, NC: Duke University Press.
Hill, C. (2007) "Digital Piracy: Causes, Consequences, and Strategic Responses." Asia Pacific Journal of Management, 24(1): 9–25.
Himanen, P. (2001) The Hacker Ethic and the Spirit of the Information Age. London: Vintage.
Hindman, M. (2008) The Myth of Digital Democracy. Princeton, NJ: Princeton University Press.
Hinduja, S. (2003) "Trends and Patterns Among Online Software Pirates." Ethics and Information Technology, 5: 49–61.
Hintz, A. (2013) "Media Activism and Advocacy: Policy Interventions in a Global Context." In: K. Howley (ed.) Media Interventions, 284–301. New York: Peter Lang.

Hirsch, E. (1998) "New Technologies and Domestic Consumption." In: C. Geraghty & D. Lusted (eds.) The Television Studies Book, 158–174. London and New York: Arnold.

Holder, H. (ed.) (2008) Alkoholmonopol och folkhälsa: Vilka skulle effekterna bli om Systembolagets detaljhandelsmonopol avskaffades? Östersund: Statens folkhälsoinstitut.

Horten, M. (2012) The Copyright Enforcement Enigma: Internet Politics and the Telecoms Package. New York: Palgrave Macmillan.

Huygen, A., Rutten, P., Huveneers, S., Limonard, S., Poort, J., Leenheer, J., Janssen, K., van Eijk, N. & Helberger, N. (2009) "Ups and Downs: Economic and Cultural Effects of File Sharing on Music, Film and Games." TNO report 34782. Commissioned by the Ministries of Education, Culture and Science, Economic Affairs and Justice; P. Rutten representing Leiden University. February 18. Delft: TNO.

IFPI (2005) "Music File-sharers Face Biggest Round of Legal Actions Yet; Many are Already Counting the Cost." Press release, April 12. http://www.ifpi.org/content/section_news/20050412.html.

IFPI (2008) "IFPI Digital Music Report." January 2008. http://www.ifpi.org/content/library/DMR2008.pdf

IFPI (2010) "Digital Music Report 2010." January 21. http://www.ifpi.org/content/library/DMR2010.pdf

Ilshammar, L. (2010) "Piratpunkten: Om det auktoritära samhällets sammanbrott och digitalpolitikens födelse." In: J. Andersson & P. Snickars (eds.) Efter The Pirate Bay, 281–300. Stockholm: Mediehistoriskt arkiv.

Ilshammar, L. & Larsmo, O. (2005) 404: Utflykter i glömskans landskap. Stockholm: Atlas.

Inglehart, R. (1971) "The Silent Revolution in Europe: Intergenerational Change in Post-Industrial Societies." American Political Science Review, 65: 991–1017.

Inglehart, R. & Welzel, C. (2005) Modernization, Cultural Change and Democracy: The Human Development Sequence. New York & Cambridge: Cambridge University Press.

Jakobsson, P. (2012) Öppenhetsindustrin. Örebro Studies in Media and Communication 13, Södertörn Doctoral Dissertations 65.

Jakubowicz, K. (2011) "Public Service Broadcasting: Product (and Victim?) of Public Policy." In: R. Mansell & M. Raboy (eds.) The Handbook of Global Media and Communication Policy, 210–229. Malden, MA, & Oxford, UK: Blackwell.

Jameson, F. (1981) The Political Unconscious: Narrative as a Socially Symbolic Act. Ithaca, NY: Cornell University Press.

Jansson, A. (2010) "Integritetsrisker och nya medier." In: S. Holmberg & L. Weibull (eds.) Nordiskt ljus, 261–276. Göteborg: SOM-institutet.

Jegers, I. & Lindgren, M. (1992) Morgondagens värderingar: För dig som tänker vara med bortom sekelskiftet. Uppsala: Konsultförlaget.

Jenkins, H. (2006) Convergence Culture: Where Old and New Media Collide. New York: NYU Press.

Jenkins, H. (2007) "Afterword: The Future of Fandom." In: J. Gray, C. Lee Harrington & C. Sandvoss (eds.) Fandom: Identities and Communities in a Mediated World, 357–364. New York: New York University Press.

Jenks, C. (2003) Transgression. London: Routledge.

Jerräng, M. (2012) "Åtta av hundra betalar för Spotify." ComputerSweden, August 22.

Jessop, B. (2004) Critical Semiotic Analysis and Cultural Political Economy. Critical Discourse Studies, 1(2): 159–174.

JO (2007) "Initiativärende beträffande den s.k. razzian mot internetsajten The Pirate Bay." Parliamentary Ombudsmen verdict, April 2. http://www.jo.se/Page.aspx?

MenuId=106&MainMenuId=106&Language=sv&ObjectClass=DynamX_SFS_Decision&Id=2275

Johns, A. (2009) Piracy: The Intellectual Property Wars from Gutenberg to Gates. Chicago, IL: University of Chicago Press.

Jordan, T. & Taylor, P.A. (2004) Hacktivism and Cyberwars: Rebels with a Cause? London & New York: Routledge.

Kaarto, M. & Fleischer, R. (eds.) (2005) Copy Me: Samlade texter från Piratbyrån. Stockholm: Roh-Nin.

Kampmann Walther, B. (2007) "The Theoretical Rationality of the Concept of the Network Society." In: N. Lehmann et al. (eds.) The Concept of the Network Society: Post-Ontological Reflections, 13–46. Frederiksberg: Samfundslitteratur/Nordicom.

Karaganis, J. (ed.) (2011) Media Piracy in Emerging Economies. New York: Social Science Research Council.

Karaganis, J., Grassmuck, V. & Renkema, L. (2012) Copy Culture in the US and Germany. New York: The American Assembly/Columbia University.

Karlsson, M. & Rider, S. (eds.) (2006) Den moderna ensamheten. Stockholm & Stehag: Symposion.

Keegan, V. (2008) "The Sound of (Free) Music." The Guardian, February 12.

Keen, A. (2007) The Cult of the Amateur: How Today's Internet is Killing Our Culture. New York: Doubleday.

Kelly, K. (1995) Out of Control: The New Biology of Machines. London: Fourth Estate.

Kelty, C.M. (2008) Two Bits: The Cultural Significance of Free Software. Durham & London: Duke University Press.

Khanna, D. (2013) "The Way Forward on Copyright Reform." Cato Unbound, January 7. Washington, DC: Cato Institute.

Kittler, F. (1999) Gramophone, Film, Typewriter. Stanford, CA: Stanford University Press.

Knorr-Cetina, K. (2001) "Postsocial Relations: Theorizing Sociality in a Postsocial Environment." In: G. Ritzer & B. Smart (eds.) Handbook of Social Theory, 520–537. London: Sage.

Kullenberg, C. (2010) Det nätpolitiska manifestet. Stockholm: Ink.

Kullenberg, C. & Palmås, K. (2009) "Contagionology." Eurozine, March 9. (Orig. in Glänta 4/2008.)

Kuprijanko, A. (2008) "Piraten från Malmö står i fokus." Sydsvenskan, January 30.

La Rue, F. (2011) "Report of the Special Rapporteur on the Promotion and Protection of the Right to Freedom of Opinion and Expression." Human Rights Council, A/HRC/17/27. New York: United Nations. May 16.

Lakoff, G. & Johnson, M. (1980) Metaphors We Live By. Chicago, IL: University of Chicago Press.

Lakoff, G. & Johnson, M. (1999) Philosophy in the Flesh: The Embodied Mind and Its Challenge to Western Thought. New York: Basic Books.

Land, N. (2011) Fanged Noumena: Collected Writings 1987–2007. Falmouth: Urbanomic.

Landes, W.M. & Posner, R.A. (1989) "An Economic Analysis of Copyright Law." Journal of Legal Studies, 18(2): 325–363.

Lanier, J. (2006) The Gory Antigora: Illusions of Capitalism and Computers. Cato Unbound, January 9. Washington, DC: Cato Institute.

Lanier, J. (2010) You Are Not a Gadget: A Manifesto. London: Allen Lane.

Lanier, J. (2011) "The Local-Global Flip, or, 'The Lanier Effect.'" Edge.org, August 29. http://www.edge.org/conversation/the-local-global-flip

Lanier, J. (2013) Who Owns the Future? London: Allen Lane.

Larsson, S. (2011) Metaphors and Norms: Understanding Copyright Law in a Digital Society. PhD Thesis. Lund Studies in Sociology of Law, Lund University.

Larsson, S. (2012a) "Conceptions in the Code: What 'the Copyright Wars' Tells about Creativity, Social Change and Normative Conflicts in the Digital Society." Societal Studies, 4(3): 1009–1030.
Larsson, S. (2012b) "Copy Me Happy: The Metaphoric Expansion of Copyright in a Digital Society." International journal for the Semiotics of Law, 26, online ed. http://link.springer.com/article/10.1007/s11196-012-9297-2
Larsson, S. (2012c) "Metaforerna och rätten." Retfærd Nordic Journal of Law and Justice, 2(137): 69–93.
Larsson, S. (2012d) "No Man is an Island': Why the 'Solitary Genius' is a too Narrow Approach on Creativity in a Digital Context." Linguaculture: International Journal of the Iaşi Linguaculture Centre for (Inter)cultural and (Inter)lingual Research, 2.
Larsson, S. (2013, forthcoming) "Conceptions, Categories, and Embodiment—Why Metaphors are of Fundamental Importance for Understanding Norms." In: M Baier (ed.) Social and Legal Norms: Towards a Socio-Legal Understanding of Normativity. Farnham: Ashgate Publishing.
Larsson, S. & Hydén, H. (2010) "Law, Deviation and Paradigmatic Change: Copyright and Its Metaphors." In: M. Vargas Martin, M.A. Garcia-Ruiz & A. Edwards (eds.) Technology for Facilitating Humanity and Combating Social Deviations: Interdisciplinary Perspectives, 188–208. Hershey, PA: IGI Global.
Larsson, S. & Svensson, M. (2010) "Compliance or Obscurity? Online Anonymity as a Consequence of Fighting Unauthorised File-sharing." Policy & Internet, 2(4): 77–105.
Larsson, S., Svensson, M. & de Kaminski, M. (2012a) "Online Piracy, Anonymity and Social Change: Innovation through Deviance." Convergence: The International Journal of Research into New Media Technologies, 19(1): 95–114.
Larsson, S., Svensson, M., de Kaminski, M., Rönkkö, K. & Alkan Olsson, J. (2012b) "Law, Norms, Piracy and Online Anonymity: Practices of De-identification in the Global File Sharing Community." Journal of Research in Interactive Marketing, 6(4): 260–280.
Latour, B. (1993) We Have Never Been Modern. Cambridge, MA: Harvard University Press.
Latour, B. (2005) Reassembling the Social: An Introduction to Actor-Network-Theory. Oxford: Clarendon.
Latour, B. (2007) "Beware, Your Imagination Leaves Digital Traces." Times Higher Literary Supplement, April 6.
Latour, B. & Lepinay, V.A. (2009) The Science of Passionate Interests: An Introduction to Gabriel Tarde's Economic Anthropology. Chicago, IL: Prickly Paradigm Press.
Leadbeater, C. & Miller, P. (2004) The Pro-Am Revolution: How Enthusiasts are Changing our Economy and Society. London: Demos.
Lee, T.B. (2011) "Swiss Government: File-sharing No Big Deal, Some Downloading Still OK." Ars Technica, December.
Lehmann, N., Qvortrup, L. & Kampmann Walther, B. (eds.) (2007) The Concept of the Network Society: Post-Ontological Reflections. Frederiksberg: Samfundslitteratur/Nordicom.
Lenhardt, A. & Madden, M. (2005) "Teen Content Creators and Consumers." Washington, DC: Pew Internet & American Life Project. November 2.
Lessig, L. (1999) Code and Other Laws of Cyberspace. New York: Basic Books.
Lessig, L. (2002) The Future of Ideas: The Fate of the Commons in a Connected World. New York: Vintage Books.
Lessig, L. (2004) Free Culture: How Big Media Uses Technology and the Law to Lock down Culture and Control Creativity. New York: Penguin Press.
Lessig, L. (2006) Code: Version 2.0. New York: Basic Books.

Levine, R. (2011) Free Ride: How the Internet Is Destroying the Culture Business and How the Culture Business Can Fight Back. London: Bodley Head.
Lévy, P. (1997; trans. R. Bononno) Collective Intelligence: Mankind's Emerging World in Cyberspace. Cambridge, MA: Perseus Books.
Levy, S. (2001) Hackers: Heroes of the Computer Revolution. London: Penguin Books. (Orig. 1984.)
Leyshon, A. (2003) "Scary Monsters? Software Formats, Peer-to-Peer Networks, and the Spectre of the Gift." Environment and Planning D: Society and Space, 21: 533–558.
Liang, L. (2005) Porous Legalities and Avenues of Participation. Delhi: Sarai Media Lab.
Liebowitz, N., Ripeanu, M. & Wierzbicki, A. (2003) "Deconstructing the Kazaa Network." Paper presented at 3rd IEEE Workshop on Internet Applications, Santa Clara, CA. June 23–24.
Liebowitz, S.J. (2006a) "Economists Examine File Sharing and Music Sales." In: G. Illing & M. Peitz (eds.) Industrial Organization and the Digital Economy, 145–174. London & Cambridge, MA: MIT Press.
Liebowitz, S.J. (2006b) "File-Sharing: Creative Destruction or just Plain Destruction?" Journal of Law and Economics, 49: 1–28.
Liebowitz, S.J. (2011) The Metric is the Message: How much of the Decline in Sound Recording? Working paper.
Linde, J. & Lindgren, S. (2007) "Sharing is Caring: Fildelningskultur, subpolitik och nya sociala rörelser." In: S. Lindgren & T. Sandgren (eds.) Unga och nätverkskulturer: Mellan moralpanik och teknikromantik, 115–128. Stockholm: Ungdomsstyrelsen/Fritzes.
Lindgren, S. (2009) "Unga fildelningskulturer." In: S. Lindgren (ed.) Ungdomskulturer, 118–175. Malmö: Gleerups.
Lindgren, S. (2010) "At the Nexus of Destruction and Creation: Pirate and Antipirate Discourse in Swedish Online Media." International Conference of New Media and Interactivity, Istanbul. April 28–30.
Lindvall, H. (2011a) "Why Grooveshark Takes a Bite out of Artists' Earnings." The Guardian, Behind the Music blog, September 9. http://www.guardian.co.uk/music/musicblog/2011/sep/09/behind-music-grooveshark
Lindvall, H. (2011b) "Why won't Grooveshark Remove my Music?" The Guardian, Behind the Music blog, December 12. http://www.guardian.co.uk/music/musicblog/2011/dec/12/grooveshark-music-site
Litman, J. (2001) Digital Copyright. Amherst, NY: Prometheus Books.
Livingstone, S. (1990) Making Sense of Television: The Psychology of Audience Interpretation. London: Pergamon Press.
Lovink, G. (2003) My First Recession: Critical Internet Culture in Transition. Rotterdam: V2_/NAi Publishers.
Löwenfeldt, J. (2006) "Eastpoint fimpar avtalet med TPB." Realtid.se, August 1. http://www.realtid.se/ArticlePages/200608/01/20060801081522_Realtid385/20060801081522_Realtid385.dbp.asp
Lull, J. (1995) Media, Communication, Culture. A Global Approach. Cambridge: Polity.
Lundell, S. (2012) "Daniel Ek: Därför ökar Spotifys förluster." Dagens Industry, April 12.
Lunenfeld, P. (2011) The Secret War Between Uploading and Downloading. London & Cambridge, MA: MIT Press.
Lyotard, J-F. (1993; trans. I.H. Grant) Libidinal Economy. Bloomington: Indiana University Press.
Mansell, R. (2012) Imagining the Internet. Oxford: Oxford University Press.
Marsden, C.T. (2010) Net Neutrality: Towards a Coregulatory Solution. London: Bloomsbury Academic.

Masnick, M. (2012) How Much is Enough? We've Passed 15 'Anti-Piracy' Laws in the Last 30 Years. Techdirt, February 15. http://www.techdirt.com/articles/20120215/04241517766/how-much-is-enough-weve-passed-15-anti-piracy-laws-last-30-years.shtml
Mattelart, A. (2003) The Information Society: An Introduction. London, Thousand Oaks, & New Delhi: Sage Publications.
Mattelart, A. (2011; trans. L. Libbrecht) "New International Debates on Culture, Information, and Communication." In: J. Wasko et al. (eds.) The Handbook of Political Economy of Communications, 501–520. Chichester: Wiley-Blackwell.
Mauss, M. (2002) The Gift. London, UK: Routledge. (Orig. 1923.)
Maxwell, A. (2007; pseud. Enigmax) "BitTorrent Survival: The Way of the Hydra." TorrentFreak, June 28. http://torrentfreak.com/bittorrent-survival-the-way-of-the-hydra/
Maxwell, A. (2012; pseud. Enigmax) "PRQ Raid Targets Revealed, Pirate Party Gets Boost, Plot Thickens. . . . " TorrentFreak, October 3. http://torrentfreak.com/prq-raid-targets-revealed-pirate-party-gets-boost-plot-thickens-121003/
May, C. (2002) The Information Society: A Sceptical View. Cambridge: Polity Press.
McCracken, G. (2006) "Of Long Tails and Fat Middles: Plenitude and the Production of Contemporary Markets." Grant McCracken's blog, November 14. http://cultureby.com/2005/11/of_long_tails_a.html
McCulloch, W.S. (1988) Embodiment of Mind. Cambridge, MA: MIT Press. (Orig. 1945.)
McKelvey, F. (2012) "We Like Copies, Just Don't Let the Others Fool You: The Pirate Bay and a Theory of Piratical Communication." Abstract proposal, M. DeSeriis (ed.) Pirate Assemblages (defunct).
Medosch, A. (2008) "Paid in Full: Copyright, Piracy and the Real Currency of Cultural Production." In: Deptford.TV (eds.) Deptford.TV Diaries II: Pirate Strategies, 73–97. London: Openmute.
Melucci, A. (1989) Nomads of the Present: Social Movements and Individual Needs in Contemporary Society. Philadelphia, PA: Temple University Press.
Mennecke, T. (2003) "SoulSeek Interview." Slyck, December 26. http://www.slyck.com/news.php?story=356
Miller, D. & Slater, D. (2000) The Internet: An Ethnographic Approach. Oxford and New York: Berg.
Mills, C.W. (1940) "Situated Actions and Vocabularies of Motive." American Sociological Review, V (December): 904–913.
Mitchell, W. (1995) City of Bits: Space, Place, and the Infobahn. Cambridge, MA: MIT Press.
Mlcakova, A. & Whitley, E.A. (2004) "Configuring Peer–to–Peer Software: An Empirical Study of How Users React to the Regulatory Features of Software." European Journal of Information Systems, 13(2): 95–102.
MMS (2009) "Hårdare lagstiftning rubbar inte attityder till illegal nedladdning." MMS press release, October 16. http://www.mms.se/nyheter/pressmeddelanden.asp?pr=8
Mol, A. (1999) "Ontological Politics: A Word and Some Questions." In: J. Law & J. Hassard (eds.) Actor Network Theory and After, 74–89. Oxford: Blackwell Publishers.
Montagnani, M.L. & Borghi, M. (2007) "Promises and Pitfalls of the European Copyright Law Harmonization Process." In: David Ward (ed.) The European Union & The Culture Industries: Regulation and the Public Interest, 213–240. Aldershot: Ashgate.
Moore, R. & McMullan, E.C. (2009) "Neutralizations and Rationalizations of Digital Piracy: A Qualitative Analysis of University Students." International Journal of Cyber Criminology, 3(1): 441–451.

Morley, D. (1992) Television, Audiences, and Cultural Studies. London: Routledge.
Morley, D. (1993) "Active Audience Theory: Pendulums and Pitfalls." Journal of Communication, 43(1): 13–19.
Morozov, E. (2011) The Net Delusion: The Dark Side of Internet Freedom. New York: PublicAffairs.
Morozov, E. (2013) To Save Everything, Click Here: Technology, Solutionism, and the Urge to Fix Problems that Don't Exist. New York: PublicAffairs.
Morrissey, B. (2012) "The Case vs Ad-Supported Platforms." Digiday, July 27. http://www.digiday.com/platforms/the-case-vs-ad-supported-platforms/
Movius, L. & Krup, N. (2009) "U.S. and EU Privacy Policy: Comparison of Regulatory Approaches." International Journal of Communication, 3: 169–187.
MPAA (2006) "The Pyramid of Internet Piracy." Graph, originally posted at http://www.mpaa.org/press_releases/pyramid_of_piracy.pdf. (No longer available.)
Mylonas, Y. (2012) "Piracy Culture in Greece: Local Realities and Civic Potentials." International Journal of Communication, 6: 710–734.
Nilsson, K. (2006) "Folket är på vår sida." Aftonbladet, June 3. http://www.aftonbladet.se/nyheter/article383250.ab
Nissenbaum, H. (2004) "Hackers and the Contested Ontology of Cyberspace." New Media and Society, 6(2): 195–217.
O'Neil, M. (2011) "The Sociology of Critique in Wikipedia." Critical Studies in Peer Production, 1 (June), 1–10.
Oberholzer-Gee, F. & Strumpf, K. (2004) "The Effect of File Sharing on Record Sales: An Empirical Analysis." University of North Carolina, March 29.
OECD (2008) "Globalisation in Services: From Measurement to Analysis." OECD Statistics Working Paper, STD/DOC(2008)3/REV1, Statistics Directorate, by I. Bensidoun & D. Ünal-Kesenci. February 12.
Olsson, S. (2006) "Pirate Bay drar in miljonbelopp." Svenska Dagbladet, July 8, online ed. http://www.svd.se/nyheter/inrikes/pirate-bay-drar-in-miljonbelopp_334410.svd
Olsson, T. (2009) "Ipred-effekten bortblåst i Internettrafiken." Svenska Dagbladet, December 4.
OpenSecrets.org (2013) "Communications/Electronics | OpenSecrets." http://www.opensecrets.org/pacs/sector.php?cycle=2012&txt=B. Based on data released by the FEC on March 25, 2013.
Oram, A. (2000) "Peer-to-Peer Makes the Internet Interesting Again." O'Reilly Linux DevCenter, September 22. http://www.linuxdevcenter.com/lpt/a/401
Oram, A. (ed.) (2001) Peer-to-Peer: Harnessing the Benefits of a Disruptive Technology. Sebastopol, CA: O'Reilly & Associates.
Oscarsson, H. (1998) Den svenska partirymden: Väljarnas uppfattningar av konfliktstrukturen i partisystemet 1956–1996. Doctoral Thesis, Göteborg University, Department of Political Science.
Ostrom, E. (1990) Governing the Commons: The Evolution of Institutions for Collective Action. New York: Cambridge University Press.
Palmås, K. (2009) "Det kulturella skiftet och den politiska mobiliseringen." 99 our 68 blog, April 22. http://www.isk-gbg.org/99our68/?p=316
Palmås, K. (2010) "The Pirate Bay-bacillen: tre spekulationer." In: J. Andersson & P. Snickars (eds.) Efter The Pirate Bay, 196–211. Stockholm: Mediehistoriskt arkiv.
Palmås, K. (2011a) Prometheus eller Narcissus? Entreprenören som samhällsomvälvare. Göteborg: Korpen Koloni.
Palmås, K. (2011b) "Predicting What You'll do Tomorrow: Panspectric Surveillance and the Contemporary Corporation." Surveillance & Society, 8(3): 338–354.
Palmeri, H.C. & Rowland, Jr, W.D. (2011) "Public Television in a Time of Technological Change and Socioeconomic Turmoil: The Cases of France and the United States. Part I, Looking Back: The Theory, The Promise, and The Contradictions." International Journal of Communication, 5: 1082–1107.

Pang, L. (2006) Cultural Control and Globalization in Asia: Copyright, Piracy, and Cinema. Abingdon & New York, NY: Routledge.
Parikka, J. & Sampson, T.D. (eds.) (2009) The Spam Book: On Viruses, Porn, and Other Anomalies from the Dark Side of Digital Culture. Cresskill, NJ: Hampton Press.
Pasquinelli, M. (2008) Animal Spirits: A Bestiary of the Commons. Rotterdam: NAi Publishers.
Patry, W. (2009) Moral Panics and the Copyright Wars. Oxford: Oxford University Press.
Patry, W. (2012) How to Fix Copyright. New York & Oxford: Oxford University Press.
Philip, K. (2005) "What is a Technological Author?" Postcolonial Studies, 8(2): 199–218.
Piratbyrån (2003a) "Porr på TPB?" Forum thread, page 1. November 23–24. http://piratbyran.org/index.php?view=forum&a=thread&id=5159&fview=1
Piratbyrån (2003b) "Porr på TPB?" Forum thread, page 3. December 10–26. http://piratbyran.org/index.php?view=forum&a=thread&id=5159&fview=3
Piratbyrån (2007) "Fyra bokbål och en begravning: En valborgsritual på vårberg-stoppen." Piratbyrån Valborg 2007 website. http://piratbyran.org/valborg/
Piratbyrån (2008) "The Bureau of Piracy Activities 2007." Online report, February 13. http://piratbyran.org/PBverksamhet2007/PB%20activities%202007.pdf
Piratbyrån (2009) POwr, □□□□, Broccoli and KOPIMI. No publisher specified. http://mackt.se/mackt.broccoli.kopimi/
Pollock, R. (2006) "P2P, Online File-Sharing, and the Music Industry." March 31. http://www.rufuspollock.org/economics/p2p_summary.html
Portnoff, L. & Nielsén, T. (2012) Musikbranschen i siffror: Statistik för 2011. Rapport 0143 Rev A. December. Stockholm: Tillväxtverket.
Post, D.G. (2009) In Search of Jefferson's Moose: Notes on the State of Cyberspace. Oxford & New York: Oxford University Press.
Pouwelse, J. (2004) "The BitTorrent File-Sharing System." The Register, December 18. http://www.theregister.co.uk/2004/12/18/bittorrent_measurements_analysis/print.html
Quinn, N. (2006a) "Secrets of the Pirate Bay." Wired, August 16. http://www.wired.com/science/discoveries/news/2006/08/71543
Quinn, N. (2006b) "A Nation Divided Over Piracy." Wired, August 17. http://www.wired.com/science/discoveries/news/2006/08/71544
Raboy, M. (2002) Global Media Policy in the New Millennium. Luton: University of Luton Press.
Raymond, E.S. (1999) The Cathedral and the Bazaar: Musings on Linux and Open Source by an Accidental Revolutionary. Sebastopol, CA: O'Reilly.
Raymond, E.S. (2000) "Don't Tweak the Geeks!" Salon.com, June 28. http://www.salon.com/2000/06/28/kakutani_3/
Reddit (2013a) "We are the Pirate Bureau, the Organization that Spawned TPB and Much More." AMA thread. February 9. http://www.reddit.com/r/IAmA/comments/187oda/we_are_the_pirate_bureau_the_organization_that/c8cc743
Reddit (2013b) "I Am Peter Sunde, Co-founder of TPB." AMA thread. February 9. http://www.reddit.com/r/IAmA/comments/187iwo/i_am_peter_sunde_cofounder_of_tpb_ama/c8cae2m
Reldin, P. (2002) "Mannen bakom succén." Ipikuré Industriell ekonomi. March. 16–17.
Renkema, L. (2010; pseud. Ernesto) "Facebook Uses BitTorrent, and They Love It." TorrentFreak, June 25. http://torrentfreak.com/facebook-uses-bittorrent-and-they-love-it-100625/
Reynolds, S. (2011) Retromania: Pop Culture's Addiction to Its Own Past. London: Faber and Faber.

Rheingold, H. (2003) Smart Mobs: The Next Social Revolution. Cambridge, MA: Perseus Books.

Ricœur, P. (1970; trans. D. Savage) Freud and Philosophy: An Essay on Interpretation. New Haven: Yale University Press.

Rigamonti, C.P. (2006) "Deconstructing Moral Rights." Harvard International Law Journal, 47(2): 353–412.

Ripeanu, M., Foster, I. & Iamnitchi, A. (2002) "Mapping the Gnutella Network: Properties of Large Scale Peer-to-Peer Systems and Implications for System Design." IEEE Internet Computing Journal, 6(1).

Rob, R. & Waldfogel, J. (2006) "Downloading, Sales Displacement, and Social Welfare in a Sample of College Students." Journal of Law and Economics, 49: 29–62.

Robins, K. & Webster, F. (1999) Times of the Technoculture: From Information Society to Virtual Life. London: Routledge.

Rose, N. (1999) Governing the Soul: The Shaping of the Private Self. London: Free Association Books. (Orig. 1989.)

Ross, A. (1991) Strange Weather: Culture, Science and Technology in the Age of Limits. London: Verso/New Left Books.

Ross, A. (1998) Real Love: In Pursuit of Cultural Justice. London: Routledge.

Röttgers, J. (2003) "P2P: Power to the People." In: A. Medosch (ed.) Dive CD-ROM and Text Collection: An Introduction into the World of Free Software and Copyleft Culture. Compiled by Kingdom of Piracy, commissioned by virtualcentre-media.net. Liverpool: Fact.

Ruskin, J. (1997; ed. C. Wilmer) Unto This Last and Other Writings. London: Penguin.

Rydell, A. & Sundberg, S. (2009) Piraterna: de svenska fildelarna som plundrade Hollywood. Stockholm: Ordfront.

Sampson, T.D. (2011) "Contagion Theory Beyond the Microbe." CTheory, January 11. http://www.ctheory.net/articles.aspx?id=675

Sandberg, A. (2006) "Den svenska politikens geometri." Research report, Eudoxa, August 3. http://www.eudoxa.se/politics/

Saroiu, S., Gummadi, P.K. & Gribble, S. (2002) "A Measurement Study of Peer-to-Peer File Sharing Systems." Dept. of Computer Science and Engineering, University of Washington, Seattle.

Searle, J. (1995) The Construction of Social Reality. New York: Free Press.

Sell, S.K. (2008) "The Global IP Upward Ratchet, Anti-Counterfeiting and Piracy Enforcement Efforts: The State of Play." PIJIP Research Paper No. 15. American University Washington College of Law, Washington, DC.

Selman, B. (2008) "Pirate Heterotopias." In: Deptford.TV (eds.) Deptford.TV Diaries II: Pirate Strategies, 19–35. London: Openmute.

Sen, S. & Wang, J. (2004) "Analyzing Peer-to-Peer Traffic across Large Networks." ACM/IEEE Transactions on Networking, 12(2): 219–232.

Serres, M. (2007; trans. L.R. Schehr) The Parasite. Minneapolis, MN, & London: University of Minnesota Press.

Shang, R., Chen, Y. & Chen, P. (2008) "Ethical Decisions About Sharing Music Files in the P2P Environment." Journal of Business Ethics, 80(2): 349–365.

Shapiro, C. & Varian, H.R. (1999) Information Rules: A Strategic Guide to the Network Economy. Boston, MA: Harvard Business School Press.

Shaver, L. & Sganga, C. (2009) "The Right to Take Part in Cultural Life: On Copyright and Human Rights." Wisconsin International Law Journal, 27(4): 637–662.

Sheckler, V. (2012) "U.S. Copyright Alert System and Other Voluntary Initiatives." RIAA report, April 26.

Shirky, C. (2000a) "Napster and the Death of the Album Format." July 1. http://www.shirky.com/writings/napster_nyt.html

Shirky, C. (2000b) "Moving from Units to Eunuchs." September 29. http://www.shirky.com/writings/herecomeseverybody/units_to_eunuchs.html

Shirky, C. (2001) "Listening to Napster." In: A. Oram (ed.) Peer-to-Peer: Harnessing the Benefits of a Disruptive Technology, 21–37. Sebastopol, CA: O'Reilly & Associates.

Shirky, C. (2008) "Why User-Generated Content Mostly Isn't." The Penguin Blog, January 30. http://thepenguinblog.typepad.com/the_penguin_blog/2008/01/special-guest-p.html

Shirky, C. (2010) Cognitive Surplus: Creativity and Generosity in a Connected Age. London: Penguin.

Silva, F. & Ramello, G.B. (2000) "Sound Recording Market: The Ambiguous Case of Copyright and Piracy." Industrial and Corporate Change, 9(3): 415–442.

Simmel, G. (1971) On Individuality and Social Forms. Chicago, IL: University of Chicago Press.

Sjöholm, H. (2009) "Partiväsendet missar frihetliga strömningar." Newsmill, December 17. http://www.newsmill.se/artikel/2009/12/17/partiv-sendet-missar-frihetliga-strmningar

Skågeby, J. (2010) "Gift-Giving as a Conceptual Framework: Framing Social Behavior in Online Networks." Journal of Information Technology, 25(2): 170–177.

Slack, J.D., & Wise, J.M. (2002) "Cultural Studies and Technology." In: L. Lievrouw & S. Livingstone (eds.) The Handbook of New Media, 485–501. London, UK, Thousand Oaks, CA, & New Delhi: Sage.

Slater, D. (2002) "Making Things Real: Ethics and Order on the Internet." Theory, Culture & Society, 19(5/6): 227–245.

Snickars, P. & Vonderau, P. (eds.) (2012) Moving Data: The iPhone and the Future of Media. New York: Columbia University Press.

Söderberg, J. (2008) Allt mitt är ditt: Fildelning, upphovsrätt och försörjning. Stockholm: Atlas.

Söderberg, J. (2011) Free Software to Open Hardware: Critical Theory on the Frontiers of Hacking. Doctoral thesis, Göteborg University.

Söderling, F. (2011) "Fildelare jagas av ny enhet." Dagens Nyheter, September 5. http://www.dn.se/kultur-noje/fildelare-jagas-av-ny-enhet

Sontag, S. (2007; ed. P. Dilonardo & A. Jump) At the Same Time: Essays and Speeches. New York: Farrar, Straus and Giroux.

Spindler, F. (2009) Spinoza: Multitud, affekt, kraft. Göteborg: Glänta.

Steiner, P. (2003) "Gifts of Blood and Organs: The Market and 'Fictitious' Commodities." Revue Française de Sociologie, 44(Supplement: An Annual English Selection): 147–162.

Stengers, I. (1997; trans. P. Bains) Power and Invention: Situating Science. Minneapolis, MN: University of Minnesota Press.

Strandh, N. (2009) "Därför uppstod Pirate Bay just i Sverige." Newsmill, February 20. http://www.newsmill.se/artikel/2009/02/20/nagra-teser-om-varfor-pirate-bay-blev-sa-stort

Strangelove, M. (2005) The Empire of Mind: Digital Piracy and the Anti-capitalist Movement. Toronto, Canada, Buffalo, NY, & London, UK: University of Toronto Press.

Strömberg, N. (2012) "Vinnare & Förlorare." Filter, 29(December): 110–118.

Suler, J. (2004) "The Online Disinhibition Effect." Cyberpsychology & Behavior, 7(3): 321–326.

Sundaram, R. (2009) Pirate Modernity: Delhi's Media Urbanism. New York: Routledge.

Sundberg, S. (2009) "Tomma ord och ett urholkat varumärke." Svenska Dagbladet, August 22. http://www.svd.se/naringsliv/it/tomma-ord-och-ett-urholkat-varumarke_3395385.svd

Sunstein, C.R. (2007) Republic.com 2.0. Princeton, NJ: Princeton University Press.

Svanell, A. (2013) "Piratkrigets förlorare." Svenska Dagbladet, February 8. http://www.svd.se/kultur/piratkrigets-forlorare_7897468.svd

Svensson, J. & Bannister, F. (2004) "Pirates, Sharks and Moral Crusaders: Social Control in Peer–to–Peer Networks." First Monday, 9(6). http://firstmonday.org/ojs/index.php/fm/article/view/1154/1074

Svensson, M. (2012) Alkoholen: En lyckad svensk liberalisering. Stockholm: Timbro.

Svensson, M. & Larsson, S. (2012) "Intellectual Property Law Compliance in Europe: Illegal File sharing and the Role of Social Norms." New Media & Society, 14(7): 1147–1163.

Svensson, M., Larsson, S. & de Kaminski, M. (2013, forthcoming) "The Research Bay: Studying the Global File Sharing Community." In: Gallagher, W. and Halbert, D. (eds.) Intellectual Property in Context: Law and Society Perspectives on IP. Cambridge: Cambridge University Press.

SVT (2006a) "Hot om sanktioner bakom fildelarrazzia" [Threats of sanctions preceding file-sharing raid]. Rapport, June 20. http://svt.se/2.22620/1.612550/hot_om_sanktioner_bakom_fildelarrazzia

SVT (2006b) "Bodström bekräftar USA-påtryckningar" [Boström confirms US pressures]. Rapport, June 21. http://svt.se/2.22620/1.613603/bodstrom_bekraftar_usa-patryckningar

SVT (2006c) "USA bekräftar Pirate Bay-samtal" [USA confirms Pirate Bay talks]. Rapport, June 22. http://svt.se/2.22620/1.614245/usa_bekraftar_pirate_bay-samtal

SVT (2006d) "Utlovad öppenhet i Pirate Bay-fall uteblir" [Promises of transparency in Pirate Bay case left unfulfilled]. Rapport, September 10. http://svt.se/2.22620/1.655850/utlovad_oppenhet_i_pirate_bay-fall_uteblir

Sykes, G. & Matza, D. (1957) "Techniques of Neutralisation: A Theory of Delinquency." American Sociological Review, 22(6): 664–670.

Takeyama, L.N. (1994) "The Welfare Implications of Unauthorized Reproduction of Intellectual Property in the Presence of Network Externalities." Journal of Industrial Economics, 42(2): 155–166.

Tan, L. (2010) "The Pirate Bay: Countervailing Power and the Problem of State Organized Crime." CTheory, November 25.

Tarde, G. (1903; trans. E.C. Parsons) The Laws of Imitation. New York: Holt and Company.

Thompson, H.S. (1998) Fear and Loathing in Las Vegas: A Savage Journey into the Heart of the American Dream, Second Ed. New York, NY: Vintage. (Orig. 1971)

Thomson, I. (2011) "BitTorrent Takes Torrenting Mainstream with Project Chrysalis." V3.co.uk, March 7. http://www.v3.co.uk/v3-uk/news/2031699/bittorrent-takes-torrenting-mainstream-project-chrysalis

Thors, A. (2008) "Sanningen om den okända piratsajten." PC För Alla, August 23.

Thrift, N. (2009) "Pass it On: Towards a Political Economy of Propensity." Paper presented at the Social Science and Innovation Conference at the Royal Society of the Arts (RSA). London. February 11. http://www.aimresearch.org/uploads/File/Presentations/2009/FEB/NIGEL%20THRIFT%20PAPER.pdf

Titmuss, R.M. (1971) The Gift Relationship: From Human Blood to Social Policy. London: London School of Economics Books.

Toffler, A. (1980) The Third Wave. New York: Bantam Books.

Tönnies, F. (2001; ed. J. Harris, trans. M. Hollis) Community and Civil Society. Cambridge: Cambridge University Press. (Orig. 1887.)

TPB AFK (2013) TPB AFK: The Pirate Bay Away from Keyboard. Documentary film, released February 8. Director: S. Klose.

Trägårdh, L. (ed.) (2007) State and Civil Society in Northern Europe: The Swedish Model Reconsidered. Oxford: Berghahn Books.

Tschmuck, P. (2013) Music Business Research. Research blog. http://musicbusiness-research.wordpress.com/
Urry, J. (2004) Small Worlds and the New 'Social Physics.' Global Networks, 4(2): 109–130.
US State Department (2009) Embassy Cable "Stockholm 09–141." March 2.
Vaidhyanathan, S. (2001) Copyrights and Copywrongs: The Rise of Intellectual Property and How It Threatens Creativity. New York: New York University Press.
Vaidhyanathan, S. (2004) The Anarchist in the Library: How the Clash Between Freedom and Control is Hacking the Real World and Crashing the System. New York: Basic Books.
Vaidhyanathan, S. (2005) Celestial Jukebox: The Paradox of Intellectual Property. Review. American Scholar, 74(2): 131–135.
Van Dijk, J. (2006) The Network Society: Social Aspects of New Media. London: Sage.
Virilio, P. (1997) Open Sky. London: Verso.
Virno, P. (2004) A Grammar of the Multitude. Los Angeles, CA, and New York: Semiotext(e).
Vogl, R. (2013) US Information Technology Law. Transatlantic Technology Law Forum. Stanford Law School. http://www.law.stanford.edu/organizations/programs-and-centers/transatlantic-technology-law-forum/technology-law/us-information-technology-law. Retrieved on May 5, 2013.
Wallis, R. (2008) "Mer konsumentmakt hotar inte mångfalden." Svenska Dagbladet, January 31.
Wark, M. (1997a) "The Virtual Republic." Paper for the Research Institute for the Humanities and Social Sciences University of Sydney. Also on Nettime mailing list, November 3. http://www.nettime.org/Lists-Archives/nettime-l-9711/msg00003.html
Wark, M. (1997b) "Rethinking Social Democracy." Nettime mailing list (header "Deleuze Contra Barbrook"), December 30. http://www.nettime.org/Lists-Archives/nettime-l-9712/msg00045.html
Wark, M. (2004) A Hacker Manifesto. Cambridge, MA, & London: Harvard University Press.
Watts, D.J. (2003) Six Degrees: The Science of a Connected Age. London: Heinemann.
Watts, D.J. (2011) Everything is Obvious: How Common Sense Fails. London: Atlantic Books.
Watts, D.J. & Dodds, P.S. (2007) "Influentials, Networks, and Public Opinion Formation." Journal of Consumer Research, (34): 441–458.
Wellman, B. (2002) "Little Boxes, Glocalization, and Networked Individualism." In: M. Tanabe, P. van den Besselaar, T. Ishida (eds.) Digital Cities II: Computational and Sociological Approaches, 10–25. Berlin: Springer.
Widlund, E. (2012) "Om den digitala marknaden." Musiksverige blog, January 24. http://www.musiksverige.org/blogg/om-den-digitala-marknaden/
Wikström, P. (2006) Reluctantly Virtual: Modelling Copyright Industry Dynamics. Dissertation, Karlstad University Studies, 44.
Williams, M. (2012) "Megaupload Shutdown: Guns, Cars and Cash Seized in Police Swoop." The Guardian, January 20.
Williams, R. (1961) The Long Revolution. Harmondsworth: Pelican/Penguin Books.
Williams, R. (1974) Television: Technology and Cultural Form. London: Collins.
Wilson, P.L. (1991; pseud. Bey, H.) TAZ: The Temporary Autonomous Zone, Ontological Anarchy, Poetic Terrorism. New York: Autonomedia.
Winner, L. (1977) Autonomous Technology: Technics-out-of-Control as a Theme in Political Thought. London & Cambridge, MA: MIT Press.
Wirtén, P. (2009) "Internetsvärmeriets 1968." Expressen. April 22.

Wistreich, N. (2006) "Disney Co-Chair Recognises 'Piracy is a Business Model.'" Netribution, October 10. http://www.netribution.co.uk/stories/26/972-disney-co-chair-recognises-piracy-is-a-business-model

Wittel, A. (2001) "Toward a Network Sociality." Theory, Culture & Society, 18(6): 51–76.

Wolfe, C. (2007) "Bring the Noise: The Parasite and the Multiple Genealogies of Posthumanism." In: Serres, M. (2007) The Parasite, xi-xxviii. Minneapolis, MN, & London: University of Minnesota Press.

Wortham, J. (2012) "BitTorrent's Plan for 2013? Go Legit." New York Times, Bits blog, November 30. http://bits.blogs.nytimes.com/2012/11/30/bittorrents-plan-for-2013-go-legit/

Wu, T. (2003) "Network Neutrality, Broadband Discrimination." Journal of Telecommunications and High Technology Law, 2: 141–179.

Wu, T. (2010) The Master Switch: The Rise and Fall of Information Empires. New York: Knopf.

WWWF (2012) "Web Index 2012: Key Findings." Report, World Wide Web Foundation, September 5. http://thewebindex.org/2012/09/2012-Web-Index-Key-Findings.pdf

Yar, M. (2008) "The Rhetorics and Myths of Anti-piracy Campaigns: Criminalization, Moral Pedagogy and Capitalist Property Relations in the Classroom." New Media & Society, 10(4): 605–623.

Yu, P.K. (2003) "Four Common Misconceptions About Copyright Piracy." Loyola Los Angeles International and Comparative Law Review, (26): 127–150.

Zerva, K. (2008) "File-sharing Versus Gift-giving: A Theoretical Approach." Proceedings of 3rd International Conference on Internet and Web Applications and Services (ICIW), Athens. June 8–13.

Zirn, T. (2011) "Motvind i opinionen för hårddiskavgifter." ComputerSweden, September 1.

Zittrain, J. (2008) The Future of the Internet—And How to Stop It. New Haven, CT, & London: Yale University Press.

Žižek, S. (1991) Looking Awry: An Introduction to Jacques Lacan Through Popular Culture. Cambridge, MA: MIT Press.

Zuckerman, P. (2008) Society Without God: What The Least Religious Nations Can Tell Us About Contentment. New York: New York University Press.

Index

For Product Safety Concerns and Information please contact our EU
representative GPSR@taylorandfrancis.com
Taylor & Francis Verlag GmbH, Kaufingerstraße 24, 80331 München, Germany

www.ingramcontent.com/pod-product-compliance
Ingram Content Group UK Ltd.
Pitfield, Milton Keynes, MK11 3LW, UK
UKHW022203190926
475702UK00003B/184
* 9 7 8 0 4 1 5 8 5 4 3 0 6 *